Joseph Engling

by Fr. Alexander Menningen

translated by
Fr. Jonathan Niehaus

Original title: *Maria ganz zu eigen.*

Joseph Engling, by Fr. Alexander Menningen, translated by Fr. Jonathan Niehaus. © 1998 by the Schoenstatt Fathers. German original © 1977 by Patris Verlag, Schoenstatt-Vallendar, Germany; used with permission. All rights reserved.

Printed by the Lithoprint Company, Waukesha, Wisconsin. Available from: Schoenstatt Fathers, W284 N746 Cherry Lane, Waukesha, WI, USA 53188.

Table of Contents

Maps and Illustrations

Introduction

It is with great joy that this completely reworked biography of Joseph Engling can be presented on the occasion of his 100th birthday.

Joseph Engling was born January 5, 1898 in Prositten, Germany. He died in the waning weeks of World War I, killed in action just north of Cambrai, France on October 4, 1918. Although his life was short, he was one of the most brilliant lights at the very beginning of the Schoenstatt Movement. He is considered the leading figure of sanctity in Schoenstatt's founding generation and made remarkable strides toward modern sanctity through the graces of the Shrine of the Mother Thrice Admirable in original Schoenstatt, Germany.

Ever since, Joseph Engling has been a guide and source of inspiration to Catholics around the globe, especially within the Schoenstatt Movement. One of his seminary classmates, Father Otto Boenki (like Joseph from East Prussia, later a Pallottine and Schoenstatt Father in the United States), already made his life available to the English reader in the 1960s in a first translation of the biography here re-presented in a new translation.

The author of this insightful biography is no less than Father Alexander Menningen. He is best known as the lifelong right-hand man of Father Joseph Kentenich, Schoenstatt's founder. Less known is the fact that he was also a contemporary of Joseph Engling in the Schoenstatt Minor Seminary from 1913 to 1916 and in the Schoenstatt Sodality from 1915 until Joseph's death in 1918. He therefore brings much personal insight into the life and times of Joseph Engling. Father Menningen later served as the first postulator of Joseph Engling's cause for beatification when it was officially opened in 1952. He served in that capacity until the process was officially presented to Rome in 1964.

The first edition of this biography appeared in German in 1938. In those years of Nazi terror it took some courage to publish such a book. The title of that edition—*Held im Werktag* (Hero in Everyday Life)—was a quiet but determined protest against the false "heroism" of Nazi-Aryan arrogance. True heroism lies not in daring deeds for self or honor but in living all things in everyday life out of love for God. A second edition was published after the war in 1952. A third edition with a number of important additions and corrections was published in 1977 under the title *Maria ganz zu eigen.*

This last edition is the basis for this translation, though some material from the first edition (omitted in the second and third German editions) has been restored. Father Menningen's policy in the third edition to replace earlier pseudonyms (used to protect the identity of living persons) with the historical names has been expanded on here. Father Menningen's death in 1994 marked the passing of the last of the living witnesses of Joseph Engling's life. Hence, the original names have been inserted wherever possible for the sake of historical accuracy.

The second half of the book (starting with Chapter 6—The New Recruit) has been abridged from the German by about a third. Most of what has been omitted involves details about the fighting and deprivations of soldier-life during World War I. They do not significantly add to the knowledge about the life of Joseph Engling and their sheer bulk tends to give the soldier years more emphasis than is perhaps their due in the "big picture" of Joseph Engling's growth in sanctity. To help the reader navigate through this "big picture," various sections have been highlighted as box articles. Single-frame boxes are material original to Father Menningen's biography. Here and there some material, denoted by double-frame boxes, has been added, most notably from the archives of Schoenstatt's founder.

May the reader find in these pages a brother and friend who gives new courage in their efforts to live the sanctity of everyday life.

Fr. Jonathan Niehaus
Waukesha, January 5, 1998
Joseph Engling's 100th birthday

1. Home and Family

Joseph's Childhood

The home of the local tailor, August Engling, was neither poor nor rich. In Prositten, East Prussia (then part of Germany, since 1945 in northeast Poland) August could get by with his earnings and the produce of their little plot of land. It was just enough to feed and clothe his family of seven children. August and Maria's fourth child was born on January 5, 1898 and baptized on January 9 of the same year. His name was entered into the baptismal register as Joseph Aloysius. Those attending the baptism could not guess the special role he was destined to play in the plans of Divine Providence.

August was respected by the villagers as a conscientious, hard-working tailor. His wife Maria was a quiet, modest woman with a good heart and unaffected piety. Their one-story home was surrounded by a few acres of land. They had a cow and a few smaller animals. By anyone's reckoning their son Joseph would live out his life in these same humble surroundings.

Maria had some concerns about her little Joseph. A childhood bout of rickets left his breastbone so malformed that his shoulders bent forward and left him looking slightly deformed. It was not bad enough to warrant calling him a hunchback; rather, he was slightly stooped. His speech also gave him some trouble. His tongue seemed heavy and the pronunciation of the letters *r*, *s*, and *l* offered insurmountable difficulties. There was no doubt that little Joseph had a speech defect. Neighbors must have thought that this poor little fellow would have it hard later on in life.

This was his mother's concern. In true motherly fashion she tried to compensate for the defects by giving more care and love to him than to the other children. The two had many things in common. Besides her cheeks and chin, he had inherited her deep emotional spirit and gentle disposition. Because his mother was deeply religious, he also gained a predisposition for religious things. Under her tutelage the little boy became quite devout. This did not require much formal instruction. On Sunday afternoons the four-year-old toddled at his mother's side to the village church were they prayed the stations of the cross. With folded hands and rapt attention he observed the actions of his mother. His big eyes went from station to station and then to the face of his mother. His youthful mind could hardly grasp the story told by the pictures, but his childlike heart quickly understood the devotion and compassion written on his mother's face. No doubt it was something sad which the many pictures portrayed. By the end of the stations he had discovered the mystery. On the way home he thoughtfully remarked to his mother, "He fell three times." The little boy had already experienced this many times and knew how painful a fall can be.

From his mother he soon learned Who it was Who fell under the weight of the cross. She told him that He had suffered for our sins, also for children's naughtiness and failings. It made a deep impression on Joseph and already in these early years his soul felt the promptings of an exceptionally tender conscience. One evening while passing by the children's bedroom, his mother heard Joseph call, "Mama." On entering she found the little one kneeling in bed with tears in his eyes and hands folded. Some childish misbehavior which she could not remember anymore filled his heart with an acute sense of guilt. He could only be calmed after his mother had taught him the act of contrition. In her simple piety, she believed that the boy might die that night and since he had not as yet made his first confession, God had given him the special grace of an extraordinary contrition in preparation for death. But Joseph was his usual happy and carefree self the next morning.

In spite of his physical defects Joseph grew to be a strong and healthy boy. With his physical strength alone he could have made himself the ringleader of the village boys. But this was not his way. It was the home—not the street—which absorbed his interest. In his early years he preferred to play with his sisters' dolls than to do "boy things." Later on he was found more often at his mother's side than with children of his age. But he was not a spoiled "mama's boy." Loving though she was, his mother was a strong woman. He acquired her boundless energy for getting things done and her resolute way of tackling the housework and chores around the little farm. From his mother he must have also gained his extraordinary ability to endure difficulties and offer all things up to God. She also

2

knew how to silently accept the hard things in life, a lesson that Joseph would apply again and again in years to come.

Nearly Drowned

In spite of his more homebound nature, little Joseph knew the meaning of resolve and courage. Once it even saved his life. One day some children came running, panic-stricken, to the Engling home. Joseph's mother soon untangled the confusion of voices to discover the cause of alarm. Joseph had fallen into a nearby pond and drowned! Her mother-heart was filled with fear as she ran to the scene of the accident. Fortunately, he had not drowned. She still found him clinging to the steep bank, half in the water and half out. The little fellow had been playing with the other children near the pond. He lost his footing, slipped down the bank, and would have drowned if he had not grabbed a tuft of grass. The boy, scarcely six years old, clung there precariously until his mother took him by the collar and pulled him out.

Shortly after Easter 1904, Joseph and about a dozen other first graders entered the village school at Prossitten. Joseph was one of the biggest and the strongest in the class. The teacher did not find him to be a prodigy, but he had a good, middle-of-the-road talent for knowledge. In learning Joseph was somewhat slow and had to think things through, but his diligence and persistence soon made him the best in the class. In Joseph's eyes schoolmates were not companions-at-arms but friends. Before long he made a solemn friendship with one of them and took it very seriously. His friend, however, was not so devoted. This was soon a source of bitter disappointment. One day in class they had to take dictation. At the end of the exercise the teacher had the children exchange their slate boards to correct the mistakes. Joseph's slate landed in the hands of his friend. Now every time his friend discovered a mistake, he laughed and pointed it out to everyone. He wanted to show the teacher how many mistakes Joseph had make. Such rudeness offended Joseph to the core. Was this loyalty to a friend? It certainly was not Joseph's idea of loyalty, and the friendship went aground. The other lad may not have thought much about it, but traces of bitter disillusionment remained in

Joseph's heart for a long time.

The perpetually willing and eager Joseph was soon a favorite of his teacher. One day, however, it nearly came to blows between the two. The good-hearted, quiet boy could take quite a lot. But when he reached his limit he could get upset and lose his temper, particularly when his sense of justice was violated. In arithmetic class the teacher assigned a new kind of problem, evidently failing to explain how to do it. Joseph thought it was unfair for the teacher to demand a solution without any previous explanation. The boy became angry and might have even struck his teacher if his respect for authority had not held him back. As soon as he got home, he told his mother about it: "Today I almost laid hands on my teacher; the other boys would have helped me, I am sure!" he burst out. It was only after his mother had corrected him and assuaged his anger that he calmed down again. Later on others, too, experienced that the good-natured Engling was no dullwit or pushover.

A Great Event

On May 1, 1910 Joseph was sitting in the living room and seemed occupied with a very important task. The twelve-year-old must have had some new idea which was absorbing his complete attention. Somewhere he had found a rough sheet of unlined paper. He was trying to fold it in such a way that it would make a little notebook. Some heavier blue paper served as a cover. He borrowed a needle and thread from his father to sew the booklet together. Now he drew lines in his book, slowly and carefully, making sure they were all parallel. Some were pretty good, while others wandered a little off course. Last of all he put a flourish at the top of the first page and it was ready for use. What was the purpose of this mysterious little notebook? He started out by putting the date "May 1" at the top. Right beneath the date he wrote the first words deliberately and in big letters befitting the important task. The first sentence revealed his purpose:

"This diary is not to serve vanity, but the improvement of my life and the preparation of my first Holy Communion. While reading the story *From the Diary of a First Communicant*, I decided to start a diary myself, because I will be a first communicant too. I thus begin

4

to write."

The boy was beginning a diary. He first kept it during his preparation for First Holy Communion and then, after an interlude, continued it until the following March. In the pages of his diary, this student with a relatively rudimentary country school education showed a remarkable talent for summing up the main thoughts from his First Communion class and later from the Lenten sermons of his pastor. This was not so much the result of having a clever mind. Rather, it came from his ability to absorb the spiritual world with his whole soul and translate it into practical consequences for his everyday life. It is the most astonishing thing about his boyhood diary.

His preparation for First Holy Communion had such a deep impact on him because his comprehension of the supernatural had made considerable strides in the last six months. In the Engling family it was customary to read from the "Lives of the Saints" on long winter nights. Father and mother did the reading, and they added suitable explanations and made applications to practical life. During this time little Joseph sat in a corner listening attentively. Yes, the saints were great men, he thought, and they accomplished great things in their lives. One day his father read about St. Francis Xavier who went to the ends of the world to convert thousands. On another occasion he related an account of the heroes of the first Christian centuries; they had opposed the mighty Roman emperors and given their lives for Christ. All this was interesting reading. His mother explained it further and told where the martyrs got such heroic courage—they often assisted at the Holy Sacrifice of the Mass and received their Lord and Savior in Holy Communion. What his mother said went deep. The hour would soon come when Joseph would receive the Eucharistic Savior for the first time. In the life of every Christian, he thought, this should be a solemn moment well prepared. To prepare the best way possible, he reckoned he should follow the advice of his mother, for she always knew how to explain service to God so beautifully.

The next day Joseph was writing in his diary again. He asked himself the important question of how he should best begin his preparation for First Communion. The answer he found was really quite simple. He only had to look to his mother's example and do everything as she did. He therefore wrote:

"The day before instruction (for First Communion) began, my mother told me to ask the Holy Spirit for His grace. This I did. Oh, I really have such a good mother! Then I made the resolution to ask the Holy Spirit before every instruction to help me be attentive during class. Because I have such a pious mother, I made the resolution to become just as devout and to obey my parents promptly. May God help me to keep these resolutions."

The Queen of May

During the month of May, Joseph directed his attention to the picture of the Blessed Mother. It occupied a place of honor in the home and during all of May her altar was specially decorated. Joseph made it a point to look for flowers and placed them in fresh water. He did this with great enthusiasm. It pleased his mother greatly to see Joseph do these things with so much love.

She was convinced that if the Blessed Mother took her children under her special protection, she would not have to worry about their future. When she knelt with the family in front of the shrine of the Queen of May, she always had one special intention for which she prayed. She never failed to ask Mary to take all her loved ones under her mantle and obtain from the Heavenly Father the grace that one of her boys have a vocation to the priesthood. Who could tell? It might even be little Joseph. His heart was always so good and devout and filled with a special fondness for Our Lady. Whenever a prayerful mother has such a conversation with the Mother of God, it is always an hour of blessing for her children.

One day during the instructions, the pastor explained the meaning of ejaculatory prayer. He had the children enumerate some of these short prayers and added others. The one which appealed most to Joseph was: "All for the love of Jesus." He realized that Jesus lovingly looked down on him as he prepared for his First Communion. Jesus saw him when he did good (this made Him happy) and when he did bad (this hurt Him). Joseph wanted to remain His loyal friend at all times and make Him happy. His ejaculatory prayer was to remind him of that. One day he made an entry in his diary and

6

reported that his little prayer had helped him:

"From May 16 to 19, I was not at home. When I returned, my whole bedroom was a mess. I almost let my anger get the best of me. However, I remembered my ejaculation, 'All for the love of Jesus,' and then I fought against my anger. I will often remember my ejaculation."

In the last days of May he had to report an incident in his diary that apparently weighed on his mind. He wrote:

"It was a bad day. I was in the big room when mother came in. She was upset and said: 'Well, Joseph, you have done a foolish thing again; you pulled out the flowers.' She showed me the plants. I saw them and had to admit that I had pulled them out. But I did not do it on purpose. I had mistaken them for weeds and that's why I pulled them out."

He judged his thoughtlessness very severely: He had upset and offended his mother and by ruining the flowers had damaged property. He must have thought he had committed two mortal sins, for he concluded his "confession" with the petition:

"Jesus, give me the grace never to commit a mortal sin again."

His still youthful conscience was not yet able to distinguish between sin and an honest mistake, but time and formation would overcome this. What this little event clearly reveals is that God's grace had awakened in him a noticeable sense of spiritual greatness. Through his personal familiarity with the Divine Savior his tender conscience became more sensitive and reacted with horror when it realized he had saddened God. This was probably one source of the urge in his soul to make resolutions and work on his self-education.

On June 29, 1910 Joseph approached the table of the Lord for the first time. Weeks and months of instruction and training had pre-pared his young heart for the Divine Friend of children. In this time he had followed the promptings of grace with an open ear and a willing heart. This hour could be nothing less than an experience that deeply touched his soul.

During the summer of 1910 Joseph had much work to do in the fields, leaving little time to think of his diary. When the long winter months resumed, however, he remembered it and around New Year's Day began to write again:

"The old year is past and I have done a lot of bad things. But what abut the good? Very little. God has pardoned my sins. Now I enter the new year, 1911, with joyful hope and with the resolutions: 1) to avoid all sins and all occasions of sin; 2) to do a lot of good."

On New Year's Day the pastor gave a sermon which seemed very important to Joseph. A summary of it earned a place in his diary for future reference. Though he forgot most of it, he managed to remember the main points. He wrote:

"January 3. Sermon on New Year's Day. Here just briefly the main points. A resolution on how to spend the year: We want to do all for, with, and in Jesus. For Jesus, by doing all our works for Him, by accepting all sufferings out of love for Jesus and bearing them patiently. We do everything with Jesus by calling on Him to lighten our burden and to help us carry it joyfully. We do everything in Jesus by remaining in the state of sanctifying grace. Thus we can do all for, with, and in Jesus."

There was a very good reason why this sermon seemed of such importance to Joseph. Some months before he had chosen "All for the love of Jesus" as his favorite ejaculation. Since that time he was united with Jesus by a close friendship. His First Holy Communion had solemnly sealed this friendship. And now the pastor's sermon was telling him how to keep this friendship all year round. The priest's words said exactly what his favorite little prayer wanted to say.

Later Joseph was again moved to write down the words of his parish priest. This time it was a wonderful little story. He remembered it so well that he could put it down almost word for word.

"February 25. A noble lady in England gave a great banquet. Among other guests she also invited her little nephew. He went and was given a great many sweets by his aunt. An officer then asked the nephew, 'Doesn't your heart now belong to your aunt?' The boy replied: 'No.' 'Well, but at least half of your heart belongs to her.' said the officer. The boy answered: 'No.' 'Does your whole heart then belong to her?' queried the officer. 'No,' was the prompt reply. 'But to whom does your heart really belong?' the officer insisted. The boy replied: 'My whole heart belongs to God.' The assembled guests were silent and from that time on many of them thought of God again. From now on my heart shall belong to God and I will not offend Him anymore."

What had happened to the boy in the story also happened to

Joseph. The great event of his youth, his First Communion, had detached his pure heart from the things of the world. Now it belonged entirely to his great Divine Friend.

God's Call

In the summer of 1911 young Joseph was working on a large farm near the East Prussian village of Landau. He was such a big, strong lad that one could have mistaken him for a regular farmhand. His exterior was a little clumsy, it is true, but his eagerness for work was simply indomitable. Whenever he stopped to straighten out for a brief rest, one could tell that he was rather young. Why was he working in the fields instead of going to school? If anyone had asked him this question, he would have stretched out to his full height and said: "Listen, in spite of my thirteen years I am already five feet two inches tall. Besides I am strong; work is really a pleasure for me. An even greater pleasure is to help my good parents earn some money. I hire out as a farmhand for the summer. My employer asked for me; he is one of my father's best customers."

The work in the fields also gave him time to think. His thoughts drifted to the future and some of them found their way into his diary. In the summer of 1911 he made the last entry:

"I have been hired here for the third summer. On St. Martin's day [November 11] I will return home to my parents. There I shall meet my brothers and sisters. I will remain at home until Christmas. Then I will graduate. From Christmas until St. Martin's day 1912, I will work for my former employer. I don't know yet what I will do after that."

Since his First Communion, the boy had been thinking more and more about his future. What was he going to do with his life? Be a farmer? This would have suited his build and temperament. Farm work gave his industrious spirit and strong build great satisfaction. His love of nature and meditative temperament would have been satisfied too. But without being fully aware of it, his decision was already going in a different direction. His parents received two mission magazines called *The Rosary* and *The Star of Africa*. Both were published by the Pallottine Fathers in Limburg on the Lahn. What he read there about the priesthood and work for the kingdom of God made such an impression on him that he could not forget it. When he was alone doing the field work his thoughts circled around the question, "Could I become a priest and missionary?"

This question eventually caused him great anguish of heart. If

Joseph's family (1913 in Prositten). Back row: Maria, Joseph, August (father), Valentine. Front row: Elizabeth, Lucy, Maria (mother), August and John.

only he could tell someone about it! His mother perhaps? It would be easiest to tell her. But to reveal his secret was more than he could manage. He tried an indirect route, saying he would like to go to high school. With a certain sadness his mother replied, "It would be too expensive to send you to the high school in Braunsberg. We cannot afford it." "That's not what I want either," said Joseph, but what he really wanted to say just would not come. His shyness kept him from speaking about his wish even when school ended for the Christmas break and he returned to work for the farmer in Landau. But the last word was not spoken yet.

In the spring of 1912 Joseph made another attempt to tell his secret to his mother. Oh, how difficult it can be for a boy to reveal a well-guarded secret! This time, too, he directed the conversation in a round-about way. First he mentioned that if the farmer in Landau would ask him to work next year, his mother should make no promises.

His mother then asked what he wanted to do. There was a hint of quiet expectation in her question. She may have long guessed what was going on in her son's soul. Was God's grace really calling one of her sons to the priesthood? But Joseph still hesitated. With one sentence he could have ended the suspense, but instead he could only say, "Wait until May. Then I will tell you." Now he was stuck again, having failed to express his heart's desire. Knowing her boy, his mother did not press for an immediate answer.

The mysterious choice of May was not hard to understand. The month of the Blessed Virgin would bring the answer, and it did. As in so many other moments of his life, Mary was there. At the end of May he was absolutely sure about his vocation. He went to his parish priest first. Having received his approval, he approached his parents and expressed the desire to become a priest and enter the Society of the Pallottine Fathers. His devout parents, especially his mother, readily gave their consent.

From then on Joseph went to his pastor for Latin lessons. The pastor contacted the provincial superior of the Pallottines in Limburg and sent in the required testimonials. On his application form Joseph gave the following reason for entering: "To become a priest and promote the propagation of the faith." The provincial superior answered in the affirmative, instructing the candidate to report to the Minor Seminary at Schoenstatt, near Vallendar on the Rhine, on September 24, 1912.

11

2. School Days in Schoenstatt

The New Beginning

For weeks the Engling family was filled with quiet expectation. Joseph was about to go on the long journey west to the Rhine River. That was the location of the school where he would study to be a priest. Such a journey required more than the usual preparations. Clothes and laundry had to be packed and other things arranged. By the time his belongings were finally together they filled a whole trunk. Before starting out there was one more concern—the travel arrangements. For such an important matter the pastor was consulted. It was decided that Joseph's father would go along, since it wasn't right for a boy to travel so far alone. Of course they had to take the lowest fare available—fourth class on the so-called "lazy train." For their money they got to see every station between East Prussia and the Rhine. It was a "pleasure" that lasted two full days. With heavy baggage and sufficient provisions, father and son set out on their long journey. It was September 1912.

When the train finally pulled into the station in Vallendar, they breathed a sigh of relief. How glad they were to walk from the depot to the seminary, so that they could at least stretch their weary limbs and get some exercise. As the two walked side by side, one could not help but notice how little father and son resembled one another. The father was small-boned and refined in his gestures; his son was considerably taller and stronger, but somewhat stiff and awkward in his bearing. His gait was heavy and he seemed flat-footed. The upper part of his body was perpetually bent forward.

At the end of the valley at the edge of town, the old monastery of Schoenstatt loomed before them. There could be little doubt about the origin of the building. Two church towers nearby were ample proof of its monastic roots. They were witnesses of a seven-hundred-year history. Devout Augustinian nuns first settled there in 1143. Archbishop Albero of Trier gave their convent the name "Schoenstatt," or "beautiful place." But how odd that the spires stood alone without a church! Long ago there had been one, but it was badly damaged by the Swedes in the Thirty Years War (1618-

48) and finished off by the French in the Seven Years War (1756-63). The building close to the towers had to be the school. It had served many purposes during its long history. From 1901 until just that spring it had been the home of the two lower classes of the minor seminary. A brand new minor seminary now stood high on the bluff, large enough to accommodate all the classes. It was home to about 180 students.

Schoenstatt in the time of Joseph Engling. Top of picture: Pallottine Minor Seminary ("New House"). Bottom of picture: St. Michael's Chapel (future shrine), "Old House", remains of Augustinian Cloister with old church spires.

When Joseph first saw the new seminary with its expansive facade and many windows, his eyes grew wide with wonder. It was so many times larger than his father's house! How would he ever find his way through that enormous building? It proved much easier than he thought. A few upperclassmen took him and the other newcomers under their wing and helped them feel at home. Soon everyone knew where the dining room and the dormitory was, how to make their beds and where to take the laundry. One of the guides was exceptionally good. Perhaps it was his particular care for the others that earned him the nickname "little papa."

The majority of the newcomers were West Germans. Several

came from big cities. Their stylish haircuts and pressed trousers gave away their origin. Compared to them, the farmer boy from East Prussia must have seemed rather old-fashioned. No matter how quietly he tried to walk, his heavy boots made more noise in the hallways than all the rest together. And when the other boys started to talk! How quick their tongues were! They spoke fluent High German while he only knew his dialect. For the moment he hung back in the background, a little ashamed. He only had courage enough to approach little Willy. Willy was very homesick and Joseph's compassionate heart made it possible for him to reach out. But he still stood so much in awe of city people that he could only speak to Willy using the formal *Sie*.

The next day his father departed. Unexpected circumstances kept them from saying goodbye. When Joseph heard that his father was gone, he felt terribly lonely. He was suddenly overwhelmed by homesickness. It was only with difficulty that he fought back the tears. Many a schoolmate who saw Joseph in those days could not help but feel a little sorry for him and think, "It won't be long before his father will have to take him home again." In the following days he had more reasons to feel depressed. Joseph expected to advance to the second year because of his pastor's tutoring. The placement test did not go well enough though, and he had no choice but to start from the very beginning. He joined the first-year class of mostly eleven- and twelve-year-olds.

"Engerling"

One morning the first-year students were waiting for the teacher to come. Instead, a broad-shouldered student at least a head taller than themselves entered the room. He seemed to be in good spirits, for his books were swinging as he walked in. The boys were taken a little by surprise. "How does he hope to get his long legs under one of these desks?" they asked themselves and began to watch. A five-foot-six-inch fourteen-year-old was indeed an unusual sight for the first-year class. The newcomer sat down in an empty desk with difficulty and somewhat awkwardly. "He must come from the sticks," most of them thought, then waited curiously to learn more about the strange newcomer.

Their curiosity would soon be satisfied. The teacher asked his name. His answer was nearly unintelligible. Boys nudged each other in the ribs and whispered, "He called himself Engerling"' (in English: "June bug larva"). Others began to giggle. The teacher asked him to spell his name out loud. More laughter! The letters seemed to come from a foreign language. In reality, they were from his East Prussian dialect. The boys could also detect a slight speech defect. Since the teacher still did not understand what he said, he asked him to go to the blackboard and write his name. The strong hand which had so steadily guided the plow now trembled at it seized the chalk and wrote in big letters: ENGLING. Some of his classmates thought to themselves, "He should have stayed on the farm." How wrong they proved to be!

The first-year class would soon have another chance to learn something about its tallest member. They had just taken their first Latin exam. For most it was a dismal failure. So numerous were their mistakes that the teacher could hardly grade the papers. Only the tests of a few could receive a proper grade. To the boundless astonishment of the class, Engling's grade was second-best. Now, that had to be due to the tutoring his pastor gave him, they thought. It was simply impossible that stiff Engling might turn out to be intelligent. Why his clumsiness showed every time he opened his mouth! He was a hopeless case, and that was that.

This unfavorable opinion seemed to be confirmed in gym class. The gym teacher would not let Joseph's stooped back and heavy gait go by without comment. He immediately tried to teach him "better posture." Joseph tried as hard as he could to follow his teacher's instructions. But there was no improvement. He had to do special exercises on the sidelines. That, too, had little effect. To top it off, his gym teacher began to say of Joseph here and there, "Oh, what a scarecrow!" This hurt Joseph very much, especially since this teacher was a priest.

All in all, Joseph's first weeks in Schoenstatt were not very promising. His spirits were at a low ebb. One day he was talking in the auditorium with one of his classmates. The two had much in common—they were both farm boys and had sensitive hearts. Suddenly an upperclassman came up to them and said to Joseph, "Listen up, Engling, you have probably noticed that you are hard to understand around here because of your terrible pronunciation. You had better look for help right away if you hope to amount to anything in your vocation. Find someone with a good pronunciation and have him practice with you. This is the only way you will gradually get rid of your speech defect." Having given his well-meaning advice, the older boy left. Again Joseph had to hear what he felt so keenly. Others let him know it, too. Even his German teacher had made a point of it. Without a word Joseph cast a sad glance at his classmate Karl Klement. He could identify with Joseph's pain and said, "Joseph, if I can be of any use, I will be glad to help you." Joseph gratefully accepted the generous offer. It was the beginning of a long and noble friendship. As long as he lived, Joseph never forgot what good-hearted Karl had done.

These difficult beginnings made Joseph realize that there were obstacles as high as mountains between him and the sought-after ideal of the priesthood. They did not cause him to lose courage, though. It was after mature consideration and not because others wanted him to that he had made up his mind months ago to become a priest. In his mind there would be no going back. He would face the obstacles with all the energy he could muster. First successes already made themselves apparent by the end of the first school year.

Honors

The 1912-13 school year came to a close. School ended around the end of July and, unlike at Christmas and Easter, the students went home for vacation. Before vacation came the all-important closing ceremonies with the announcement of the prizes. It was not just the ceremonies marking the end of the school year, but a moment that the boys eagerly awaited for weeks in advance. Before the assembled student body, the three best students of every class would be awarded for their achievements during the year. As a rule the prize consisted of a valuable book with a congratulatory inscription from the rector. In the lower classes it was also customary that all students would be announced by rank as determined by their grades. To the underclassmen it made a world of difference whether one was "the first of thirty-eight" or "the thirty-eighth of thirty-eight." The greatest honor was, of course, to be ranked first in the class. This young man could claim the title "primus" (Latin for "first"). The battle for this coveted prize stirred the ambition of many a boy, and there were more than a few who had "ambitionitis" by year's end. One boy even thought it necessary to invoke God's aid after his natural talent came up short. While praying the rosary he prayed after every decade, "Dear Lord, let me be the primus of my class."

On the last day of classes, teachers and students assembled in the auditorium of the minor seminary. The little fellows in the front seats were nervous and fidgety. To them the orchestra's selections were much too boring. The talk by Father Rector seemed to go on forever. At last he came to the real order of business—the distribution of prizes! All held their breath as the "primus" for the first-year class was announced. It was Joseph Engling! The students in the other classes were dumbfounded. With the eyes of his surprised fellow students trained on him, Joseph rose and with his heavy gait walked up to the front. "What? The slow farmer boy from the east, the fellow with the heavy tongue is supposed to be primus?" None of them would have guessed that. When Joseph got to the platform he made an awkward bow, received his prize and, a little embarrassed, trotted back to his seat. His classmates from the first year class were not astonished, however. They had suspected as much. Afterwards, when they crowded around their "primus" to congratulate him, one could see that they sincerely shared his joy without any envy. They felt the choice was just. How much their opinion had changed of him since the beginning of the year! Some had passed him over disdainfully, others were annoyed by his awkward manners, still others felt sorry for him, but most were sure that he would soon be heading back home to work on a farm. And now he had become their "primus." What happened?

Joseph's rise to first place had something to do with the history of that first-year class. It had not been an easy year. Their morale had reached a low ebb around the end of the school year. This was not because they were bad. They had many talented and spirited young men bubbling over with enthusiasm. But such a group needed a strong hand to guide them in the right direction. And such leadership was precisely what they lacked. Sickness among the teachers had led to many substitutes, meaning no one teacher was continuously at their side to keep them on task. Worse still, many hours of classtime were lost outright, and the boys did not know what to do with so much free time. They looked for diversions and eventually grew careless and neglected their studies. The homeroom teacher, a former military officer, was not the right kind of man to deal with such a delicate situation. The things he did only made things worse. There were, of course, a number of students with enough maturity and self-discipline to keep their nose to the grindstone, but they were in the minority.

Joseph belonged to this minority. For him the temptation to idle or dream away the many study halls was not very strong. The view he had of his high calling would not allow it. His strong drive for knowledge urged him to seek out books. It was almost a passion for him to read and concentrate on his studies. Others, meanwhile, were busy dividing their subjects into "interesting" and "dull." During the former they were all ear; during the latter they made a habit of yawning at the teacher. For Joseph there hardly seemed to be any difference. As a blotter absorbs every kind of liquid, so Joseph avidly absorbed every kind of useful information. His classmates wondered at how he could be interested in every subject. His eyes were always riveted on the teacher during class. There were many in his class who were a thousand times better at giving glib answers. Others raised their hands more often than he. It took him time to think and still more time to express his thoughts in words. On the other hand, he often said more in one sentence than others in a lengthy discourse. He was used to thinking and digesting what he had heard. This was characteristic of his thoughtful disposition. This was also the reason why, in the long run, he mastered the material more profoundly than his quicker classmates. Because he applied himself to his studies, he outdid those who were more talented than he, and became the best in his class.

Joseph Tames the "Wild West"

At one point the situation of the first-year class became especially precarious. With glib tongues and worldly manners, a small group of reckless boys started to exert a bad influence on the others. Given the conditions in the class, it was not hard for them to gain the upper hand. A Wild West atmosphere ensued. Some made wooden daggers, painted them red and carried them under their coats. They ambushed their classmates during the outdoor recreation time, pulled them into the bushes, and gave them an "Indian" licking. When Father Prefect[1] heard of it, he severely reprimanded the whole class in front of the student body. They were said to be the worst and most undisciplined class in the school. He threatened them with severe measures and even expulsion if the abuses continued.

Joseph took this deplorable condition of his class very much to heart. Shortly after the public reprimand, first-year students could be seen standing together in small groups. They were trying to think of ways to regain their tarnished honor. Joseph took an active part in these deliberations. In fact, as time went on he became the soul of the reform effort. In those days the groundwork was laid for his becoming the spiritual leader of his class. It was not until the following year, however, that a complete change for the better took place. Some of those responsible for the unwholesome atmosphere left the seminary of their own accord; others were advised to look for more suitable occupation.

Why was it that Joseph became "primus" and the others rejoiced without a trace of envy? In such matters boys have a logic all their own. Others in his class stood out because of their intelligence or talent. But these were not as unanimously liked. If the prize had gone to John Greven, for instance, the acclamation would have been less. John, too, was much respected, and his ability to keep his cool in front of a crowd was something the other boys admired. Some, however, detected a streak of pride and haughtiness. He was the best longball hitter in baseball, but his home runs were always accompanied by a dramatic pirouette, as if to bask in all the wonderment of those around him. If he had won first prize, he would have been even more insufferable. Joseph was liked because he never acted that way when he won a prize. He behaved so naturally and unaffectedly that everyone knew he was not conceited.

If Peter Busch had been "primus" he would not have received

---

[1] The priest in charge of discipline.

19

everyone's sincere congratulations either. He was a fine boy, but somewhat inclined to unbridled ambition and boasting. Next year's first-year class would have heard right from the horse's mouth that he was the reigning "primus." No one could imagine Joseph acting that way. Evidence of his freedom from ambition and fame had come on several occasions in the past year. One of these was especially impressive. Joseph was so consistent in his homework that as time went on the teacher began to take for granted that he always had a perfect "100%." Given the large size of the class, the teacher would skip over Joseph's paper now and then and move on to the the the next one. As he handed the papers back one day he said to Joseph, "I did not correct your paper but gave you an 'A' right away. I know there aren't any mistakes on it." They went over the papers in class. No sooner were they done when Joseph raised his hand and said plainly, "I *did* make a mistake." His classmates looked up in disbelief. Some thought, "Boy, is he dumb!" Others considered him truthful to the point of fanaticism. Deep down in their hearts, though, they could not help but admire him. And the more mature ones even said so. That's how he was. Honesty and plainspoken openness were written in his face.

Like John and Peter, Francis Pelzer would not have been as accepted as "primus" either. He was generally well-liked, for he was a quiet sort of fellow who hardly stepped on anyone's toes. He had a good head on his shoulders, too. But some suspected him of being a "schemer." There were times when the class would be racking its brain over a difficult arithmetic problem. Francis would find the solution long before the rest. But he would keep it to himself and not help the others find the solution. He wanted to show off the next day that he was the only one able to work out the problem. Joseph acted quite differently. He couldn't stand seeing anyone in need. He was always willing to help others, even when they took advantage of him. This cost him a great deal of time which he could have well used to his own advantage. Some began to just take for granted that he would help them whenever they needed it. What one of his classmates would say a year later was already true, "He especially gained the confidence of the less talented." One came to ask for help with Latin vocabulary, another sought advice about a composition.

20

Everyone seemed to assume that Joseph was there only for him, and his readiness to accommodate everyone strengthened their assumption. In spite of sacrificing so much of his time for the good of his fellow students, he remained first in his class. He was not a "schemer."

The fact that Joseph led his class at the end of the year was due to his earnest striving for the priestly ideal. It was not just an ethical motive that inspired him to want to do his best. His classmates sensed this and were glad that he had won the prize.

The Spiritual Director

Fall 1913. Summer vacation was over and a new first-year class, thirty-eight strong, moved into the Schoenstatt seminary. They soon knew their way around every nook and cranny of the house. Only one door still left them half curious, half puzzled. They slowly spelled out the words: "Conference Hall." Not far away they discovered a room which had a name that sounded just as mysterious: "Spiritual Director." No wonder the new students showed more excitement than usual when it was announced that the spiritual director would be giving a conference to the two lower classes that evening. Now, in a single stroke, they would finally discover the meaning of these two mysterious words.

When the first-year class arrived, the second-year boys were already in the conference hall making a terrible racket. Before classes things were entirely different; there was absolute silence then. A little surprised, the newcomers asked if they were permitted to talk. "No," was the answer, "but the spiritual director doesn't say anything." Would he report it to the superiors? "No danger. He keeps quiet. He never takes part in the meetings when the teachers discuss student behavior because he doesn't teach and he doesn't supervise a study hall either." They asked what his job was and received the reply, "He hears confessions every Friday and gives a weekly conference. In addition, students are free to go to him at any time, even after night prayer, in case they have important problems to discuss." One of them, who was repeating the first year, added with an important air, "For example, if you are homesick or have doubts in matters of faith." With that the conscience of the newcomers was formed and they joined in the ruckus.

The conferences were really something out of the ordinary. They dealt with the priestly vocation and self-education. But the approach

Joseph Engling in 1913.

was different from all other classes including religion. His predecessor had given spiritual talks in the customary manner with a three-point outline and piously edifying content. But the present spiritual director, Father Joseph Kentenich, approached the matter differently. With a few skillful questions he started a discussion. At times these became so lively that they developed into regular arguments. This gave the students a chance to express their opinions and be active rather than remain passive and listen all the time. The spiritual director made sure that something beneficial resulted from the debate. He also knew how to close every discussion with a very interesting story, and it always fit the conclusion of the discussion. In the course of time he even encouraged the boys to give little impromptu talks about the matters being discussed. It seemed a little too daring to most, but one had the courage to give it a try. It was little Arnold, a member of the second-year class. Later during World War I he was given a citation for bravery in face of the enemy. At this time, however, his courageous attempt hit a road block. While trying to sum up his statement, his mind went blank. The little fellow was rather embarrassed, but with some prompting the spiritual director helped him out of the tight spot.

During the conferences Joseph was in his element. The things he learned in the very first conferences about the beauty and dignity of the priesthood were already part of the deepest experiences of his soul. The spiritual director expressed thoughts and sentiments which had moved him since early childhood. He had the same feeling in the next conferences when the discussion was about persevering in one's vocation even when faced with the greatest difficulties. That touched on what he had gone through himself during the first year in Schoenstatt. Father Kentenich now read the story of "Boy, Stick It Out." A cabin boy was placed over a barrel and roughed up by the sailors again and again. During this rude treatment he gritted his teeth and recalled his captain's motto: "Boy, stick it out." He made this motto his own in every difficulty. It became the secret of his success. Joseph identified with this story. When he thought of his initial difficulties, when he considered the little incidents brought about by his speech defect and physical limitations, he could not help but think he was like the cabin boy. He, too, felt "taken over the barrel" at times and roughed up. In these conferences he learned to say as the captain did: "Boy, stick it out."

Joseph listened with more than the usual attention one day. The conference was about preparing for the priesthood while they were still young. This could best be done by working on their personality. A program was worked out for how each boy could educate himself. The conferences were now touching an unspoken drive which had long been tugging at Joseph's heart. He had felt it from early childhood and it was getting stronger as the years went by. By now it acted in him like a rough-hewn, inordinate force of nature. All this pent-up energy could at last be put to positive use.

The conferences dealt with delving into the mysterious land of one's soul. In this connection the spiritual director spoke about the "little angel" (the appetite of the intellect and will) and the "little animal" (the appetite of the senses and the emotions). The little angel makes itself felt in one's enthusiasm for all things great and beautiful, and in one's resolve to become a great person who accomplishes great things. The little animal, on the other hand, manifests itself in the life of the drives, so often disordered, and in the tendency to seek things pleasing to our senses, which gets us into all kinds of trouble. The two are engaged in a constant battle for supremacy. Whoever helps the little angel win will become a real man. Father Kentenich backed this up with examples from the lives of youthful saints and heroes. He also showed what happens when the little animal gets the upper hand. He read the tragic story of a boy who always yielded to his animal inclinations. He sank lower and lower until he became a sacrilegious thief. Joseph did not have to look long to find the little animal in himself. He had been aware of it for a long time already. It was his inclination to sudden anger. Somewhat later he found another character weakness—the tendency to brood and be moody.

When personally slighted, as when he was teased or given a cold shoulder, his temper was not likely to flare up. But he could very quickly reach the boiling point if his sense of justice was wounded or others intentionally interfered in some task he was eagerly performing. Of course there were enough wags who noticed this weakness in him. They practically made a sport of trying to get the otherwise so even-keeled Engling riled up. They were successful on more than one occasion. Wednesdays and Saturdays were cleaning days. The boys were assigned various tasks. Joseph, who liked working around the house, did his cleaning energetically and thoroughly. There wasn't work for all the boys, so there were always a few idle hands on the lookout for a good practical joke. Engling was considered an especially good target. One "accidentally" tripped over Joseph's bucket. Another made the mop mysteriously disappear. It went well for a while, but soon the "target" was angrily chasing the troublemakers down the hall with a wildly swinging

24

mop! This time the taunters were quick enough to make good their escape.

The Mud Fight

Another time the teasers weren't so lucky. On Thursdays work in the yard often replaced the afternoon hike. A big garden was being prepared and much loam soil (a mixture of clay and sand) had to be moved. Such earthwork was practically a treat for big Engling. He was glad to be able to put his muscles to use. His schoolmates were less enthusiastic. In such things some were downright lazy. Instead of working, they decided it would be more fun to make balls out of the moist earth and start a mudfight.

Most of their missles were aimed at Engling who was happily doing his job. They could hardly stifle their laughs when he suddenly turned, expecting to find the culprit. Every time he looked, he only saw innocent-looking faces and was thoroughly puzzled. All at once his patience snapped. With a quick motion he made a mudball. An instant later the mudball was dripping down the face of one of the main culprits who couldn't get out of the way.

The sudden rage sobered up his classmates quite a bit, but Joseph most of all. For days he was filled with deep remorse for such undisciplined behavior. It also came back to haunt him from time to time as his schoolmates were not inclined to let him forget it.

He could become angrier still if his sense of justice was injured. This was his Achilles' tendon. If it had not been for his innate sense of obedience and respect for authority, his temper would have burst out even in his dealings with superiors and teachers. Schoolmates observed on more than one occasion how he had to physically control himself to keep from doing something rash in the face of an injustice, real or imagined, from a teacher or superior. One day during the long recess, Joseph correctly asked for permission to do something. Father Prefect then forgot he had granted it and sharply scolded Joseph and some others for what they had permission to do. As further punishment they had to stand against a tree during the rest

25

of recess. Joseph felt so provoked by this injustice that he trembled with wrath and could barely control his anger. It was quite some time before he calmed down again.

Joseph could now see a wide-open door for his self-education. It was the battle to give his "little angel" the upper hand over his "little animal." Father Kentenich's conferences turned out to be a good instruction in how to do this. The spiritual director told about the use of special resolutions called the "particular examination." He explained it like a battle, quoting a famous poem in which a certain "Marshall Forward" declares:

"Where is Paris?"
"Paris is here!"
"Then go to work. Let's take Paris!"

Joseph directed his first attempts to apply this "military wisdom" to conquering his sudden fits of anger. He certainly had enough opportunities, given the rascally schoolmates who could not resist tempting Engling's fury. At the time Joseph hardly realized how important the particular examination would later be in his striving for sanctity. And no one could have guessed that these first halting steps would eventually develop into a level of mastery of self-education worthy of any great general in history.

A somewhat provocative topic in the conferences was the debate about the "mass-man." When this characteristic was discussed, it hit a raw nerve in everyday life. Exposed were those who followed the rules of the house or went to Holy Communion only when and because their superiors and schoolmates were watching. Those just "going with the flow"—howling with the wolves but never having an opinion of their own—were taken to task. The discussion was summed up in the sentence:

"The mass-man is someone who does what others do because they do it."

They concluded that the educational task they needed to work on was this: How can I use the rules of the house and our life in the seminary for my self-education? Joseph took the suggestions they worked out very seriously. Together with a close friend he even went a step further. They wrote down on a piece of paper the important exercises of their daily routine. In a written control they checked how they kept them. For an omission or carelessly kept act they imposed some small penance on each other.

The story of the "whipping boy" had a similar effect on the discussion. In one of his talks the spiritual director told about a method once used to educate the royal princes of the French court. If the prince misbehaved, he was not beaten. After all, he was the prince! Instead, a whipping boy was beaten while the prince looked on. Seeing the innocent boy punished was meant to deter the prince from committing his fault again. When the boys heard this, they could hardly control their indignation. "What an injustice!" they burst out. But the wind was soon taken out of their sails when the spiritual director convincingly showed them that they all not only had one whipping boy, but more than they could count. Everyone who suffered under their character weaknesses was a whipping boy. Someone else was constantly paying the price for their shortcomings. Now was the time to start working on brotherly love. The lessons that Joseph learned in these discussions corresponded to some of the strongest tendencies of his own heart. It was always alert, kind, and filled with the urge to lend a helping hand to anyone in need. A year later this trait would develop into the great ideal that shone out over his life: "To be all things to all men."

In this way the conferences touched on all the aspects of daily life: prayer, Communion, confession, Marian devotion, etc. All of them had some impact on Joseph. This is attested to by his diary entries in years to come. There we often find expressions, resolutions, examples and other lessons which go back to these conferences. How much he had absorbed them and applied them to his life is shown in a particular episode.

In the last conference before Easter the spiritual director had a surprising suggestion. He asked if the first- and second-year boys would be willing to write an essay during Easter vacation about what they had learned in the conferences. Of course, all were willing to do it just because it was not mandatory. Besides, the discussions had been most interesting and the stories had been great fun. Their topic was: "How do I receive and foster the grace of my vocation?"

When they finally took pen in hand and faced the blank sheet of paper, though, many were at a sudden loss. What had Father really talked about? The examples and stories he told were freshest in their minds, but it hardly seemed appropriate to just write down stories. What else had he said? Oh, it was so long ago! Surely he couldn't expect them to write all that! One of the more inventive ones found his way out by remembering a pious book his aunt had given him when he joined the minor seminary. It contained lots of good ideas on the subject. They were not exactly what Father had presented but they were somewhat similar and that was good enough. So the forgotten book was dug out from the bottom of his desk, dusted off, and put to work. He copied from it extensively and was soon finished. At least it sounded pious. He signed his name and added a decorative flourish and said to himself, "Hans Ritten, you have done a fine job again!"

Others did not have such bright ideas. They tried to recall what the spiritual director had said and, not finding very much, simply made use of thoughts they had heard in their religion classes and mixed them up with pious exhortations learned from their good parents. This gave them an inexhaustible source of material to write about. That some of what they wrote was scarcely identifiable as coming from the conferences was a minor detail soon overlooked in their enthusiasm to write the essay. Wasn't the main thing that it sounded pious? That was certainly the main thing Father would be looking for in such a report!

When the spiritual director read what the youngsters had written, he could not help but smile. Had he really taught all these things? There were certainly some who had to be admired for having a fertile imagination! Others had been more sparing with their words but only managed disconnected fragments of the discussions. But when he came to Joseph Engling's composition, he could not help but be impressed. It was a brief, concise, and for the most part all-encompassing summary of everything they had covered. There were no repetitions, no wordy digressions, no products of his own imagination. Every sentence brought a new essential thought, even though the discussions had sometimes drifted to trivial and second-ary matters. Joseph's paper was without any doubt the best of all. Father began to ponder the possible reasons for it. Was the sixteen-year-old gifted with such an extraordinary memory that he could faithfully recount the entire subject matter of the year? No teacher, however, had yet discovered traces of such an extraordinary memory. He asked himself further if an extraordinarily bright mind had enabled him to always grasp the essential points and reproduce them correctly. This was not a satisfactory explanation. Engling was considered a good student, but by no means a genius. His judgment was sound, as his answers during the conferences indicated, but not one to match Hans (a new classmate since the beginning of the second year) in intelligence. And while Wormer had produced a good paper, it was considerably inferior to Engling's. The reasons why Joseph had written the best essay were not to be found in his talents. The spiritual director realized that the reason lay elsewhere.

The rapt attention and thirst for knowledge that Joseph brought to his regular classes was even greater during the conferences. This quiet thinker would thoroughly consider what he heard and independently work them out. They became his own personal conviction. Even more important was the fact that he immediately set out to seriously and persistently realize them in practical daily life. What he heard in the conferences did not remain sterile doctrine, merely stored in his mind or learned by heart. It immediately became honest-to-goodness lived experience. The program of the conferences practically became the program of his soul's history. That he was able to so perfectly reconstruct the contents of the conferences was certainly in part due to his mature judgment, but even more so because he only had to consult the development of his own spiritual life. The thoughts he wrote in his essay were not just learned but lived! Such thoughts could not easily be forgotten.

That year's conferences also resulted in something else of major significance. In the course of time the spiritual director increasingly became the man of his confidence. How quickly Father could win over the youthful hearts! And how delicately he knew how to interpret the dark, ill-ordered urgings the boys wrestled with in their souls! Joseph also immediately sensed the fatherly kindness which Father Kentenich showed him during his weekly confession, and how he helped him find the right next step in his self-education. In the process, his East Prussian soul with its natural reserve dared to open itself up and place its entire trust in the spiritual director. From then on he followed the thoughts and suggestions of his spiritual director with a readiness that seemed to know no bounds, and he made them the object of his love.

Under Father Kentenich's direction, he grew up to be the champion of a great cause. His first two years in Schoenstatt had sowed vital seeds for his future growth.

Class Prefect

The seminarians were eating supper. No sooner had the reader finished the usual Scripture reading when Father Prefect rang the bell. As if with a single stroke, the rattling of knives and forks abruptly stopped and, just as abruptly, 180 boys looked up. No doubt there was a special announcement. Father Prefect had a piece of paper in his hand. He read off a list of names. It was plain that they all belonged to the second-year class. Hesitating, they stood up. Some of them suddenly blushed. Almost all of them dropped their heads in embarrassment and stared at the floor. In a flash the whole student body began to suspect, "They must have done something wrong!" Even the class prefect was among the culprits. What had happened? Soon Father Prefect answered their unspoken question, "At the recent class excursion to the Marksburg[2], these boys went off by themselves without permission, secretly purchased cigarettes and smoked them." The rest of the boys did not know whether to be serious or to laugh. So young and already craving for tobacco! Even little Albert, one of the smallest in the school, had joined the prank. Their punishment was meted out at once. They had to "kneel one out," as it was called. They had to kneel next to the piano near the priests' table for nearly the whole meal while the others enjoyed their supper. This was the standard punishment for more serious infractions of the rules. Seminary slang dubbed this dreaded fate with a meek-sounding euphemism. It was called "playing at the piano."

The occurrences of the evening had another repercussion on the second-year class. The class prefect who had so shamefully neglected his duties was relieved of his office. Who would be his

[2] A famous castle along the Rhine River near Schoenstatt.

successor? There were two main candidates: Joseph Engling and Hans Wormer. Hans had joined the class only at the beginning of the school year. Because of his extraordinary talents and outstanding character, he quickly earned a place of high respect in the class. At the close of the school year he would wrest the rank of "primus" from Joseph. Nevertheless, the choice of the superiors fell on Engling. Future events bore out the wisdom of this choice.

As class prefect, Joseph's "perch" was at the teacher's desk during study halls. From there he could best keep an eye on his charges. His first duty was to maintain order and silence during study hall. Since the beginning of this school year, the class had shown signs of genuine improvement. This was chiefly due to the influence of the new homeroom teacher, a man who finally knew how to handle the class. Eagerness to study increased and class performance visibly improved. Joseph lent his whole-hearted support to the efforts of the homeroom teacher.

Silence in Study Hall

In spite of the improved attitude of study, the new class prefect still saw a major flaw: Too many questions were being asked in study hall. These whispered questions created a constant restlessness which made it hard to concentrate. Many questioners came to the prefect. Engling's readiness to help was thoroughly taken advantage of. If this restlessness were to be overcome, he, the prefect, would have to take the first step. He first tried putting off the questioners until the break. But this was doomed to failure. Finally he had to apply more radical means. Instead of answering the question he made a little sign of the cross on his lips to say that silence must be observed during study hall.

Some laughed, others made sarcastic remarks, still others grew angry and growled at him. They did not succeed, however, in changing his mind; he stuck to his little crosses. Like-minded classmates soon noticed that Joseph was swimming against the stream. They had the courage to support his policy. Soon a regular movement developed which insisted on unconditional silence in the study hall. Not immediately, but in the course of time, they attained the end for which they were striving. Behind it was the tenacious and unyielding will of the class prefect.

As prefect however, Joseph believed that he should not restrict his endeavors to merely keeping order and silence in the study hall. He wanted much more, namely to form his class's attitude and their striving for the priestly ideal. There he admittedly faced quite a difficult challenge. To reach this goal, more than anything else he would have to win the hearts and confidence of the majority of his classmates. It was true that he was already respected by them but this alone would notd move the majority to an increased and enthusiastic striving for the priestly ideal. How should he proceed?

When he looked around him, he saw that some of his classmates had ways of exerting a sustained influence on the others. One of his classmates knew how to impress others by his polished appearance. He attracted a whole following that put great stock in his words. Joseph did not want to imitate his way. Such an attempt would have been doomed to failure because of his stiff, rustic manners. It would also have been against his innermost nature to impress others by his exterior bearing. Again he saw others in the class who were admired because of their clever words. One classmate with an extraordinary imagination attracted many friends by telling Karl May's famous cowboy stories. Joseph could not follow this course either. He was a slow East Prussian with a clumsy tongue. In his quest to win over the class he could not throw the power of the spoken work in the scales. His sound judgment told him that he could not put on the armor of others if he wanted to fight for his ideals. He had to be true to himself and use whatever talents and powers God had given him.

Joseph therefore remained the plain country boy. He was the son of ordinary parents and would not have it any other way. He kept himself neat and clean. He did not get angry when others teased him about his old-fashioned pants. Nor did he go along with things just because others were doing them. An example was how the boys wore their school caps. They liked to remove the wire that gave the cap its stiffness and bend the cap into a different look. Then they cocked it over their right ear. It was supposed to imitate the "up-to-date" look of high school boys outside Schoenstatt. Joseph did not go for this at all. He did not consider himself an "up-to-date" man of the street and did not want to look like one. When he got a new cap, he first thought of his parents back home. On their next bill would be an additional 2.50 Marks. He thought of how long his father would have to work and how his mother carefully pinched every penny. As a result, he treated his cap with great respect. He wore it straight like the cap of a train conductor. Some laughed at him and thought he was old-fashioned and unprogressive. There were even some who were ashamed to walk with him on the hikes because of it. Joseph let it be and didn't himself be swayed just by what people thought.

As a matter of fact, Joseph's loyalty to self gave him a hidden advantage. While his classmates did not think much about why they liked him as their leader, they all clearly sensed that Engling was always genuine. He did not push himself into the limelight or try to make himself important. When he now became the champion of an ideal spirit, they took him seriously. And when he had to scold some little ruffian, the latter listened without protest. They might make fun of Joseph's stiff gestures, but they attached great value to his words. Little episodes document this.

On special occasions the school orchestra performed in the dining room. Joseph often took part playing the bass violin. After a lot of practice he became quite good at it. The youngest ones in the house always thought it was a funny sight to see Joseph playing his instrument. He was so taken up with the music that his whole body seemed to become part of the act. He vigorously tapped his foot, his head went up and down, his lips counted the rhythm and the upper part of his body rocked back and forth. The little fellows poked one another in the ribs and slid on the benches for sheer pleasure. When a piece was finished, they gave an uproarious applause. The breast of many an orchestra member swelled with pride to hear such enthusiastic approval from the youthful audience. They never guessed that it was directed at one player in particular—Engling and his "bass fiddle." Especially little Kiefer was enthusiastic for days afterward. On one of the next hikes, Kiefer trotted alongside the class prefect. Joseph gave him a fatherly admonition because he had talked so much during study hall.

Another time a different mischief-maker, with a similar appetite for teasing his class prefect, was sitting next to Joseph during the evening break in the gymnasium. Joseph duly scolded him for jumping over the beds. Especially in the dormitory all mischief was forbidden. The guilty took their scoldings from Engling without contradiction. This would not have been the same with others. If the scolding had come from someone else, he would have been branded a fault-finding and nagger. Joseph simply had an authority that the others accepted.

Besides his simplicity and genuineness of character, Joseph had another trait which made his efforts successful with his classmates. It was his sincere and faithful kindness. The office of prefect sometimes meant extra work which took a lot of time. He was in charge of fetching the needed classroom materials, of distributing paper, pens, ink, etc. in class, and was the liaison between the teachers and the class. He performed these and similar tasks with an undying and upbeat enthusiasm. Those who had to struggle with difficulties in their studies became especially devoted to him. During the recesses or walks they came to him. At such times he reviewed the irregular Latin verbs with them or explained certain rules of grammar. No one was ever refused when the busy prefect was asked for anything.

What his classmates valued most was his patience with the character fault of others. When others were criticized in his presence he remained silent or said a kind word excusing the individual. In his discrete reserve he went so far that, when conversing with his fellow students, he hardly ever used any nicknames, although they were in vogue and his class had been very liberal in bestowing them. Joseph was neither narrow-minded nor scrupulous in this habit; rather he was genuinely concerned that such names might offend or hurt his classmates. When he was the target of laughter, he was generally quite tolerant. They could give him a hard time, but he mostly ignored it with a good-natured smile. Often, when it helped to pass the time pleasantly, he even laughed with them. He was an unusual blend. Outwardly he was a man of strong build, heavy fists, and jutting bony features. Inwardly he was a man of tender feelings and of motherly kindness. Bodily strength was given him to help and not to hurt others. He was often teased by those around him, and yet he stood in their midst as an accepted authority.

Joseph and Sports

In the course of the year the second-year class earned the reputation of being good sportsmen. Whenever there was a game between the classes, they put together a formidable team. This had not always been the case. It was not so long ago that they had been the proponents of the "wild west." The prefect had taken a decisive part in this change for the better and now he enjoyed the victories it brought. He liked games requiring physical exertion. This was so much in line with his nature that he could hardly stand being without a game during the recess periods. Handball, hunter ball, baseball, and "baste the bear" (or "prisoner's base") were his favorites. In those days soccer was still unknown. Joseph let neither wind nor weather stop him from starting a game. He went around trying to organize a team until he had enough players. He could be so captivated by a game that he forgot everything else. Outwardly, his moves were not those of a polished athlete. When he lumbered down the playing field, the ground trembled under his feet. His friends teased, "No grass grows in his footsteps!" They called his big shoes "beetle-crushers" and "clod-hoppers." Others, who wanted to describe his distinctive run, shouted, "Engling, you trapper!"

Given his indomitable spirit, he inevitably had success in games. Whenever his class played for a championship, he was on the team. As a runner he was untiring; he kept on going even when the more adept players had to catch their breath or began to tire. In open-field games he was even called to lead the charge. On more than one occasion he proved himself a smart but innovative player. Their awakening interest in games influenced the class' turn for the better more than they realized at the time. It cleared the air and gave their excess energy a field in which they could use it to their advantage. The reputation of being one of the good players increased Joseph's prestige. Somehow his classmates felt that their prefect represented a piety free from any stuffy or "sissy" overtones.

In those days, thanks to the efforts of the homeroom teacher and the exemplary prefect, the second-year class enjoyed some of its best times.

3. A Year of Sowing

The War Breaks Out

Joseph Engling's second year at the seminary in Schoenstatt was drawing to a close. During the last week of July 1914, the week before the students returned home, everyone had vacation fever. No sooner did a class finish when it was solemnly crossed out on the big schedule. The choir director was already practicing the songs for the closing ceremonies. Again and again the words of the well-known hymn rang through the halls:

> "Gentle Concord, Heavenly Peace,
> Hover ever friendly o'er this place.
> Never may that day be dawning
> With the lords of battle swarming."

This passage from Schiller's "Song of the Bell" was fresh in the boys' minds. If they had only known how quickly these strains of peace would turn to refrains of war! Neither teachers nor students could foresee the dramatic exit the school year would make.

One morning the first class period was suddenly interrupted. By order of the rector all students were immediately assembled in the dining room. Surprise was plainly written on the students' faces, and they wondered what had happened. When the rector appeared, he looked more serious than he had ever looked before. The students listened breathlessly as they heard for the first time about the most recent events in the political life of the nations. "There is grave danger that a great war will break out," the rector explained. "The order of mobilization can be expected at any moment. All students must get home before the railroads are closed to civilian transport." All would have to pack their belongings at once and leave for home on the next train. Not only that. If war did break out, the seminary would become a hospital for wounded soldiers. Students would have to wait for later notification about when and where classes would resume.

Indescribable excitement broke out following the announcement. In moments boys were racing through the corridors to their bedrooms and lockers to pack everything for the summer. As soon as they had packed, they left the school that had become so dear to

36

them. The younger ones looked up with wonder at the upperclassmen who would soon be wearing the Kaiser's uniform and going to war. As they shook hands in farewell, the older students, soon to be drafted, said in deathly earnest: "Who knows if we will meet again?" The same night Joseph and some of his fellow students boarded a train for East Prussia.

What followed was a period of great agitation. Right after the outbreak of hostilities, the legendary "Russian Steamroller" began its march toward the German border. Two Russian armies invaded East Prussia, forcing back the weak German border guard. The vanguard of the Russians soon reached the immediate vicinity of the Engling home. On Sunday, August 23, the pastor of Prossitten announced that the Russians were coming. They were pillaging the villages and towns, killing the inhabitants and burning homes. He advised them to be ready to evacuate the village, since a battle in the vicinity was likely. The military authority ordered all men ages seventeen and eighteen to report to Heilsberg to enlist. All the cattle had to be driven farther inland, away from the invading enemy. The pastor declared that he would remain at his post as long as any of his parishioners were left. Joseph became his right-hand man and helped him however he could. They placed the most important and valuable church utensils in a safe hiding-place. One little incident angered Joseph very much. He noticed that the first person to leave the village was a local official whose responsibility would have been to help the rest. Justly indignant, Joseph considered him a coward.

In the meantime, Field Marshall von Hindenburg advanced with his army to turn back the invading Russians. German troops marched through Prossitten all day long. Joseph was much occupied with supplying drinking water to the soldiers, who were thirsty and ex-hausted from the forced marches. In his great eagerness to help, he even gave away the last apples he could find in the house. On August 26, the booming of cannons could be heard to the south. The historic battle of Tannenberg had begun. The people of Prossitten anxiously awaited its outcome. In the evening the skies were reddened by the glow of burning villages. It marked the destruction and retreat of the Russian Narew Army. The very next day Joseph hastened to the site of the battle—villages only some ten kilometers distant. He saw great numbers of captured Russians. For the first time he also saw the devastation of modern warfare.

The victory at Tannenberg did not yet mean the Russian armies were repelled. From the northeast a second mighty army was moving across the border. Soon its approach was noticed in Prossitten. Again they heard the roaring of cannons in the distance. Toward the end of August a first Russian patrol appeared in the woods near the village. There was a brief skirmish with some German patrols on horseback. Those that were still in the village were anxious about what would happen next. At the same time a rumor began to circulate that the Russians were taking all young men and carrying them off as prisoners. This caused great anxiety. Joseph's mother feared for her sons. At her urging Joseph remained hidden, but only for half a day. During the night he was again one of the guards whose duty was to alarm the villagers in the event of the enemy's approach. On Sunday he attended Mass with only a handful of people. After days of high nervous tension came signs of a change for the better. Once more German troops marched through Prossitten. In early September von Hindenburg fought the battle of Masurian Lakes. As a result, East Prussia was definitively freed from the invaders for the coming winter.

The exciting weeks had shown Joseph to be a brave and courageous young man. In the midst of the general confusion he remained calm. He stepped in resolutely whenever the passing troops needed a helping hand. He even found time to keep a little diary. There he wrote in brief words the important events of those days. Judging from later remarks, the impressions of these events remained with him for a long time. He gratefully remembered the good soldiers who fought to protect his home from the enemy.

In the meantime September passed and with it the normal date for the end of vacation. Joseph's thoughts went longingly to Schoenstatt, but it was not until late October that he finally received the summons to return. How many things had changed in Schoenstatt! Two-hundred to two-hundred-fifty wounded soldiers were in the seminary building on the bluff. In every classroom, in the gym, in every available room there were long rows of beds. The students asked themselves how a regular seminary life could go on. The superiors, however, had an answer and made provisions accordingly. In the valley below, in the one part of the ancient Schoenstatt convent still standing—usually called the "Old House"—a provisional home had been prepared for the students. Of course, it could not be compared to the "New House" on the hill. Until recently the Old House had been used for workshops. Now provisions were hurriedly made for dormitories and classrooms. The general opinion was that the war would end within a quarter of a year. They estimated that for this short time the students would have to be satisfied with the makeshift quarters.

It did not take the new occupants of the Old House long to find out how makeshift it was. Without a good coat of paint the walls looked rather gloomy. This impression was heightened by the bad repair of the floors, doors and windows. And how unpleasant it would be in the winter without steam radiators like in the new building! The makeshift character was especially evident in the dormitories. There long rows of straw mattresses were laid in close succession on the otherwise bare floor. The wash basins were at the end of the hallway on the third floor. The straw mattresses became favorite nesting places for mice and the boys knew the damp basement was not free of rats. For chapel services and meals they had to walk up to the new building. Not less than four times a day they had to walk up the hill. "Well, it is war," was the brief and simple explanation which helped them to adjust to the new conditions and hardships. Here in the second half of October 1914, the school year began for about eighty to one-hundred students.

A Memorable Day

Among the astonishing changes in the Schoenstatt Valley was one that especially caught the attention of the boys. It concerned the chapel of St. Michael located just a few steps away from the Old House. This chapel had a long history of its own. It was once the cemetery chapel of the Augustinian nuns who founded the cloister in the 13th century. In later years it experienced the same travails as the cloister. Most recently, it had been just plain ignored. Many years had passed since its last Mass. It is doubtful that the rickety, old altar would have stood up to a Mass. For all practical purposes, the former cemetery chapel had become a tool shed. A few old pews were stored there along with the garden equipment used to maintain the surrounding shrubs and lawns. There was even a garden roller there. Just the year before a few rascally underclassmen had conducted some "experiments" with the unprotected electrical wiring in the chapel. Several short circuits resulted and, to the dismay of Father Prefect, burned out the fuses in the adjacent Old House. But during the last vacation the chapel of St. Michael began to look like a church again. The water-seepage under the floor was stopped and the floor replaced, the altar was repaired, and the ceiling of the apse was painted sky-blue. But what was the newly restored chapel for? The house chapel in the New House was still used for the seminary's daily Mass. Here the upperclassmen were better informed. The chapel was going to house the religious gatherings of the Marian Sodality. The Marian Sodality! These words had caused such an uproar among the upperclassmen just the year before! It would soon affect the other classes as well.

The Marian Sodality was a relatively new innovation in the upper grades. It had just been founded in the spring on April 19, 1914. By then it had quite an agitated history. The instigator was none other than Father Spiritual Director. The basis of his whole work with youth was the simple principle that personal initiative in one's own character formation is the best way to a self-reliant personality. It was precisely this self-reliance that priestly life would later demand. His conferences on self-education had been received by his youthful charges with enthusiasm. Now he had to secure the fruits of this labor and give the activity of self-formation a permanent form. The Sodality of our Blessed Lady seemed to be the most suitable way to reach this goal.

When the spiritual director presented his plans to the boys there was an immediate difference of opinions. Many of them had a very unflattering image of the sodality. They thought of it as an organization which was basically old-fashioned and stagnant, coated with a little flowery piety. They had seen more than enough of such caricatures of the sodality in their home parishes. The boys heatedly discussed the pros and cons of the sodality, and genuine debates ensued over the issue. This was exactly what the spiritual director wanted. The founding of the sodality was not to be ordered by a decision from on high, nor was it to be tossed into their laps as a free gift. It had to be the fruit of their own hard work. They were to express their ideas and to clarify them in discussions until they became convinced that the sodality should be introduced. It should become their work. This was reenforced by the structure of the sodality itself. It was a free realm which the boys could govern by freely chosen leaders and shape according to their own plans. No one was forced to belong to the sodality; it was the individual's free choice. Teachers and superiors alike expressed serious misgivings about such a new-fangled approach which gave students so much room for free initiative. They opposed it. Despite the opposi-tion, the discussion ended with the successful official establishment of a Marian Sodality in Schoenstatt on Low Sunday (the Sunday after Easter), 1914.

Only scanty information about the events preceding the founding of the Sodality of the Blessed Virgin Mary trickled down to the lower classes. The upperclassmen who founded the sodality felt so strongly that it was their work that they wanted its founding to be celebrated solely among themselves. They zealously guarded the doors of the house chapel to keep out any unauthorized guests. In spite of this precaution one—and only one—underclassman suc-ceeded in slipping in. It was Joseph Engling. He could sense when something was afoot involving greatness and ideals. Not incor-rectly, he also sensed the hand of the spiritual director behind this new founding. This was reason enough for him and his friends to be interested.

A similar thing happened at the beginning of the 1914-15 school year. When underclassmen learned that the recently renovated chapel was for the sodality, they tried to penetrate the cloak of secrecy surrounding it! On October 18, 1914, the first Sunday after the students' return from the long summer vacation, the first "ecclesial" meeting of the Marian Sodality was scheduled to be held in the chapel. On this day the seminary celebrated the feast of Mary as *Mater Puritatis*, the Mother of Purity. It was the patronal feastday of the house. Here was a chance to get behind the secret and learn what the sodality was really all about and what its plans were concerning the little chapel. But the sodalists wanted to keep unauthorized guests away and shut the door right in front of their noses. Not admitted to the chapel, they crowded next to the window and listened attentively to what was going on inside.

Within the chapel an event of great importance was taking place, the full import of which would only become clear with the passing of the years. The spiritual director gave a talk which would later come to be known in the history of the Schoenstatt Movement as the *Founding Document.* In the talk he proposed a daring plan to the boys. His starting point was a little practice which he had suggested some weeks before and had met with a favorable reaction. It consisted of the sodalists showing their love for Mary by especially giving her—as a free sacrifice—all their prayers, work, and sufferings in fulfilling their daily duties and in their self-education. Through her intercession Mary would transform these gifts into a shower of graces for the spread of God's kingdom here on earth. In the language of the boys this practice would later be called "contributions to Our Lady's capital of grace." The aim of the spiritual director's grand plan was to draw this practice into intimate connection with the little chapel. Through their prayers and sacrifices the students would storm the Blessed Mother to set up her throne of grace, as she had in so many other pilgrimages places, in their little chapel in Schoenstatt. In this way her mediation of graces would be connected to this place in a special way. Towards this end they would place at her disposal as large a "capital" of grace as possible (through their sacrifices, etc.) so that she could bless them abundantly in this very place. So it was that through the grace of the Blessed Mother and through their cooperation, the chapel would truly be transformed into a spiritual home for the sodalist family and into the focal point of its life and work. It remained for the future history of the sodality to verify whether Mary had truly accepted this offer.

The hearts of the young listeners were immediately set afire for the proposed plan. None of them probably had the slightest idea that they were experiencing a great moment in history.

Joseph was not present on October 18, 1914. In the makeshift conditions of that fall, the upper classes began school two weeks earlier than the lower classes. Joseph and his class returned only about two weeks after the memorable event. Here and there he learned about its content, perhaps even from Father Kentenich. For him the plan was summed up by the idea of "contributions to the capital of grace." After all, he had a natural talent for taking the ideas and teachings that captivated his heart and translating them into everyday life.

"I Want to Become a Saint"

Joseph Engling was sixteen going on seventeen and beginning his third year at Schoenstatt. It would be a crucial year, and one influenced by his growth in a group he did not yet belong to—the Marian Sodality.

The echoes of the important meeting of the Marian Sodality of October 18 were fading. In the everyday life of the older students who belonged to the sodality it seemed to have left almost no traces. Their enthusiasm for the grand plan of the spiritual director soon gave way to more sober sentiments. In fact, for a while the plan hardly seemed to leave a ripple in the public awareness of the sodality family. It seemed totally forgotten. But this was not the case. What was happening was like a seed in the ground. It must first rest in the protecting folds of the soil. There, unseen by anyone, it silently germinates and unfolds its vitality. Its life and vigor can only be detected when it reaches a later stage of maturity.

Meanwhile, the regular routine of everyday life and studies engrossed the new inhabitants in the Old House. As before, they sat behind their books and studied. They tried to get accustomed to the uncomfortable conditions of the Old House and hoped for a quick end to the war. The attention of the boys was totally absorbed by the gigantic events of the war, with its communiques and reports from the battlefields. There hardly seemed to be room to think about or experience anything else, including October 18.

Interestingly enough, the proposed plan played no noteworthy role in the subsequent conferences of the spiritual director. In the middle classes—third and fourth year—he turned to an entirely new topic, and spoke about a subject which really moved their young hearts: the momentous struggle between the nations. The world war was given a deeper meaning. It marked the onset of a gigantic and decisive struggle between divided ways of thinking. It was ultimately a battle between the kingdom of God on earth and the evil forces of darkness paired with our aroused passions. Then he described what this means for the Church's youth. With daring synthesis he summed it up in the simple assertion: "Our time needs saints." He did not mean this as a pious platitude. He meant it in all earnestness. They needed to become real saints as Holy Mother Church had always understood the term. He reminded them of so many of the Church's canonized saints.

The spiritual director's motto caught his young listeners off guard. As long as he had interpreted the conditions of the time they had readily followed along. But now many felt they had to contradict this sudden and extraordinary conclusion. Yes, they wanted to become true boys, every inch men and ideal priests. But saints? That was going too far! How could he think such a thing? He was usually such a sensible man. Last year his conferences were so different. He had stirred their youthful hearts for the priestly ideal. But now they were to suddenly become saints?

Joseph's friend Karl Klement best described what went on in the hearts and minds of many of the boys. He had an old copy of the "Lives of the Saints" he had once borrowed from his godparents. The yellowing pages of the venerable book told him all he needed to know about what a saint was and how he looked. His imagination painted a picture that he described this way:

"When I heard the word 'saint' I always thought of a deeply serious, fearsome figure with a hair shirt and a guant face, protruding cheekbones, and sunken eyes. In his left hand was usually a crucifix, in the other a terrible whip."

Others associated similar images when they heard the word saint.' They felt that this ideal meant they had to practice an outdated and unhealthy piety. Would that not make them fanatics living life without excitement or joy? This could hardly be what their spiritual director wanted! Or was he perhaps using the same strategy he had followed to establish the sodality? At that time the mere words "Marian Sodality" had a similar effect. But in a short time the new ideal had won over their hearts because, in the course of his

44

instructions, he gave the word an entirely new meaning.

The spiritual director stuck to his motto no matter what. The detractors had to admit that they had overlooked something he had been saying. Father Kentenich was not just talking about "saints" but "saints needed for our times." He now presented an ideal which everyone ultimately agreed on. A saint was defined as the summation of all greatness and strength, as the outstanding God-filled person. Not extraordinary gifts—like visions, ecstasies, miracles, or even extraordinary penances—make the saint, but a heroic love of God which proves itself in the little things of everyday life. The idea of a saint was clarified and exemplified in the person of St. Francis de Sales. In his person he united godliness and ethical nobility, the wonderful education of a scholar and the spirited determination of an apostle, an unyielding character and an extremely kind and winning personality.

The conferences dealing with the ideal of holiness made an extraordinary impression on Joseph. They unleashed something in him that could be compared to the cascades of a high mountain stream. How long he had already felt an indomitable energy and longing in his breast! Only superhuman accomplishments could give him peace, he thought. Now he knew his great life's task. It was not only the priesthood that now stood before him as his life's goal. He must be a priest who is a modern saint! During these days he made a decision he never took back:

"I want to become a saint."

Such a resolution may not seem too out-of-the-ordinary. Which true Catholic boy, having been shown the pinnacle of greatness and strength in the ideal of sanctity, would not say the same? How many have not made the same resolution in a moment of youthful enthusiasm or devotional exultation? In Joseph's case, however, it was truly a moment of decision, for from this day forward his resolve to strive heroically for the ideal of sanctity formed his entire life. It would never perish from his soul. Its effect was not that of a pious daydream. It took deep root in his strong masculine will, and not even the most severe tests of later army life could break it.

Friends in the Cause of Sanctity

In this series of conferences there was one which impressed Joseph most profoundly. It was held around Christmas 1914. He was so enthused that he wanted to share his excitement with someone who felt it too. But who? What took place in his soul was so tender and sacred that a modest reserve urged him to silence. He could at least try to speak with his friend Karl Klement.

He started with a broad question, cautiously trying to find the right approach: "Say, how did you like the conference?" he inquired. In the meantime Karl had been completely cured of his preconceived notion of a saint. The conferences had deeply impressed him. So now both met on the basis of the same conviction. It did not take long for them to agree to make a kind of covenant. They would help each other in this battle for the high ideal. They would support one another, admonish one another, point out each other's character faults, and remind each other again and again of the great ideal they had in common.

Joseph remained faithful to this agreement as long as he lived, even keeping it in the agitated life of the front lines.

In the ensuing conferences, the spiritual director saw to it that the growing enthusiasm for the ideal of the modern saint did not end in empty dreams. He dealt extensively with the question: What does the spiritual development of such a saint look like? It became clear to them that it was not born of a desire for the extraordinary, for the conspicuous, or the strange. Rather, saints are formed in the middle of the working day. A sentence was used which became a frequently repeated watchword: A saint is someone who faithfully fulfills his daily duties! Sometimes it was described with the words *ordinaria extraordinarie*—to do the ordinary things extraordinarily well. The latter version became so much a part of Joseph's vocabulary that we find him using it again and again until the end of his life.

Moreover, for Joseph a happy circumstance helped turn the ideal of sanctity in little things into an impressive experience. It happened this way. At about this time the common spiritual reading in his class was the biography of a young Jesuit student from Croatia, Peter

Barbaric. It was Joseph's duty as prefect to read the book out loud. Whenever he read publicly there were always a few rascals who made sport of it. Because of his heavy tongue he would stumble over difficult phrases. Such embarrassing stumbles always seemed funny and entertaining to them.

But with this book something else caught their attention. They noticed how he read with more enthusiasm than normal. It was plain from the excited tone of his voice. Many a drowsy fellow looked up with amazement and observed the prefect with surprise. What was the matter with him? The things he read were ordinary occurrences. They were nothing to get excited about. In fact, they considered it out of line to be too enthusiastic about reading. They wanted to hear the thoughts of the book, not the feelings of the reader. This was not the case this time. Without knowing why, there was something in Joseph's fascination which commanded their respect. Then another thing happened. When Joseph finished the book, he read the table of contents and began to sum up the contents of the different chapters with remarks of his own. "Does our prefect want to repeat the whole book in his own words?" the surprised listeners asked themselves. The young Croatian seems to have been a big deal for Joseph. Some were tempted to tease him about it. But in the end they let him be and accepted his fatherly counsels without contradiction. When the true-hearted and well-intentioned Engling discharged his duties in this way they had enough brotherly love to know not to tease him. For some weeks, though, he had another nickname—Peter Barbaric—and when they said it, the more clever ones could even imitate Joseph's voice with surprising accuracy!

But why did this book have such a big impact on Joseph? Peter Barbaric's life was not marked by strange and out-of-the-ordinary events. It was a different trait that set him apart: He mastered everyday life. He mastered prayer and the interior life, the duties of his vocation, his dealings with others, the unavoidable burdens of life on this earth—in short, the sum total of daily life in all its detail. And he did so with remarkable faithfulness. Here was the reason his example was so attractive to Joseph. In him Joseph suddenly found an example of precisely what he had been seeking for weeks and which, at times, had left his soul very restless. No wonder this biography retained a special place in his heart. He would still refer to it now and then in years to come. From now on his life stood under the sign of this specific ideal of modern sanctity: the everyday saint and hero of perfect faithfulness in little things.

Other little experiences helped Joseph's newly discovered ideal to take deep root in his soul. There was his habit of immediately applying what he learned to his everyday life. He had done it the previous year during the conferences about the ideal of priesthood. These lessons became such a part of his heart and mind for the simple reason that he earnestly tried to put them into practice. It was in the tedium of everyday life that he first realized what these lessons were really about. This time, too, he faithfully used the same approach. The uncomfortable conditions of the Old House, daily duties, the constant close contact with his peers—all of this offered a cornucopia of opportunities to take everyday sanctity seriously. At times there were even little incidents which especially put his striving for holiness to the test.

At the beginning of his third year at Schoenstatt, Joseph was not only reappointed class prefect, but also given the job of class orderly. This meant he had to take care of the pot-bellied stove in his classroom. If his duties as prefect took up much time, his new task took up even more. The war dragged on and shortages began to be felt. Coal was in short supply. Now and then there were fights among the orderlies of the different classes over the coal allotment. The clever ones were known to shortchange the slower ones. This was hard for Joseph to bear. He found himself in a tight spot for another reason, too. His stove was stubborn and had a mind of its own. At times it would belch smoke and soot, at others it refused to function altogether. This, however, was not the worst. With more than forty students, Engling's class was the largest and had to occupy the largest classroom. It was on the ground floor and had large windows—some of them reaching all the way to the floor. And it was a cold stone floor. To heat such a room to the satisfaction of all was nothing short of impossible.

The fire had to be going before the early study period began, so Joseph began his work before his schoolmates gathered. In most cases he succeeded in having the room warm. At other times he was not so fortunate. Then the students would sit at their desks, shivering in their overcoats, while he worked hard to get the fire going. Some know-it-alls criticized him, but none of the critics would move a finger to help him. When the stove finally got red-hot, those at the end of the room near the stove could not stand the heat, whereas those sitting at the other end were still freezing. The ones said, "Engling, don't make it so burning hot!" The others cried, "Engling, when will the room finally get warm?"

The poor orderly was caught in the middle. He sincerely tried to do his best and his only reward was criticism. But Joseph kept doing his work without complaint. He did not waste any words over how he had to do this unpleasant task all alone. He did not even become ill-humored or irritated by the unjust reproaches. He did not complain about the ingratitude of his classmates. Every day he began his menial task anew and performed it with plain, unaffected loyalty.

There was another job that put Joseph Engling's ideals to the test. One day Father Prefect added a new job to the list of tasks the boys did in the Old House. It was cleaning the toilets. In the New House the boys did not have to do this job. But with the war there was no one to take the job except the boys. The boys considered this an especially embarrassing job and some even made sure they were out of the house when jobs were assigned rather than risk getting this one. Father Prefect also seemed to know that this was a hard task and looked for someone who would do it willingly and well for the first month. The choice fell to Joseph Engling. It was even hard for Engling. Inner resistance could be read in his face, but he gritted his teeth and did it.

The jobs were reassigned every month. Father Prefect hoped to find a volunteer for the toilet cleaning. No one stepped forward. To the relief of all, Joseph volunteered again. In the end Joseph would volunteer again and again for over two years, until he was drafted into the army. When he left, the successors in this job may not have been happy, but at least the boys' attitude had changed. In later years the toilet cleaning was simply considered a normal job that had to be done. It was not a service that won Joseph much honor, however. On the contrary, there were upperclassmen who looked down on

Joseph because they thought he was naive or stupid. There were even some of his own classmates who felt that way about him. Joseph was not blind to this contempt. But no one ever heard him complain about it or speak bitterly. Most of his classmates knew better, too. From their daily contact with Joseph they knew that it was not stupidity that stood behind his deeds, but manly striving for a high ideal. He had the courage to take it seriously, even at the cost of many sacrifices.

These sacrifices bore much fruit. With the help of his spiritual director he had progressed from the ideal of his vocation to the ideal of sanctity—and from the ideal of sanctity to everyday sanctity.

Sodalist of Mary

For the third- and fourth-year classes the Marian Sodality was still shrouded in mystery. Uninvited listeners no longer stood by the chapel windows eavesdropping on the conferences of the spiritual director. An order of Father Prefect had stopped that once and for all. But even without this prohibition the practice would have soon ended, for one day Father Spiritual Director announced that a new branch of the sodality would be founded for the middle classes. The branch for the upper grades would be called the Senior Sodality; the branch for the middle grades the Junior Sodality. The announcement was received in the lower grades with visible satisfaction. In some way they felt raised to an equal footing with the upperclassmen. This did more than a little to lift their self-esteem. Members of the fourth-year class (the grade ahead of Joseph's class) founded the Junior Sodality on December 8, 1914. At the same time, members of Joseph's class (the third-year class) began their probation as candidates. The prefect of the newly founded Junior Sodality assumed the task of introducing the candidates to the sodality. Here was their chance to find out what they wanted to know for so long.

They first heard about the history of the Marian Sodality. Special emphasis was placed on its fruitful activity during the Counter-Reformation. The candidates were more than a little surprised to hear the sodality's real aims. It was not some saccharin-sweet "blue ribbon society," but a true spiritual army which already had won great victories in some of the most difficult periods of Church history. They became acquainted with its three fundamental principles:

self-education,
apostolate,
and Marian devotion.

They were interested in all of this. But what they really liked was the organization and methods of the sodality. It was directed by a leaders' circle called the "magistrate." The membership of the sodality elected the first three officers of the magistrate, who in turn appointed the remaining magistrate officers. The sodality was divided into two sections—the Eucharistic Section which focused on self-education, and the Mission Section which focused on promoting apostolic spirit. Marian devotion was worked on by both sections. The Eucharistic Section occupied itself with questions of self-education in close connection to the life of Christ. It consisted of three groups. The Sacred Heart Group concerned itself with the person of Christ. The Prayer Group imitated Jesus at prayer. The Courtesy Group considered Christ in his dealings with others. At the beginning of the year the sections worked out a plan of action. This included the topics for the talks which were to be given and discussed at the weekly meetings.

Needless to say, the sodality and its way of doing things greatly interested Joseph. His heart, receptive for great ideals, quickly caught fire. He soon recognized that the sodality offered him an outstanding opportunity to further his personality formation. His spontaneous drive to serve community also found new and wide-open vistas. He had a hard time deciding which section to join. His inclination toward great ideals and tireless apostolate urged him to join the Mission Section. His inclination for the interior life and personality formation called him to the Eucharistic Section. The latter inclination prevailed. Within the Eucharistic Section he joined the Courtesy Group, a decision which was not surprising. How often was his clumsy exterior brought to his attention whether he liked it or not! And how painfully he felt his deficiencies! That was where he had to start.

While the third- and fourth-year classes were engaged in organizing the Junior Sodality, the regular conferences of the spiritual director turned to a new but closely related topic. Starting in early 1915 he circled primarily around Mary as "Sodality Queen." The talks were all about Marian devotion. Their effect was to breathe the soul, as it were, into the new Junior Sodality. For Joseph the spiritual director's talks always had a great impact. This time the conferences practically wrote a whole chapter in the story of his soul. They began by portraying the Mother of God as the Queen adorned with the royal dignity of her grace and purity. God has entrusted to her a veritable kingdom, for she is the official Christ-bearer and patroness of the Church. The sodalists are her knights who share in her tasks. Before all else they must conquer the holy land of their soul. The most effective way of doing this is to contribute to Mary's capital of grace. Such thoughts struck a familiar chord in Joseph's soul. What the Sodality Queen was asking was really no different than the ideal of modern sanctity. He was very much at home with that.

Soon the spiritual director approached the matter from a different angle. He presented Mary as the Mother of the Sodalists, always ready to help. His point of departure was the experience of the boys. He described their past battles in the interior life. They then realized how often their energy flagged in the face of mountain-high difficulties, how often their will-power lapsed, or was overcome by inordinate passions, or even overpowered by sin. Joseph scanned the battlefield of his heart. Yes, he had to admit: Anger sometimes got the better of him. And momentary pleasures had too often carried the day. When he looked up to his high ideal and then down at his weaknesses and faults, he felt the heavy weight of an oppressive helplessness.

But then there stood before him the Mother of God as depicted by the conferences—the powerful and sympathetic helper. By using examples from the lives of saints, the spiritual director showed that she is the most powerful intercessor before the throne of God and that she leads weak children to the heights of sanctity. She wants to make of her sodalists useful instruments in the hands of God. That's why they dedicate themselves totally to her service. In this context the words *Mariae specialiter mancipatus* came up again and again. They were a summation of what it meant to be a sodalist of Mary:

to be *Mary's very own*[1]. The term was taken from a papal encyclical on the Marian Sodality.

The effect these talks had on Joseph were similar to the effect of the series on sanctity. At that time he had made the irrevocable and earnest decision, "I want to become a saint." Now he specified: "I want to enter the service of Our Lady and remain entirely devoted to her." Striving for the ideal of modern sanctity and total dedication to the Sodality Queen came together to form an indissoluble unity. This new far-reaching resolution was to be given its solemn seal on the day of his admission to the sodality.

Shortly before Easter 1915, the magistrate of the Junior Sodality met to make important decisions. The candidates from the third-year class were to be solemnly admitted into the sodality on the Sunday after Easter. Now they had to decide who was to be admitted. The candidates were on pins and needles. The magistrate seemed to have had a hard time reaching its decisions. They even called on two of the more mature candidates to counsel them in their deliberations—Joseph Engling and Hans Wormer. The other candidates had no objection for they knew that these two would be impartial. The decision of the magistrate would greatly disappoint some. The officers had been strict in their selection and turned down some candidates who thought they would surely be accepted.

On April 11 the Junior Sodality gathered in the little sodality chapel for the solemn admission ceremony. In his talk Father Kentenich explained the meaning of the Marian consecration. He pointed out two sentences in the sodality consecration prayer which deserved special attention—*"Eligo te hodie in Dominam, Advocatam et Matrem meam..."* (I choose you today as my Queen, Advocate, and Mother) *"...tuere me servum, clientem et filium tuum."* (Protect me as your servant, client and child). The mutual contract between the sodalists and Our Lady was expressed in this brief formula. For

---

[1] *Mancipatus* means a hand-picked servant or slave. In this context: the sodalist is no mere day laborer serving Mary from "9 to 5", but someone who totally belongs to her around the clock with all he is and has and does. Hence *Mariae specialiter mancipatus* (literally "a servant specifically to Mary") is translated "Mary's very own."

Joseph such a contract could have only one meaning: He placed his life unreservedly into the service of the Mother of God for the realization of her tasks, and trusted firmly that she would form him into a saint for our times.

Deep emotion gripped the sodality family as the candidates prayed their consecration at the altar steps. Then one after the other, they approached the sodality banner and, placing a hand on it, declared: "This is the banner I have chosen, I will not desert it. This is my solemn pledge to Mary." Some made the pledge with beating heart and quivering voice. Others were so moved that they could hardly speak the words. Was it really a pledge that would seal their fate? Only one endowed with the gift of prophecy could have guessed.

"I will not desert it." Three of them—Engling, Wormer and Paul Reinhold—remained loyal to this pledge until they gave their lives for the Sodality Queen on the battlefields of World War I. Others would die shortly after the war because of its privations.

"I will not desert it." A good number, confident of victory, would carry it into the priesthood and pass it on to future generations.

"I will not desert it." There were others whose raised hands the prophet would have stayed: "Do not speak these words of fidelity, for in a few years' time you will prove unfaithful."

The "Mother Thrice Admirable"

About two weeks after their admission into the Junior Sodality, the sodalists were surprised to see something new in the Chapel. A picture of Mary was hanging in the sanctuary! It had been placed there by the Senior Sodalists. The thought of adorning their chapel with a Marian image was nothing new. If it were to be their spiritual home, it would need a picture of the Sodality Queen. One of the upperclassmen had written to a well-known painter, but the letter was never mailed. Father Prefect could not see how the sodalists would pay for an original painting. At this time Professor Huggle, a secular priest and teacher at the seminary, offered to donate a picture he had seen in an antique shop. One day the sodalists held the gift in their hands. Some did not like it and thought it too Oriental. A

Madonna with Germanic features and garments would have appealed to them more. But they could not offend the well-meaning donor by refusing the gift, so they placed it in their little chapel and gave no further thought to its artistic value.

It was not long before the Senior Sodality had named the picture. In their chapel it was to be venerated as the *Mater Ter Admirabilis*—Mother Thrice Admirable, or MTA for short. The younger sodalists shook their heads and wondered where the older ones came up with such an name. But their choice had a reason. It lay in a book called *Father Rem and His Marian Conferences*. It had fallen into the spiritual director's hands and was now making the rounds of the Senior Sodalists. The book told about a high school sodality that flourished in 16th century Ingolstadt, Bavaria. Under the direction of the Jesuit Father Jacob Rem it became a real school of leaders. At a time of great religious upheaval, it sparked a movement which helped to revive the Catholic Church in Bavaria. The members of the Ingolstadt Sodality had venerated Mary as the *Mother Thrice Admirable*. The fact that a group of exemplary young men could become champions of a movement for the renewal of religious spirit naturally appealed to the boys and prompted them to do likewise. Under the protection of Mary they, too, were willing to educate themselves to be leaders who labor as priests for God's kingdom. It seemed natural to give the recently acquired picture in their chapel the title *Mother Thrice Admirable*. This would most surely remind them of the model which had made such an impression on them. The reference to Ingolstadt would be of great significance for the further development of the Schoenstatt Sodality. In the Junior Sodality this fact is directly tied to the name of Joseph Engling.

At the beginning of May 1915, the sodalists of the third-year class had an important matter to resolve. The class above them was going to advance to the Senior Sodality. This meant Joseph Engling's class would soon be filling key openings on the magistrate. Of greatest importance was the question of who to elect as prefect of the Junior Sodality. The majority nominated Joseph Engling without the least hesitation. A small but vocal minority favored Hans Wormer.

"Hans," they argued, "is entirely different from the stiff, clumsy Engling. He cuts a good image, is much more talented, and will keep things moving." Hans was too noble to take any pleasure in the publicity being made for him against Joseph. He was visibly uncomfortable with how they made him and Joseph look like rivals. This actually improved Hans' chances of getting elected. But when the sodalists handed in their ballots on May 13, Joseph Engling won by a landslide. With that he became prefect of the Junior Sodality. Hans was elected his first assistant.

Champion of an Idea

In the days that followed, the new sodality prefect visited the spiritual director many times. He needed to know what was expected of him in such an important position. He could not build much on the experience of his predecessors. They themselves had been insufficiently trained and almost made the sodality more of a debate club than a school of self-education. But other considerations also played an important role in these consultations with Father Kentenich. He told Joseph what was going on in the Senior Sodality and revealed some of his plans and deliberations. Nearly eight months had passed since that memorable October 18. What had become of the grand plan? After all, through contributions to the "capital of grace" they had intended to move Our Lady to erect her throne in the little chapel and make it into a blessed home for the sodality family.

The chronicler could report flourishing life in both sodalities, increasing fervor for the idea of the "capital of grace," and a new springtime of Marian devotion. Could not these facts be taken as a sign that Mary had accepted their offer? For many months the plan had been dormant, but in the Senior Sodality it was now beginning to awaken. The example of the Ingolstadt Sodality gave it a new and daring turn. So far the sodalists had hoped the Blessed Mother would make their little shrine the focal point for the life of the sodality. Could they, inspired by their confidence in her, not go a step further? No doubt it was within her power to choose their chapel for the starting-point of a movement of religious and moral renewal for broad and broadest circles of the Church and world. In short: Could not Schoenstatt become another Ingolstadt? The thought had begun to catch on with many in the Senior Sodality. For now the spiritual director did not consider it opportune to bring such a plan of unprecedented proportions into the public discussion of the whole seminary. Since the sodality's founding, its "new-fangled" ideas had attracted many critics within the seminary. Such far-reaching objectives would surely have caused new storms. Without the sodalists quite knowing why, Father Kentenich dubbed the new plan the "Ingolstadt-Schoenstatt parallel." This code name became well known among the Senior Sodalists; occasionally it was mentioned at the gatherings in the chapel. But most of the boys only had a vague notion of what the phrase really meant.

The consultations with the spiritual director gave Joseph a deeper understanding of these questions and events. He was also able to hear from Father Kentenich himself what he really meant by the "Ingolstadt-Schoenstatt parallel." Whether Divine Providence had actually chosen the little shrine as the center of a movement of moral and religious renewal remained to be seen. The future course of events would have to speak. For the moment it was enough to know that the Blessed Mother had richly blessed the young sodality. The sodalists should continue to serve her faithfully and confidently entrust the future into her hands.

For Joseph the full significance of this parallel may have only been a glimmer on the horizon. He had no idea of how it would come about. How could an insignificant high school sodality presume to lay claim to such a mission? But why worry? The spiritual director, under whose guidance everything had progressed so admirably thus far, would know the right time to take the next step. For now one point caught fire in Joseph and gave him no rest. The blessings which the sodality family had thus far received from their little chapel were evidently meant to go beyond the narrow confines of their school. If this were true, did not the Blessed Mother expect new and greater contributions from her loyal children for her "capital of grace"? And did she not expect of him that he place everything, his whole life's work, at her disposal for this great blessing? The thought so stirred him in the depths of his soul that he arrived at another important determination about his mission in life. In an act of faith and will he made the "Ingolstadt-Schoenstatt parallel" his own. Even though he had not as yet grasped its full significance, this much he did know—that from her little chapel the Sodality Queen wanted to bless not only the sodalists themselves but also people beyond the walls of their school. Moreover, he realized that for this purpose his whole life must become one great contribution to Our Lady's capital of grace. He felt the Blessed Mother calling him to a great mission. He was to assist in making the little shrine the headwaters of a great river of grace flowing into the whole world for the religious and moral rebirth of our times. With this a new essential element was added to his life's ideal. From now on he was not just to be "a saint for our times" or even "a saint in the service of Mary," but "a saint in the service of the Mother of God of Schoenstatt."

Where did Joseph get this inner clarity to reach out and make this ideal his own? Was it perhaps his inborn drive for accomplishment that perceived an unlimited field of endeavor? Was it perhaps the trust he had in his spiritual director, whose thoughts and plans he always followed with greatest willingness? Or was his decision inspired by a certain intuition telling him that Divine Providence had laid the foundations here for a great undertaking? Who can say? It may well have been a combination of nature and grace. In any case it was a turning point of decisive importance for his whole life.

Meanwhile, Joseph had other matters to attend to. The recently formulated ideal had to be put into practice. Only one month remained before the students went on vacation. During their long vacation every member had an excellent opportunity to live the ideals of the sodality outside the seminary. Under no conditions should such an opportunity be wasted. After consulting with Father Kentenich, Joseph came up with a plan. Vacation would be a harder time to work on self-education, but that was precisely when the sodalist must show his worth. The fact that it was harder would make it a greater contribution to Our Lady's capital of grace. In order to make the plan more concrete, Joseph made a very tangible and practical suggestion. Every member of the Junior Sodality should make a schedule of spiritual exercises for his vacation. Every evening he would check off in writing whether he did them or not. The schedule should include suitable spiritual practices and acts of self-denial. Furthermore, the sodalists were to be apostles. In every possible field they were to devote their strength to God's kingdom. The Mission Section was to deliberate and discuss how this could be done. If their vacation program could be realized by the whole sodality, it would be the first step towards their goal: Schoenstatt—another Ingolstadt. The sodality prefect was visibly pleased, but much had to be done before vacation started.

Interior of Schoenstatt Shrine around 1916.

In the coming weeks Joseph was extremely busy. During each recess, each evening recreation, each walk, at all times, he tried to contact one of his fellow sodalists and talk to him privately. Through the "little work" of personal contacts he wanted to win over everyone for the vacation plan. Hans Wormer, the leader of the Mission Section, agreed to take charge of the vacation apostolate in his own section of the sodality. The leaders of the Eucharistic Section were equally willing to become loyal promoters of their spiritual daily exercises as "contributions to the capital of grace." Soon the work planned for the approaching vacation was the subject of every sodalist's conversation.

Toward the end of the school year the Junior Sodality held a meeting to discuss the striving for the upcoming vacation. They all agreed that they should spend it differently from that of former years. Later Joseph summarized the results of the meeting in a report:

"In our vacation work we want to adhere to a twofold purpose. The first and more important is to obtain by our sacrifices and acts of self-denial a great treasure of graces for our Mother Thrice Admirable, so that she can dispense them from our own little chapel, if we or others ask for help or are in need. We want to realize our Ingolstadt-Schoenstatt parallel.' The second purpose is to find a sure means to continue more successfully in our self-education."

Inspired by his spiritual director, Joseph was perhaps the only one who saw the vacation effort on such a grand scale. For the other sodalists the predominant idea was more that a Sodalist of Mary should enjoy vacation and do some apostolate. As a result, their attention during the meeting focused almost exclusively on practical suggestions.

A member of the Mission Section took the floor and suggested that they collect aluminum foil to benefit the missions. Another suggested that they sell mission calendars at home. A third proposed that they sell a little book containing instructions on how to make an act of perfect contrition daily. Then, too, they did not want to overlook the sale of holy cards, especially of our Blessed Lady. One well-meant suggestion after another was added. More difficult was the question: How can one do apostolate in one's family? Giving a good example was mentioned first. Then followed a particular recommendation to promote prayer together as a family, to spend time with one's younger brothers and sisters, and to get people interested in frequent Holy Communion. Finally came the most important question: "Do we keep a written examination of conscience about our daily spiritual schedule?" It was clear to everyone that they had to make special sacrifices for the "capital of grace." But why have a written spiritual schedule? Why shouldn't they be sincerely glad to have a few weeks off from the strict daily order of the seminary? Why should they deprive themselves of this precious freedom? It took some time before the objectors were convinced that there is never vacation from self-education. If a vacation is spent in a disorderly and dissolute way, it does not make anyone happy. Almost all the sodalists drew up a schedule for their spiritual exercises before leaving for home.

The sodality prefect was satisfied with the preparations for vacation, but would all the resolutions be kept? The fact that the young company went home with the determination to conquer souls, to accomplish something, already showed a marked difference from former years. They regarded themselves as heralds of the Mother Thrice Admirable, sent out into the battle of life. When they returned six weeks later, the sodality prefect and the sodalists reviewed their efforts. In the sodality chronicle he summed up the results of the entire vacation in a detailed report. With great satisfaction he expressed his conviction that the sodality had really done what it had set out to do.

He could also honestly say the same for himself. An extensive schedule of spiritual exercises became the soul of his vacation activity. It contained the following: punctual rising, morning prayer, sodality prayers, particular examination, Holy Mass, Holy Communion, spiritual reading, apostolic deed, hour of adoration, perfect contrition, evening prayer, punctual retiring, speech exercises. At the top of the sheet for checking off these exercises he wrote in big letters: "Contributions to the Capital of Grace of the Mother Thrice Admirable." In the sodality chronicle we can read how he tried to carry out his apostolic work:

"One sodalist [he meant himself] worked in his parish quite successfully to promote frequent Holy Communion. First he won over his mother. He asked her to distribute a pamphlet about frequent Holy Communion. He also distributed the pamphlet and talked to people about it. By the end of his vacation at least a few women went to Communion on weekdays. One man was of the opinion that frequent Holy Communion was all right; he, too, would go daily provided other men went. So the sodalist suggested it to his father. In order to keep up the practice he encouraged his mother to keep promoting it. He asked her to let him know how things are going and in his letters continues to awaken further interest in it."

In this way Joseph remained faithful to his resolution. He wanted to clear the way for graces to flow from the little shrine into the world. He had promised it to Our Lady of Schoenstatt. His vacation work proved that he really meant what he promised.

Joseph Engling's spiritual life made great strides forward in the year 1915. The two previous years had prepared the garden of his soul; this one sowed the seed. The ideal of the modern saint became clear to him and remained an inalterable aim in his mind. He wanted to become a real saint marked by consummate faithfulness in little things. He was trained in the school of the Blessed Mother. Since then his resolve was to become a modern saint through Mary's intercession. In loyalty and love his whole life was to belong to her. Finally, the "Ingolstadt-Schoenstatt" parallel attracted him. From then on his little ideal took on new meaning to be a saint in the service of Our Lady of Schoenstatt and her cause. It is true that Joseph was not conscious of all these processes in his spiritual life. They slumbered like dimly recognized figures deep in his soul. The moment would soon come for them to enter his full awareness.

1915 was truly a year of sowing.

4. Spiritual Combat and Growth

A Plan of Self-Conquest

The beginning of December 1915 was set aside for the customary annual retreat at the Schoenstatt seminary. Joseph always took part in these days of solitude and prayer with great interest and attentiveness. But this time he was especially alert. The talks on the eternal truths no doubt left their mark, but it was something else that captured his attention. There were so many experiences to look back on! All the events of the past months now suddenly came to life again. His soul was dogged by a confusing number of ideas and feelings that he could not yet put in words. The time had come to put them in some kind of order. The best way to go about it would be to write them down.

He sat behind his desk, steeped in thought. Before him was an open notebook. He was trying to discover the "key signature," the common thread of all the experiences of the past few months. Slowly and carefully he entered a first sentence into his notebook: "I want to become a saint." Now he thought a little farther. What kind of a saint did he mean? It had to be about *greatness* and superhuman accomplishment—that much was clear. But also *radicality*, the daring to give it his all. He wrote down a second sentence: "Dear Lord, let me die rather than offend you by committing a venial sin."

He continued his search by looking for the characteristics of the ideal that motivated him most. Now he noticed something new. He wanted to be in the service of Our Lady of Schoenstatt and consume himself entirely for her cause. He had always liked the way it was said in the little phrase *Mariae specialiter mancipatus* (Mary's very own). He thought of it just now. And what should his battle for the kingdom of the Blessed Mother of Schoenstatt look like? Brash or noisy? No, that was not his style. His gentle heart and Samaritan spirit constantly urged him down another road. He wanted to serve others, be attentive to the little things, win over the hearts of all. St. Paul probably said it best when he wrote, *Omnibus omnia*—"I must become all things to all men" (1 Cor 9,22). Joseph took his pen for the third time and wrote, *Volo omnibus omnia fieri, Mariae specialiter mancipatus*—"I want to become all things to all men, and Mary's very own." And he added a fourth sentence, too: "I want to be faithful in even the littlest things." Faithfulness in the little things, the characteristic of the everyday saint, could not be forgotten! Peter Barbaric's life reminded him of it. Furthermore, the little things of everyday life were some of the most important things he could contribute to Mary's capital of grace.

Now there were four prominent sentences in his notebook. To him it was like the outline of a grand plan of life. Along these lines he would shape his whole future. Every sentence was a program of its own. He clearly felt it as he read them again. But he did not just want to *feel* their meaning, like some kind of intuition. No, he wanted to *know* it with complete clarity. So he started to take each sentence apart. He rewrote them in the form of questions. As he considered the first two sentences, his thoughts turned to tireless striving, persistent work in the little things of self-education, fostering a life of prayer. Come to think of it, his life had always been this way. He did not stop there. With dogged determination he fleshed out the meaning of his sentences for every duty of his daily life. Now the pen seemed to write of its own accord. Thinking about the first two sentences we wrote:

"Have I always seen my aim clearly?— Have I persevered in my striving for perfection?—Has confession helped me to improve?—Have I made my daily examination of conscience thoroughly?—How have I kept my particular examination? How was my prayer life?—Have I consistently practiced self-denial at dinner and supper?—Have I freely made some other sacrifices each day? Have I conscientiously avoided all sin? all imperfection?—Have I always followed my conscience?"

The questions concerning the third sentence being "all things to all men"—were particularly numerous. After a few questions about giving a good example he wrote:

"Have I made community life hard for anyone?—Have I offended anyone?—Have I acted unjustly?—Have I ever been rude or moody?—Have I distracted anyone during their studies?—Have I endured the faults of my fellow students in the right spirit?—Have I been courteous in my dealings with them?—Was I ever too free?—Was I always ready to help?—Did I help others with their

64

studies?—Did I make sacrifices for them?—Was I always obliging?—Have I fulfilled all their requests?—Have I had an eye for the sufferings of others?—Have I been compassionate?—Have I tried to console them?—Have I tried to entertain everyone in an interesting manner?—Have I been apostolic among my fellow students? everywhere else?—How has my behavior been toward my superiors? my teachers?—Have I loved them?—Have I been obedient to them?—Have I prayed for them?—Have I regarded them as representatives of God?—Have I caused any trouble to my parents?—Have I prayed for them?—Have I helped them to educate my brothers and sisters?—Have I been grateful to everyone?—Have I always been respectful?—Have I made everyone happy?—Have I been entirely unselfish?"

Why did he unfold the third sentence of his plan of conquest so extensively? There was a very good reason. Loyal, helpful love was his strong suit, the fundamental strength of his soul. It was the inspiration behind most of these thoughts. In the future it would become the main motor of his interior life.

He dealt with the fourth sentence in the same way he had the other three. He emphasized every part of his daily routine. Among other things, he phrased questions about his duties: "Did I rise promptly?—Have I been punctual everywhere and at all times?" Then he reviewed his behavior in study hall to see if he had, for instance, preserved silence and promptly went out for recess at the bell. In still other questions he considered his classroom participation: "Did my mind wander during class?—Did I study for all subjects?—Did I make use of every opportunity to learn more?—Did I waste any time?" etc.

After he had analyzed all four sentences he could heave a great sigh of relief. Finally, the confusion which had raged in his soul was brought into a clear order. Before him lay a comprehensive program for life, a plan of spiritual conquest. It encompassed every phase of his life and focused every detail towards a clear aim. Only one question remained unresolved. How should he translate this wonderful plan into tangible actions which would form his everyday life? It was not enough to commit it to writing and then forget about it. Without any doubt he had to hold a self-examination every so often in order to compare his deeds with his resolutions. He immediately wrote down his intent to repeat this examination of conscience monthly and put the results in writing. The object was to know how he had kept his resolutions. Now his plan of self-conquest seemed complete. The coming weeks would have to show if it would really take hold.

About four weeks later, during Christmas vacation, Joseph took out his notebook again. He was making a three-day recollection to review his resolutions. How was he doing with his plan of self-conquest? Using the questions he reviewed the state of his interior life. The result did not quite satisfy him. His plan was fine. But how often he had forgotten it in the demands of everyday life! He had to make it more concrete!

Joseph and Confession

Now a new thought came to him. What was his weekly confession really for? Like all boys he had his troubles with it. From his earliest childhood he felt sincere sorrow for every, even the least, sin. In the course of the years this sentiment deepened and became more tender. In his plan of self-conquest, when he expressed the desire to die rather than offend God by a venial sin, it was no empty or exaggerated claim. At that time his confessor could have attested that Joseph was no longer committing willful venial sin. He deplored and felt a keen need to confess faults of omission or other shortcomings. When he went through the Ten Commandments for his examination of conscience, the result almost always the same: distractions at prayer, impatience in dealing with others, carelessness in observing the rules of the house. Since he had to confess more or less the same things every week, confession was soon an uninspiring routine. Even the act of contrition and true amendment failed to touch his heart.

In his plan of conquest he resolved to make good use of his weekly confession. But that alone was not enough. How would it be, he thought, if I make my plan of conquest my examination of conscience for confession? This would make it much more personalized than to go through the Ten Commandments. In future the question in his examination of conscience would not merely be: "How have I failed against the Ten Commandments of God?" but rather: "How have I followed the will of God shown

> to me in my life's ideal and in the concrete demands of my plan of self-conquest?" This idea met with his approval. He wrote down the resolution to review his plan of self-conquest before every confession. As his personal writings testify, in the coming months he would do just this almost every time.

By connecting his plan of self-conquest with the weekly confession, Joseph made a significant step forward in his striving. From now on his examination of conscience had new standards. He no longer judged himself merely along the lines of duty and obligation. Instead he appraised himself according to the standard of the heroism he had freely chosen. For him the Christian life now encompassed the striving for religious and moral perfection, not just the observance of God's Law under the pain of sin. As a result he became less self-occupied. He did not focus overly long on weaknesses and failings, wallowing as it were in his limitations. Instead, his eyes were fixed on his great ideal. Against this background even the least fault would plainly, and sometimes painfully, come into view. According to him, there was guilt not only in every sin but also in every infidelity against the clearly perceived demands of his ideal. Under the influence of this new way of thinking, the lofty enthusiasm of his soul and the tenderness of his conscience became even more refined.

Three elements were now fused in the alloy of his striving—a clearly defined ideal, weekly confession, and examination of conscience according to his plan of conquest. But one more element was still needed. For over a year now he had practiced the particular examination[1]. He chose a troublesome fault and then focused all his strength and attention on overcoming it. Could he not make this a part of his plan of conquest too? Soon he had the answer. He already knew that he could not tackle all of the many resolutions in his plan

---

[1]   The particular examination (or special resolution) involves choosing a point of one's character formation to focus on "particularly" during a given period of time (a week or a month). To prevent forgetfulness (and therefore ineffectiveness), one "examines" the point at least once a day—preferably in writing—and in one's regular confession.

at once. He would have to proceed in a well-ordered manner and take one at a time. This would be the task of the particular examination. The plan of conquest presented a practically inexhaustible list from which to choose his particular examination. He gradually worked his way through the whole list, picking out certain areas for immediate attention—

"prayer life, posture, good manners, language, conscientiousness, community (including helpfulness to schoolmates, considerateness, taking part in activities, willingness to make sacrifices, cheerfulness, promoting good conversation, work for the sodality)."

From now on his particular examination would be the heart of his weekly examination of conscience. To be as thorough as possible, he decided to check his particular examination in writing every day. His plan of self-conquest was complete. At its head stood his life's ideal. The questions in his plan of conquest vouched for its practical application in everyday life. They would be his personal examination of conscience for the weekly confession. At the heart of his plan was the particular examination, to be checked off every evening.

And what became of his plan? Joseph himself became the "reporter" of this conquest. In the first days of January 1916, lying on his straw tick at the end of a tiring day, he reviewed the day's events before he fell asleep. "How would it be to keep a diary? To record everything that has a special impact on my soul?" he thought. The very next day he started his diary. In it he related the ups and downs of the battlefield of his heart. He was a brutally honest reporter, as honest as his down-to-earth nature was, and with the plainspoken innocence of his keen eye.

A Day in the Life of Joseph Engling

Every morning at 5:30 Father Prefect sounded the bell to wake the boys. It was well-worn by the years and had a somewhat tinny clang. For many this wake-up call was a most unpleasant disturbance. Strictly speaking, a few seconds after it sounded the whole dormitory should have been as busy as a beehive. That is how it would have been, if things had always gone according to the will of Father Prefect. At least it always looked that way when he came to check up on the boys. But those winter mornings! It was extremely

68

cold in the drafty dormitory and snug and warm in the beds, i.e. on the straw ticks on the floor. Jack Frost had already decorated the dormer windows with his icy flowers for days. The one or the other boy was invariably taken hostage by his pillow. Portly Paul Pabelmann, for instance, phlegmatic as he was, would stretch and wax philosophical. He would meditate on how everything in life is turned on its head. At night when the bed was cold, you had to get into it; in the morning when it was warm, you had to get out of it!

Not far from this sleepyhead Joseph Engling was already up, partially dressed. His neighbors thought he was the model of punctuality. His own judgment was more severe. He considered it a failing if he did not jump out of bed at once. In his diary he noted that he had not been quite punctual on one or two occasions in January; in February he even failed three times. Now he gave his straw sack a few whacks to try to restore its shape. It was hopeless. Under his weight the unruly sack spread during the night. The same thing happened to the neighboring sacks. They tended to gobble up all the spare room between them. Eighteen-year-old Joseph did not like the arrangement.

Now he went to wash up! But when he got downstairs he found the water in the wash basin covered by a thin layer of ice. No wonder! The whole house was freezing cold. How could it be any different? The only heating (and that used very sparingly) was in the classrooms and only during the day. Little Titus was standing next to Joseph. He buried his hands more deeply into his pants pockets and sleepily gazed at the ice in his wash basin. His teeth were chattering. How could he wash himself? How pleasant and comfortable it had been in the well-heated seminary on the hill! While Titus daydreamed, Joseph took the sheet of ice from his basin and broke it in the sink. After rolling up his sleeves, he unbuttoned his shirt and courageously dipped his hands in the ice-cold water. He wanted to toughen himself for the future. He had decided to wash his chest on even the coldest days. Washing was made more complicated by the lack of real soap. They had to use a war substitute containing more clay than tallow. If it wasn't carefully rinsed off, there would be a fine clayish residue behind the ears.

Personal Morning Prayer

When Joseph returned to the dormitory, the stragglers were finally out from under the blankets. As usual, Paul was last. Joseph knelt down at the end of his straw mattress and said his prayers. Morning prayer was said in common but he had decided to have a personal morning prayer, too. Anyone looking around the dormitory could see that Joseph was the only one kneeling at his bed. The story of morning and night prayer was a chapter in its own right. When Joseph started this custom, some of his schoolmates were a little taken aback. Others were annoyed and teased or ridiculed him. Naturally, his friends asked why he acted so conspicuously. His answer: community morning and night prayer are obligatory. A real man has to be able to stick to his daily prayers even when they are not obligatory.

To practice this, he had decided to say his sodality prayers (three Hail Marys and one "My Queen, My Mother") as his private morning and night prayer. At first it took quite a bit of self-denial to keep the resolution. He knew that some would shake their heads and that others would ridicule him. Finally he overcame the fear of what others would think and said his prayers anyway. He even made them part of his plan of conquest. His reasons made sense to some of his friends, and a few followed his example. The meaning of a private morning and evening prayer even came up for discussion in one of the sodality meetings. The sodalists then realized how sensible their prefect was. After that the number of those who followed his example grew steadily.

Of the twenty minutes allotted for washing and dressing, Joseph devoted at least five to calisthenics. At that time there were no directed morning calisthenics. So Joseph helped himself as best he could. Outside the Old House he would do jumping jacks in the gray of dawn. When it was time to go to Mass in the New House, he tried especially hard to walk straight and tall. Throughout Mass he knelt in his pew as immoble as a statue. Daily Mass and Holy Communion were sacred to him and the focal point of the entire day. He dedicated each morning to giving thanks and each afternoon to preparing for the next day's Mass. In order to make it the center of his whole day's work, he observed a "Sacred Heart Hour" every morning and afternoon. It had long been a personal custom of his. During this hour he would briefly stop what he was doing every so often and think of Christ in the Blessed Sacrament or God dwelling in his soul. He would let an ejaculatory prayer arise in his heart, or some devout sentiment.

When Joseph received Holy Communion, he was deeply recollected. It was a moment that filled his soul with tender mystery. Here and there he briefly alludes to it in the pages of his diary. If one were to express the general tone of what went through his heart, it might look like this: "My Savior and I have been inseparable friends ever since my first Holy Communion. I will never forget that solemn day. When I decided to become a priest, I promised to follow him and remain faithful to him until death. Following his example I want to be all things to all men. In the last year I have come to know how I can share in his redemptive activity and work for his kingdom. I want to invest my whole life's strength so that a stream of graces may flow from the chapel of our Sodality Queen into the whole land for the renewal of the world in Christ. The contributions to the capital of grace of the Mother Thrice Admirable have taught me the secret of quiet, constant sacrifice in the service of God's kingdom. Here the Blessed Mother has opened my eyes to the meaning of the sacrifice of the Mass. Was it not by Christ's sacrifice on the cross that the world was redeemed? Do I not share in his redemptive activity when I participate in his sacrifice and death through contributions to the capital of grace? Nowhere do I more profoundly experience my life's ideal which moves me so deeply than during Holy Mass. That is why they have both become the center of my daily life. I talk over all the plans, worries, and the events of my life with Our Lord. Since I made myself Mary's very own, I feel especially close to her. I especially place my particular examination on the paten as a daily offering. Holy Mass is indeed a sacred moment without which I would not want to begin the day."

This is more or less what Joseph would have said. Perhaps he would have added that the thanksgiving after Mass was too short for him. This might explain why, as soon as there was some free time after the beds were made, he hurried to the shrine. There he often prayed until the first class period in the morning.

There were others for whom the prayer time each morning was quite long enough. They were glad to finally be able to go to breakfast. The walk from the chapel to the dining room became a bit of a race. Hunger was the reason. Two thin slices of bread—no more, no less—were waiting at each boy's place. Food rationing had been going on for a long time already because of the war. At no time did these growing boys feel the privation of war more keenly than when they saw the two thin slices of bread. Even though this grayish-black "war bread" smelled oddly like potatoes and had the consistency of sawdust, it was a much coveted delicacy. This was probably because the boys brought a ravenous appetite to every meal. It was rarely satisfied. Nothing else was served with the dry slices of bread except a cup of black coffee. Paul Pabelmann was always the first to reach the dining room. With a sharp eye he quickly sized up the slices. If he discovered more on his neighbor's plate, he deftly switched the plates. He was not the only one. Some of their victims protested, others did not. Joseph was among those who kept their peace when cheated out of a bigger portion.

In the classroom the fourth-year men were waiting for their teacher to arrive. He was late again. Did this mean he was having a bad day? If so, he could be very testy. The class consisted of translating the authors of antiquity. Joseph felt a sincere admiration for these great statesmen and military leaders. They stood for greatness, and greatness always appealed to him. But in his eyes St. Francis de Sales and St. Francis Xavier were incomparably greater. They were spiritual giants who did mighty deeds for the kingdom of God. He would have enjoyed translating the ancient writers if his teacher had not made the exercise so miserable. This man's explanations of the texts were complicated and hard to understand. How could they possibly learn anything? Anger and ill-humor began to stir in Joseph's soul. How different it had been with their former teacher! Under his guidance learning had been a pleasure.

In the meantime the teacher called on one of the students. Schmitz was taken to task for being insufficiently prepared. Joseph began to boil with rage inside. "It's his faulty teaching method that is to blame. This never happened with our old teacher. And he shouldn't be showing his authority so quickly when the mistake is really his." The teacher's actions offended his sense of justice. At recess he would have liked nothing better than to explode with anger. But the teacher was someone in authority. And there were enough others who vented their anger. He had said in his plan of conquest that he would always be respectful. So he said nothing. The shrine was close by, so he paid a little visit there and offered it up to the Our Lady for her capital of grace. Somewhere, however, his communicative nature needed to express itself, so he wrote about it in his diary. At the end he drew a useful conclusion: "From it I want to learn how to avoid making the same mistake if I ever become a teacher."

The class was on better terms with the math teacher. He really mastered his subject. At times funny things happened during class which made for rollicking conversations afterwards. Nor was it just about the students' antics. The teacher had his share, too. One day during recess, just before math class, word got around that a teacher had passed the masters exam at the University of Bonn. No one knew who it was, but popular opinion quickly guessed the math teacher. Did he not go to Bonn regularly to the university? In reality it was someone else, but this guess soon turned into a "fact." A few wags immediately saw the chance for a practical joke. Soon the whole crowd was mobbed around Joseph Engling, the class prefect. "Engling, you have to congratulate math Professor R. in the name of the whole class before the next period begins." They explained the reasons, to which the prefect cautiously responded, "Is it really true?" "Without a doubt," said some who were "sure" of their information. Of course, the prefect was willing to do his duty. But the country boy had to blush a bit and admit that he didn't know what to say. One of the rascals had a ready answer: "In the name of the class I congratulate you on your professorship." The crowd agreed that this was the right thing to say.

Class began. The students waited expectantly to see what would happen. Sure enough, the prefect walked to the front of the room. He tried to make a polite bow which didn't quite work. He then recited his memorized line. For an awkward moment the two just stared at each other with undescribable looks on their faces. Neither teacher nor prefect understood the action of the other. The rest of the class had to bite their lip to keep from laughing. "What is going on?" Professor R. finally inquired. Joseph made his bow again, even more awkwardly than the first time, and repeated his congratulations. Then the puzzled teacher directed his question to the whole class, "What is going on? What does he want?" Someone gave an answer, but it did nothing to solve the mystery. By now he may have begun to guess that unsuspecting Engling was the victim of a trick. The look on his face was so sincere that he was clearly not the source of the joke. The teacher finally said with a smile, "Go back to your seat. I won't ask about it today." This event was talked about over and over in the coming days, even in Joseph's presence. In fact, Joseph laughed too. He did not make a big deal out of a harmless practical joke. On the contrary, he was glad to contribute to a little fun around the house.

The students heaved a sigh of relief when the bell rang at the end of the morning's classes. That miserable hunger had been torturing their stomachs for some time already. How could one possibly remain focused all morning with so little to eat? Still, in Joseph's plan of conquest stood the question: "Was I always attentive during class?" His natural thirst for knowledge helped to rivet his attention to every subject, even those which seemed quite boring to others. But the natural urge was not enough to keep his resolution. Quite often he had to help it along with an energetic act of the will. Fortunately, during recess he could always go to the shrine of the MTA. These moments of recollection helped him to focus everything on his high ideal and to summon new strength. Such a source of strength was truly necessary, for living conditions were getting worse and worse. One could clearly see that some of his classmates were undernourished. During the last class period they suffered from severe headaches and were hardly capable of doing anything. A substantial meal would have quickly put them back in shape. But such things were now relegated to the memories of days gone by. In Schoenstatt, like elsewhere in Germany, food was rationed. Not only breakfast was impacted, but dinner and supper as well. Only sauerkraut and rutabagas were exempt from rationing.

The issue of food in the dining room was strictly regulated. There was a serving bowl at each table for every four students. It was their task to divide the contents evenly between them. But hunger corrupted all sense of measurement; the task became as hard as the quadrature of the circle. At intervals the groups of four were reassigned. One day one of the younger students was so happy he nearly did a handstand. He had been assigned to the group with both Joseph Engling and Hans Wormer! In their company he knew he would not be shortchanged like he was in the previous group. He was not disappointed. When they took their share, neither Joseph nor Hans took all the "substance" of the barley soup for themselves. They didn't go "fishing" for the pieces of rutabaga or potatoes.

One could not help but notice that Joseph went hungry. The tall, strong fellow had a good appetite on account of his size. The diet, deficient in fat, did not appease it. At times the spoon or fork would tremble in his hand from sheer weakness. In order not to cheat his three neighbors, he would always take a little less than they did. One of the boys who noticed this even had the impression that Joseph wanted to fast. This fellow thought it was a most imprudent mortification and decided to stop the foolishness. He reported Joseph to the spiritual director. In his heart, however, he was greatly impressed. Anyone who could go hungry out of love for his fellow students, not only once or twice, but day after day, had to be a real man. He thought how easy it is to misjudge someone. This fellow was not far off the mark about Engling wanting to fast. As we know, Joseph's plan of conquest included the resolution to perform at least one act of self-denial at each of the main meals. And even more importantly, he could tell his diary that he had done it.

Once again, the long noon recess seemed rather boring. Most of the students did not feel like a game. For some, the weather was bad; others felt dejected because of setbacks in school; still others didn't really know why. Joseph appeared on the scene. He could not imagine a recess without some kind of game. Soon he had his trustiest companions on their feet. He could always count on Fritz Esser, Hans Wormer, Karl Klement, and a few others. "Let's play prisoners' base," someone yelled across the playground. If getting the game going was not enough to coax those that still hung back, he made a direct appeal to them personally. His coaxing was not always successful, but he almost always managed to get a good game going with most of those present. He himself got into it, heart and soul. He was not the picture of grace with his heavy step and stooped posture. In fact, during gym class he was once told, "Fellow, you are as bent as if you had to carry the whole war debt of the German Empire." Since then it was often said, "Engling, watch out for your war debt!" Then he would straighten up and try to better his posture.

Good posture was one of his more frequent particular examinations. He even asked some of his schoolmates to remind him when his posture flagged. Others, too, heard of his request. Now Joseph had more than enough "help." These rascals would throw the ball at his back in the middle of a game or catch him off guard with an unexpected slap on the back. Then they would put on an innocent face and say that they only wanted to remind him of his resolution!

The afternoon study hall for finishing the day's homework was nearing a close. Joseph put the finishing touches on an essay. Now his homework for tomorrow was done. He had worked long and hard on this composition, even being especially meticulous with his penmanship. What would his professor think? "Regardless of what he thinks, it was good exercise for me." He let his mind rest for a moment. He looked at the picture of the Mother Thrice Admirable on his desk. His thoughts turned to his "holy hour" and tomorrow's Mass. He spent a few moments in quiet prayer. Then he pulled out his watch. Study hall was almost over. How much he had planned to study today! As he looked over his books, an insatiable thirst for knowledge came over him. It was as if he wanted to know and discover everything. How often he had said to himself that he wanted to become "a holy and learned priest!" He hurriedly took a little index card file out of his desk. He used it to record his "discoveries" while studying. Now he added a few new entries, carefully writing them down on cards and filing them away.

In the study hall it was obvious that the last quarter hour had begun. Not far from Joseph, younger students began to cause some disturbance. Joseph gave them a whispered admonition. "We're done with our work," the two replied. "Then study your German grammar or try to solve some geometry problem to pass the time,"

Joseph suggested. Instead of giving an answer, one of the two pointed a finger at his forehead. This Engling is crazy! After a little while he poked his neighbor in the ribs and said, "Look at Engling! He really is studying his German grammar." Engrossed in what the textbook had to say, Joseph sat there as if reading a novel!

Suddenly Rolf appeared at Engling's desk and gave him a little manuscript. Joseph knew at once what it was about. It was the academic magazine they were planning. In a sense Joseph had started the project. A few days ago he had talked with Rolf about starting an academic circle. This gave Rolf the idea to produce a magazine with boys writing literary, scientific and general articles. Now he gave Joseph the first issue. While he read it, an expression of disappointment swiftly covered his face. Not a single page held any serious academic work! It was more like a satire magazine. He was especially displeased to find one of his schoolmates being ridiculed on the last page. Under no circumstance would he write anything for this magazine! He told Rolf so in no uncertain terms.

"Fresh Fish in the Kitchen"

During the recess after the final study hall there was a commotion behind the house. Three voices were yowling like cats: "Fresh fish in the kitchen!" What was going on? A whole gang of jokesters had cooked up a new way to tease Joseph, of course. He even seemed to be the ringleader of this off-key chorus, though in reality he wasn't. Quite the opposite, in fact! Joseph was following a teacher's suggestion to do some speech exercises to correct his impediment. His teacher had advised him to clearly pronounce certain combinations of words which were especially helpful. One of these combinations was "Fresh fish in the kitchen." While pronouncing these words, he was to shake his fists to give some vibrato to his voice. His secret place to practice was behind the Old House. He was soon discovered, though, and often had to put up with an annoying crowd of mimics. They showed what comedians they were and pretended to help Joseph recite his exercises, causing a deplorable racket. Finally, they offered to help him shake his fists and did it so vigorously so that they got into a regular scuffle with Joseph if he resisted.

If his patience had not been so great, he would have beaten the whole gang to pulp with his strong fists. Instead he pleaded with them—with a certain sadness in his voice—to leave him alone. If they did not, he quietly went away. At least this is the way he acted with younger students. If, however, he noticed an older fellow among them who acted so rudely, he would defend himself very courageously. The next day he stood again in the customary place and continued his exercises. In later years some of these "humorists" had to admit with shame and sorrow, "We sometimes went too far in the way we treated our good Joseph Engling!"

For the evening recreation some of the fourth-year men announced a little surprise. Paul Reinhold had composed another "hit." Happy-go-lucky Paul was a veritable comedian and could be counted on for some good fun in the recreation. Last week he presented "The Song of Nicholas Buschmann," a schoolmate who was quite a daredevil. It had everyone doubled over with laughter. Who would be tonight's "victim"? Some of those with inside connections knew it was Professor Huggle, the French teacher. Professor Huggle was a nervous man who constantly adjusted his glasses, tugged at his goatee, and liked to say, "It's not that way in any class!" It had recently been discovered that he said this in *every* class—ideal fodder for Reinhold's clever humor.

When evening came, the song did too. Every verse ended with "It's not that way in any class!" as Paul mimed the teacher's famous gestures. They laughed so hard there wasn't a "dry eye in the house." But Joseph felt torn inside. On the one hand he did not want to spoil the fun. He was wholeheartedly in favor of good fun. He also knew that the spoof was not motivated by any ill will. On the other hand, he could not quite reconcile himself to the fact that a professor was being made the object of ridicule. The lines were so funny he could not help but laugh, and he joined in singing the refrain once or twice. But others could clearly see that he was not completely at ease. He was too patient and broad-minded in judging the personality of others. Such a song could hardly have come from his lips.

After evening recreation, the day ended for the residents of the Old House with night prayer. In the large dormitory the boys soon

78

got ready for their night's rest. Joseph knelt by his straw mattress and said the sodality prayers. Once more he offered up his day's work and placed it into the hands of the Blessed Mother and Queen of Schoenstatt—his prayers, his striving for self-improvement, his studies, and the unavoidable trials of everyday life. Every act was a contribution to the capital of grace so that Schoenstatt would eventually become another Ingolstadt. His life's ideal demanded it. Then he directed his thoughts to the next morning's Mass and Holy Communion. After that he could retire in peace. Within minutes, the dormitory was usually enveloped in the deep peace of the night. Sometimes, though, things turned out a little differently.

While the weary sleepers sought their well-deserved rest, the mice would have their fun in the nearby storeroom. It happened occasionally that some of these little creatures wandered into the dormitory and sought refuge in one of the straw mattresses. But how to sleep with a mouse nibbling and gnawing in one's mattress! Some of the boys were thick-skinned enough to ignore it. Others, however, went into a frenzy and angrily pounded their straw sack. One smart aleck thought he found the perfect solution. He put his pocket watch in his bed, believing that the ticking would send the four-legged creatures scurrying the other way. Not long after, he had to disappointedly admit it didn't work. One night the peace of sleep was interrupted by the shout, "There goes a mouse!" It triggered pandemonium. Clad only in nightshirts and pants, an excited mob descended on the errant beast. Soon a regular chase was on. Joseph let himself be drawn into the general commotion. Afterwards, when he was lying on the straw mattress again, his conscience bothered him. Was what he had just done compatible with the rule of the house? One rule called for strict silence in the dormitory after night prayers. The killing of the mouse was, of course, not against the rule. But it certainly was not in keeping with the rule to make such noise and commotion. And he, the sodality prefect, by giving bad example, was responsible for the disturbance together with the others. Before falling asleep, he decided to ask his schoolmates' pardon the next day for the scandal he had caused.

It was on days like this one that Joseph's plan of self-conquest had to pass the test of everyday life.

Helplessness and Mary's Help

More than three months had passed since the drafting of the plan of self-conquest. In that time he had surveyed the battleground of his heart more than once, evaluating his progress. Had the workday with its many duties and events really been mastered and shaped as his plan intended? Pondering this question, he became totally dissatisfied. To him the past months seemed an uninterrupted chain of failure. Since deciding to use his plan of conquest as the examination of conscience for confession, his eyes had been opened. Only now could he see how many failings he still had. And because he measured the gravity of his faults in the light of his high ideal, they seemed all the more grievous to him.

His plan of conquest included the solemn promise to die rather than commit a venial sin. But what had happened not so long ago? He could no longer say exactly how, but he knew for a fact: he had clearly lied twice. Both times it came rather suddenly. Before he realized it, it was done. Deeply sorry, he entered in his diary, "Offended God again. Mother, obtain complete forgiveness for me!" Even now remorse filled his heart. And how had he followed the other directives of his plan? What about the particular examination, for instance? It was supposed to be the focal point of his efforts. In the past few weeks he wanted to concentrate on cultivating an especially good life of prayer. The religious exercises of the day —especially Holy Mass, his holy hour, and morning and evening prayers—were to be performed as religiously as possible. That he had kept his particular examination could be seen from his written control. Each evening he wrote down how he had done. But he was still not satisfied. It was not much better with his daily studies. He wanted to become a saintly and learned priest. But how slow was his progress in his studies! At times he could not even finish his homework. He wanted to master the German language perfectly, but he was struggling to even gain control of his pronunciation! Although he did his speech exercises daily, there was hardly any noticeable improvement in his speech. To become "all things to all men" was one of his favorite resolutions to win the hearts of his schoolmates for the great cause of the Blessed Mother. But how clumsy and awkward he was with others! He noticed it especially when the others teased him. How often he made efforts to stand up straight and how often he studied good manners in the books of etiquette! And yet how little success he had in spite of all these almost desperate attempts.

There were times when the feeling of dissatisfaction became so strong that it became an agonizing, oppressive burden. In fact, in the last weeks he had gone through a time of turmoil in his soul. His moods changed like the rising and falling of the tide. At times he was full of enthusiasm, at others he felt so depressed he could have died. Scanning the pages of his diary, he found the strangest contradictions. For instance, at the beginning of February he found entries about his newly awakened zeal and energetic work for the sodality. A week later his feelings were exactly the opposite. He wrote about being annoyed and disgruntled and discontented with everything. A short time afterwards the picture changed again. He called the most recent days "days of grace." He could still remember it well. His life's ideal suddenly stood before him in all its overwhelming greatness! In his inmost being, the urge to become a real man came to life again. He wanted to accomplish superhuman things for the Church and for science, as his diary said. These lines were written in a moment of great enthusiasm. And yet a week later he wrote down under the date of February 18, 1916, "Yesterday and today I was full of fiery determination and now I am in turmoil inside over basically nothing." Thus his moods swung from one day to the next. He felt like a paper boat on a stormy sea. These unpredictable moods simply swirled around him, doing with him as they pleased. He no longer understood himself.

And if he had asked those around him at that time what they thought of him, he would have been even more puzzled. Their impression of him was altogether different. Of course they saw that he had to control himself when his passions suddenly took charge. It might happen during a game or when his friends talked about things that happened in one of the classes. It was also evident when the teasing during his speech exercises went too far. But changing moods? Not that they could see. On the contrary, they thought he enjoyed a well-balanced, cheerful emotional life, and an unbroken, resolute will-power in tackling his self-education. Years later one of his schoolmates said, "I often asked myself with amazement: How can he always be so happy?" Could *he* experience failure in *his* efforts to reach the ideal? If so, he would not have been their esteemed prefect and a recognized leader of the sodality.

Joseph would have been at a loss to reconcile these opinions with his own. He suffered terribly from the broad discrepancy between his high ideals and the undeniable reality of where he was. When he reflected on his failures, a paralyzing discouragement threatened to overcome him. When he thought about the tempest swirling around his constantly changing moods, he felt even worse. Then he felt uprooted, as if there were no ground under his feet. And in spite of it all he should believe in his high ideal? Even see it as his life's task—that Mary's realm from Schoenstatt spread over the whole world? So many of his schoolmates seemed so much more qualified than he. Hans Wormer was so gifted and could speak so well in public! Fritz Esser had such a charm in dealing with others. And himself? Should he give up his ideals? No, his whole interior revolted at the thought. But he found it equally difficult to believe in his ideal. He was hindered by an indescribable helplessness. Was there any way out of the dilemma?

Then he happened to remember a conference his spiritual director had given to the sodality a few weeks ago in the shrine. He liked it so much that he wrote down the main thoughts in his diary. It went this way: The Son of God carries out his plan of redemption here on earth with the help of his creatures. He has assigned the greatest task to his Blessed Mother. She is the official Christ-bearer and protector of the Church. To accomplish her task she needs human instruments. Who does she choose through her intercession? Surely the sodalists! After all, in their solemn consecration they made with her a contract, as it were. They wanted to work for her cause, while she implored for them the graces they needed to become useful instruments of God. But the sodalists included yet another "clause" in their "contract." They offered to make their contributions to the capital of grace so that Schoenstatt might become a second Ingolstadt. So one might ask: Has the Blessed Mother really accepted the sodalists' consecration—also with regard to being a second Ingolstadt? Only time would tell. But anyone familiar with the abundance of graces already showered on this sodality must be inclined to believe that she has already accepted it. Be that as it may, Mary let no one outdo herself in generosity. If we therefore devote ourselves wholeheartedly to her task, she will accomplish great things even with insignificant instruments.

The thoughts of this talk showed Joseph the way out of the difficulty. What his spiritual father said was true. Was he permitted to doubt in the least that the Blessed Mother had accepted his consecration as a sodalist? Certainly not. Had she not also included him in the "contract" which the sodality had made with her? Any doubt would have been a lack of confidence in her motherly love and care. Hence he could entrust himself to her with unlimited confidence. She would enable him to carry out his life's task. She would give him a share in realizing her work in spite of—or rather *because of*—his own evident weaknesses. How she intended to do it was up to her. One thing was certain—he wanted to follow her blindly. A month earlier similar thoughts had passed through his mind. At that time he entered in his diary:

"I want to and must become a great man in every respect. My Mother cannot deny me this favor because I have totally dedicated myself to her and she has placed me at the head of her elect. Our dear Lord cannot deny His Mother any petition."

With this awakening confidence in Mary, he felt solid ground under his feet again. His interior life became calm again. At the same time a profound change began to take place. From now on his titanic striving for an ideal was based less on his own strength. The last month had freed him of the notion that he could do all things by himself. Now he rooted his striving all the more deeply in a boundless confidence in the Mother of Grace of Schoenstatt. This gave his idealism—this he felt quite unmistakably—a new, greater fervor, and his will a greater impetus.

In addition, it had been good that he had recently followed the suggestion of his confessor and changed his particular examination. Since then he was reading something daily about Mary. To deepen what he read, he tried to discuss it whenever possible with his friends. He discovered what tender confidence was beginning to take root in his soul under the influence of his reading. Now his trust totally came into its own. From the time he entrusted himself blindly and unreservedly to the Blessed Mother, it seemed as if a magic wand had transformed his interior life. A grateful attachment and fervent love welled up in his heart. His devotion to Mary received new life. A rich emotional life seemed to have awakened in him and urged him into the arms of his Heavenly Mother. He would never separate himself from her. Without her he would have felt entirely helpless. This experience had such an impact on him that in the midst of spiritual struggles he would appeal to her almost instinctively for help. For the days ahead he chose a particular examination to fight against his moods. But his resolution was not simply, "I want to fight against my moods." He formulated it this way in his diary: "In order to prevent my moods from hindering me in my work, I want to fight against them; I want to specifically call to mind the kindness of my Heavenly Mother three times a day."

This was not yet enough for him. He wanted to visit the shrine of the Queen of the Sodalists more frequently each day, to greet her and spend a few moments in prayer. What else could he do to increase the love of his heart? Then he recalled that the month of March is dedicated to St. Joseph, his own patron saint. He immediately decided to say a prayer to him each day, asking for the grace of a more fervent love of Our Lady. He thought some more. The Blessed Mother must be the absolute Queen of his Heart. Was it perhaps possible to find an outward expression of this covenant of tender love? He soon found it in a vow of holy chastity. On March 12, 1916 he vowed virginal chastity to his Heavenly Mother for the first time. He could offer her a heart which up to then was untouched by any serious sin. He renewed his vow from one confession to the next. When he closed his eyes in death, he held in his hand the unbroken lily of purity. His Heavenly Queen granted him the grace of sparing him serious temptations against this virtue.

May Blossoms and His Personal Ideal

The culmination of his glowing love of Mary came, however, in the month of May. At the start of April, Father Prefect appeared at the noon recess. He pulled out his whistle and sounded a shrill blast. In a few minutes all of the seminary's students were gathered around

84

him. Slowly, almost solemnly, the school prefect took a pinch of snuff. The students sensed there was an important announcement. "Because it is so difficult to get enough food," he began, "you will not spend your Easter vacation at Schoenstatt this year but at home [2]." The announcement was followed by great jubilation. For Joseph, however, it was semi-sweet news. It would not pay for him to make the long trip home. So with a handful of other classmates from Eastern Germany he stayed in Schoenstatt during Easter vacation. He already had a plan. A time of solitude suited him very well. During Holy Week he would make a private retreat. They would be days of thorough spiritual renewal. First he meditated on the eternal truths, then the future was put in order. Again he carefully deliberated: Where are my greatest weaknesses? What particular examinations can practically and effectively keep me moving forward? However, the most beautiful fruit of his meditative and prayerful solitude was to come just a few days later.

God's nature was aglow and spring was in the air. The pussy willows were blooming in the valley where the brook rushed down the hills past the shrine. On the fresh green slopes the primrose was blooming. Hill and vale were radiant with Easter sunshine. Joseph could no longer stand being inside. He had to go out into the beauty of God's springtime. The budding, blooming life about him put him in a happy mood. Soon the Queen of May would come. Her month was only a few days away. That's why the grass and every kind of flower were diligently at work. When she came, they would honor her with their fragrance and blossoms of a thousand colors. Did he too not want to join the flowers in singing her praises? Was he not a chosen child of Mary? Did not his heart cling to her with tender, affectionate love? He did not need to be asked a second time. Of course he wanted to help honor the Queen of May! He, too, would prepare a bouquet of flowers for her as lovely as the loveliest blossoms of spring! He would make his soul into a beautiful garden of Mary! Hurrying back to his room, he took a sheet of paper and began to write:

---

[2]   Easter 1916 was on April 23.

"May blossoms

from the garden of my heart presented to the Queen of May in May 1916. Mother, the whole garden of my heart is dedicated to you. For you I will plant and cultivate in it:

"I. The rose of love and esteem.   At the same time the rose symbolizes you, O Mother. As the rose is the queen of flowers, so be the Queen of my Heart. I place everything at your disposal, my Queen. In particular:

   1) acts of surrender to you,
   2) increasing your honor,
   3) reading abut you,
   4) speaking about you,
   5) reverence to your picture,
   6) visits to your shrine,
   7) rosary,
   8) communion,
   9) spiritual communion,
  10) apostolic deeds,
  11) efforts to make you the center of my day,
  12) ejaculations.

"II. The forget-me-not of faithfulness in your service. I want to be faithful to you by:

   1) the proper recitation of my sodality prayers,
   2) preparing for sodality meetings,
   3) being attentive at spiritual reading,
   4) studying attentively,
   5) keeping silence in the study hall,
   6) observing silence at the sound of the bell,
   7) doing my little chores well,
   8) making my bed properly,
   9) keeping order in my desk,
  10) following the inspirations of grace and of my conscience.

"III. The violet of humility and modesty. I will cultivate this flower by:

   1) accepting corrections patiently,
   2) forgiving offenses,
   3) obeying cheerfully.

"IV. The passion flower of crosses and love of sacrifice. It thrives amid:

1) patient acceptance of unpleasant things,
2) considerate behavior,
3) obligingness,
4) mortification at table,
5) faithfulness to the particular examination,
6) reading from the book of etiquette,
7) reading from the rule book,
8) kindness to others,
9) other sacrifices.
"V. The lily of purity:
1) guarding my eyes, especially in the dormitory,
2) silence in the dormitory,
3) praying for purity before Holy Communion."

All this was to be his gift to Mary and his homage to Our Lady—an all-inclusive program of little sacrifices taken from everyday life for the capital of grace. How inventive love can be! This May became the springtime of his youthful love. Day after day he went into the "garden of his heart" and prepared a bouquet for the Blessed Mother. He put a tally mark behind the proper category for each gift he made. If we add them up we come to a remarkable 1712 tallies—in a single month! Again and again he hastened to the shrine to visit the Queen of May and greet her. There he prayed with ardent love the prayer he had placed at the end of the "May Blossoms":

"Mother, I offer myself entirely to you. I give myself to you with all that I am and have. Mother, do with me as pleases you. I ask nothing for myself, only let me love you. Let me love and honor you without end."

The more his love increased, the more the shrine became the center of his thoughts and feelings. A mysterious charm seemed to emanate from this simple chapel and attract his soul with irresistible force. During the month of May, he visited the chapel of the Mother of Schoenstatt six or seven times daily on average. Could he guess it was destined to be the starting point of a great stream of grace and the center of a mighty movement of renewal? For him it had already been holy ground for a long time, land which the Our Lady wanted to take into her possession. He saw the shrine was the visible symbol of a daring idea and of a great undertaking. The history of his own spiritual life was intimately associated with it. All the important developments of his interior life were somehow connected to it. Here he had struggled with himself until he came to the decisions which had molded his life thus far. No wonder that it was increasingly becoming his spiritual home, the place where he felt rooted with every fiber of his heart. Hardly at any other time did he feel it as strongly as now. His heart was filled with a tender and intimate love of Mary. The shrine was his Tabor where he conversed intimately with his dear heavenly Mother.

May Visits to the Shrine

Every Saturday afternoon the sacristans of the shrine, two of Joseph's classmates, gave the chapel a thorough cleaning. The shrine was scrubbed and decorated for Sunday. Especially the blue and white tile floor had to be spic-and-span. It was the pride of the sacristans. No sooner did they finish their work when Joseph Engling appeared on the scene. He took his place in the very front by the communion rail, immediately in front of the picture of the Mother Thrice Admirable. Engrossed in devout prayer, he knelt there for quite awhile.

"Piety is fine," thought one of the sacristans, a little perturbed, "but he does not have to walk over our freshly mopped floor."

The next Saturday Joseph stood again at the threshold of the chapel. The strict sacristan stopped him and told him quite frankly, "Engling, you cannot do that. You have to wait until the floor is completely dry."

Joseph pleaded. He had just cleaned his shoes and they were absolutely clean.

"I don't care," said the sacristan. "They will make spots on the floor anyway. You have to come back later."

But he kept begging them: What if he walked only on his tiptoes, making really long steps? If he would make any spots on the floor, he would clean them up himself. He said this in such a winning, sincere way that the sacristans could no longer refuse. After that he became a regular customer. Eventually they even wanted him to come although they did not know why. But when he knelt there, there was so much natural devotion in his whole being. They always felt greatly edified by it.

At the end of the month of May, Joseph offered the sacrifices he had made in the course of the month to the Blessed Mother in the shrine. In his heart was the burning desire: If only this place would become the fountain of a stream of graces flowing into the whole world. In his mind he formulated a prayer which he wrote at the end of his "May Blossoms":

"Mother, accept all the good works I have done to honor you during the month of May, especially those I have marked down. It is true that in the beginning of May I offered all to you so that you might dispose of it as you see fit. But now I have a wish. Please accept it so that the idea may be realized: Schoenstatt a second Ingolstadt. But it is only a modest wish, I leave it absolutely to you, O Mother, to do with as you please. *Ave Maria.*"

The approaching end of May gave Joseph an opportunity to review the past weeks. As was his custom, he measured himself according to his life's ideal. He felt that he had done nothing special during May, in fact, little. When he probed the experience of these last weeks more deeply, though, it appeared to him as if he were now first beginning to correctly comprehend the meaning of his ideal. In little more than a month his love for Mary had increased tremendously and reached even into the deepest corners of his heart! He noticed the turning point—and since then mysterious forces had begun to stir that he scarcely knew existed. It was an elemental urge to love, to devote himself to others. He wanted to give himself to Our Lord and Our Lady, to consume himself for the kingdom of God like a pure, blessed votive light. He wanted to serve others unselfishly. He felt so gripped by this urge to give of self that it seemed as if an irresistible, primitive force had taken hold of him. And he saw very clearly that it had all come about since he had learned to truly love the Sodality Queen. The thought had begun to dawn on him during his private retreat in Holy Week. At that time he entered in his diary that the urge to devote himself to others was the strongest fundamental force of his soul.

His experience during May completely unfolded this natural drive until it became an all-dominant power. It absorbed, as it were, all the other contents of his life's ideal. Joseph discovered that his life's ideal was now both greater and much simpler. Before, when he tried to describe his ideal he listed several components: the ideal of a priest, the ideal of a modern saint. By that he meant a man who has overcome sin and is totally gripped by God and Christ. He saw in himself the inclination to be great, the inclination for superhuman accomplishments. He also saw the faithfulness in small things and everyday sanctity. Other facets of his ideal were confident, generous love for Mary and unselfish devotedness to neighbor. Again others pointed to the Mother Thrice Admirable of Schoenstatt and her shrine as a symbol of a great idea. His ideal also told of tireless work for Our Lady's capital of grace so that Schoenstatt might become the center of a movement of Christian renewal.

He made an attempt to simplify his plan of conquest and to express it in fewer sentences. Through his experience of the last weeks he sensed that everything could be captured in a single thought. He found it best expressed in the sentence *Omnibus omnia, Mariae specialiter mancipatus,* "To become all things to all men, and Mary's very own." He also coined a new word for this sentence. From then on he called it "my motto." With his motto he could concisely summarize all the events of four years of interior growth. When he renewed his motto, his spiritual "ear" also heard all the things which had taken place in his soul in the past. But it also pointed to the future. It said in one sentence the most unique and specific task in life given to him by God. From now on all his thoughts and feelings were to revolve around it. As a man of a single, great idea he became a man of real character. *To become all things to all men, and Mary's very own* was his personal ideal.

The month of May 1916 brought him many blessings. It awakened and strengthened in him an intimate love of Mary. Confidence in the Blessed Mother gave him firm footing to control his ups and downs. It taught him to believe in his ideal again. Most of all it was during the month of May that he found his personal ideal.

5. Standard Bearer

An Apostle in Daily Life

A few years after the First World War, some former members of the Junior Sodality were together, reminiscing over old times. "You have to marvel," said one, "at how the sodality could awaken and maintain such an ideal striving among us students in spite of the extreme adversity of the times."

Another added, "It would have hardly been possible without a Joseph Engling to victoriously carry its banner."

The first half of 1916 was the period in Joseph's life when seeds long sown began to sprout. He experienced a springtime of tender love of Mary, which in turn helped many other seeds to germinate. A similar thing could be observed in the school at large. The Junior Sodality experienced its first and most memorable "golden age." It was no coincidence that the springtime of Joseph's interior life coincided with the flourishing spiritual life in the sodality. Since he became prefect of the Junior Sodality, his sincere enthusiasm for the sodality ideals urged him to win over others to the same greatness. He was well on the way to becoming the prime advocate and standard-bearer of the sodality's ideals.

Toward the end of 1915 a few third-year students gathered around Joseph, then in the fourth-year class. One asked, "Say, Joseph, if the sodality is not just for your class, when do we get to join?" The relationship between the two classes had always been a bit strained. This was not surprising, since Joseph's class was noted for its energetic and enterprising members who always claimed the top positions. Not that the third-year class lacked leaders—in fact, it had more than one articulate and determined young man—but they resisted the "over-achievers" in the class ahead of them. They had to admit, though, that their fourth-year brethren had been a good deal less uppity since their admission to the sodality. Joseph was glad to hear of the third-year men's interest in joining the sodality. He smiled. In a very short time they would have weekly instructions to tell them about the sodality. At that time they could begin their candidature. The spiritual director appointed Joseph the master of candidates. He now had two difficult tasks—being master of candidates and sodality prefect—at the same time. His great life's ideal would lead him.

Giving the instructions was no easy task for Joseph. His efforts were not masterpieces of oratory and clever thinking, but they were carefully prepared. His listeners could tell at the beginning of a talk what he was going to say, how the discussion questions would be ordered, and which answers he expected. This was very different from the conferences of the spiritual director. With Father they could rarely guess where it would end. Because of this difference, some did not like Joseph's instructions. They were too much like "school." But everyone had to admit one thing: Joseph Engling lived everything he said. His words about the sodality's ideals were visible in his everyday life.

It was similar with his work as prefect. He did not speak up too much at the meetings. It was not his talent to be a public spokesman or popular orator. For that matter, he did not consider any kind of public teaching to be his strong suit. Following the urging of his temperament, he used a different approach. He dubbed it "the quiet apostolate." It would be the longer and more laborious road to success, but also the more certain one.

Joseph did not have to think long about the right way to start his "quiet apostolate." He sought out closer contact with the members of the magistrate and with the most eager and hard-working sodalists. Looking around him, he observed quite a few who seemed well suited to work together for the aims of the sodality. Joseph sincerely admired his assistant, Hans Wormer. Whatever he said was well thought-out. Once he knew a thing was right, he would carry it out energetically and undeterred by what others might think or say. But so far Joseph had not succeeded in establishing a closer rapport with Hans. Hans was no socialite. Somewhat closed and not very talkative, his words did not radiate much warmth, but rather objective thinking and resolute will. If sodality work had to be done, the prefect could count on his energetic cooperation. But it did not quite satisfy Joseph that their conversations rarely went beyond the facts. He wanted a heartfelt, human relationship. It seemed necessary if their sodality work together was to be fruitful. In any case, he wanted to try and make progress in this direction.

The rapport was better with Fritz Esser. Deep down in his heart Joseph had to envy him sometimes. He exemplified the social graces that Joseph so missed in himself. To be sure, the poor fellow had a terrible time with his studies. It was always a battle of life and death to pass into the next grade. But this weakness was more than compensated by his heartfelt approach to others! He had such a winning and happy-go-lucky nature. He was also perceptive of their hidden worries. Without saying much he could radiate to others the sincere empathy that filled his good heart. If he needed something from a schoolmate, he did not do so bluntly. He patiently waited for the right moment and the right way to ask. This made him liked by many and many confided in him. Yes, Joseph would have to get to know Fritz even better. There was much he could learn from him. He was a master of apostolic "little work."

Joseph also took note of Karl Klement. They had been friends for quite some time. Karl had a keen eye for the little shortcomings of everyday life. In the field of self-education Joseph had benefited more than once from his assistance. Only recently Karl called his attention to the fact that he was constantly picking his face while studying. In addition Karl told him to keep his desk in better order and remove a few spots from his suit. Karl was always willing to help and he found opportunities for little services where others did not see them or think of them. If Brother Gardener left a wheelbarrow full of vegetables at the foot of the hill, Karl, of his own accord, pushed it up the hill and brought it to the kitchen entrance. He cleaned many a washbasin whose owner had carelessly left an ugly black ring, and no one knew who did it. No doubt Karl could be of great help in the sodality.

Then there were the leaders of the various groups of the Eucharistic Section. Their heart was in the right place and they were eager to promote the sodality. They just had to get over their shyness and come out of themselves a little more. Then they would be sturdy associates in the apostolate. Joseph had enough "good timber" all around him for the sodality. But there was no teamwork yet. Everyone was doing what he felt best. They needed to become a team, and for this Joseph's first step was to win each of them over to a closer personal rapport.

His approach with the candidates was very similar. Having sized up the situation, he clearly saw where he had to begin. It was with the three third-year men who were at the heart of the class. If he stayed in touch with them, he would be in touch with the whole group. They were Alfons Hoffmann, Joseph Schnierer, and Alex Menningen. Alfons had been elected by the candidates as their representative to the magistrate, and Joseph already had a good start in getting to know him. But Alfons was still a little bashful and closed; at times he was easily discouraged, especially when things went wrong. In recent weeks Joseph helped him in word and deed. Since then their relationship had warmed up. Alfons was held in esteem by his class for his genuine piety and for already winning first chair in the violin section of the school orchestra.

Engling got along well with Joseph Schnierer, a gifted, mature student who was a little older than his classmates. Their hearts found something in common when Engling noticed in a conversation that Schnierer had a tender, ardent love for Mary. He was delighted by this discovery and entered the little incident in his diary.

Joseph was also looking for ways to get closer to Alex Menningen. He had been class prefect in his first year. His strictness as prefect had upset his classmates and this was not completely forgotten. But being sharper and more articulate than most, he knew how to keep the opposition down. It was important for Joseph to win over Alex because he was one of their top students and because he had a considerable following. Alex considered a small circle of them to be his friends and companions. It was with them that he shared his packages from home. The others were regarded as satellites; they depended upon his help in their studies, for he helped them with their homework and prepared them for tests. Joseph would have a difficult time with him. In the beginning Alex was much more impressed by Hans Wormer than Joseph. That's why he joined Hans' section in the sodality. He looked on Joseph Engling critically, almost contemptuously, and only paid him any attention by teasing him. But in the end Joseph won him over. It happened very simply. The more Alex became familiar with the ideals of the sodality, the more he used them in measuring Joseph. In the end he began to admire him, and finally became his ally.

In this way a circle of faithful followers, consisting of the most talented students of both classes, gradually formed around the prefect. All of them had a good reputation with the faculty and the respect of their classmates. Joseph now had his work cut out for him. He was constantly doing his "quiet apostolate." He managed to arrange his free time in such a way that he was nearly always able to speak privately with one of his assistants. He did not just engage in "shop talk" either. He concerned himself with each one's personal well-being, the things going on in class, and sodality business. At least that was how the conversations began. Then Joseph began to guide the conversation to other matters: how to show proper devotion to Mary, how to make a good particular examination, Schoenstatt as a second Ingolstadt, etc. It was remarkable how the boys took to his little lessons, even those who had a reputation for being quite headstrong. Of course, if Joseph had not been so totally genuine and transparent, if he had not lived the ideals he taught, they would not have stood for his "lectures." But it was plain that he was totally sincere. He worked for Our Lady of Schoenstatt and not for himself. He was motivated by sincere, heartfelt love of neighbor. It showed so much in everything he did that the others simply could not oppose him even those who were sometimes annoyed by his awkward manners.

Joseph sensed that his efforts to build up a good rapport with the "leadership potential" was only a first step. They in turn would need to be motivated to do the same with their friends. If each one gathered a circle of cooperators, the whole school would soon be influenced. Most of his friends were already reaching out. But he still had to help the younger ones. They needed encouragement and an occasional word of advice. Eventually even Alex Menningen, who initially opposed him, became his willing disciple.

Promoter of Quiet Apostolate

Alex and Joseph were sitting together one evening at recreation, when Joseph suddenly asked, "Alex, do you know what quiet apostolate is?" His friend had no clear idea. Joseph explained: "You get along quite well with Peter Jakobson, Paul

---

Raikes, and Ewald Fahr. You know each other quite well and are acquainted with each other's faults. Couldn't you try to win them over to self-education? You have to show them how to make a real particular examination and how to make contributions to the capital of grace." Alex thought it over. Surely he could do it. The three were decent fellows. They would probably even be glad if he would discuss such sensible things with them. "And then," Joseph continued, "look at some of your classmates who are not sodalists. Paul Pabelman, for instance, does not have too good a reputation because of his laziness. Unless he changes his attitude, he might even get expelled. Ted Kobler's foolish pranks are also in danger of costing him his vocation. The same goes for Alois Paitz. He is not too good in his studies and pretty lukewarm. I doubt they could be won over for the sodality. But that does not make any difference. We must not drop them by any means. After all, they are our schoolmates. As sodalists we must take them into our care and try to lead them to better ways." Alex was not yet convinced. "They won't let us convert them," he objected.

Joseph did not give in. "You have to find the right approach. Try to be kind and friendly with them; for instance, don't tease Alois or call him 'Schnoz' because of his big nose. That makes him angry. Do little favors for him. Then you will win his confidence and that of the others. You remember what we discussed at the meeting of the Mission Section concerning the indirect missionary method. Later you can put in a good word." This was more or less what Joseph said. Alex promised to give the quiet apostolate a try.

Soon Alex could happily report to Joseph that everything had gone well. His three comrades were now making a particular examination. He and Peter Jakobson even wanted to win over non-sodalists. On the next hike Peter walked with Paul Pabelman and helped pull him up a steep hill. Alex was with Alois, who looked pretty glum. Their conversation about the weather turned to school matters. Alois revealed that his last Latin test was a disaster. He just didn't get the *conjugatio periphrastica* and *oratio obliqua*. "Listen," said Alex, "it is not really so hard." He began to explain it but could not finish before the end of the hike. It took many weeks before Alois, testing Alex's patience and endurance, discovered the secrets of Latin grammar. But in the end their efforts proved quite successful. After the next test was handed back, Alois reported with a big grin that he had gotten a "B." Now Alex remembered the advice Joseph had given him. The hour had come to put in a good word.

"Do you know, Alois," he began, "you are not only expected to write good tests, but you are expected to become a modern saint?"

Hearing this, Alois turned up his nose and scratched his head with embarrassment. The extra help now seemed to be taking a dangerous turn. After a little reflection he replied, "Alex, I think I can manage the *oratio obliqua* by myself now."

Alex hastily dropped the dangerous subject and started talking about something else. On the following day, however, Alois sought him out, scratched his head exactly the same way he did the day before and said, "Say, what did you mean by *modern saint?*" They were on the desired topic after all. In the future they changed off, sometimes discussing the modern saint, sometimes the *oratio obliqua.*

Joseph was happy with Alex's success. It even helped them become better friends, and Joseph took him into his confidence more and more. One evening he spoke with him about a topic he had rarely mentioned before. It concerned the Blessed Mother. Alex listened in silence. He would not have known much to say about this topic to his schoolmates. But for Engling it was so natural to talk about Mary that he liked to listen to him. He had a very solemn sense about him that evening, and from then on he did not tease or play tricks on Joseph anymore. Nor would he let anyone else do so either. If he caught anyone doing it, he made him stop at once.

The whole student body could soon notice a mysterious influence radiating from the prefect. Whatever he experienced deep down in his own heart flowed over to the other sodalists. Without their knowing it, he communicated his striving for the sodality ideal and influenced them to do likewise.

His work with the enthusiastic was going well. But there were problem children as well. Given his kind heart and sense of duty,

Joseph could not just give them a cold shoulder. In the study hall, not far from Joseph, sat Willy Schmitz. What a unique mixture of talent, carelessness and kindheartedness he possessed! During recreation he was often very comical, providing entertainment and laughter. One of the teachers could not stand him and reprimanded him many times during class. It was the general opinion that this was often done unjustly. Willy had more good will than appeared on the surface. Joseph's sympathetic heart sensed this quickly. One day when Willy was severely reprimanded and excessively punished, Joseph felt sorry for him and decided to help him. Joseph spent more time with Willy at recess. Willy began to confide in Joseph. One of the tallest boys in the whole school, Willy received Joseph's advice like a little child. If only he had not been so careless! On account of it, his best resolutions ended in failure. Joseph did not lose his patience with him, and so Willy had the courage to try again. He was even one of the candidates for the sodality. At the end of the candidature, the magistrate recognized his sincere striving and decided to admit him as a sodalist. Admissions, however, were only valid after they were confirmed by the moderator of the sodality, the seminary's Father Rector. Joseph spoke with the rector about the matter and the admission was confirmed. Joseph and Willy were quite happy. But not long afterwards Joseph got a summons from Father Rector. He had reconsidered and felt it necessary to with-draw his approval. Joseph felt struck by lightning. Now he had to ruin Willy's happiness. He could hardly muster the courage to do so. His heart went out to Willy and the disappointment he would feel. The matter affected Joseph so much he even developed a headache.

About a month later he wrote a few lines in his diary, casting light on his sorrow and thoughtful concern:

"Yesterday three schoolmates, Kalen, Landar and Schmitz, were expelled. When I heard it, all kinds of thoughts came to my mind. Is it really true that all our efforts have been in vain? Could we have done any more?' I asked myself. I felt sorry for all, especially Schmitz. Well, we did almost all we could do. God alone knows why it happened the way it did."

In May 1916 the sodality had a celebration. While the sodalists were practicing the songs for it, a little incident occurred. Three of them stayed away from the rehearsal because they had an argument with their schoolmate who was the choir director. In order to make him angry, they sang war songs near the choir during rehearsal. Naturally the sodalists were upset and appealed to Joseph. He could not be won over to immediate action. He calmed them down and convinced them it was best to ignore the mischief-makers. He did not want to take strong action before the celebration, spoiling the atmosphere of the celebration. On the other hand, the disobedient troublemakers would not go unpunished. After the celebration he would give them a piece of his mind. If they did not repent of their wrongs and make amends, he would take measures against them. He was firmly resolved to approach the magistrate and ask for their immediate expulsion from the sodality. The three rebels were quite upset when they saw they were being ignored. They sat in the back row at the celebration. They would have liked to see the choir get stuck. When it became noticeable that the choir was having trouble with some difficult passages, they made nasty remarks. But they felt strangely unhappy. This became quite apparent when Joseph called them in and gave each of them a stern lecture. It hit home. The rebels acknowledged their guilt and did penance "in sackcloth and ashes." This was fortunate for them, since Joseph would certainly have carried out his resolve to have them expelled from the sodality.

Joseph was involved in resolving more than one conflict in his class. Two of his classmates couldn't stand the sight of each other. One glance was enough to light their short fuses and set them at each other's throats. It could not go on like this; something had to be done. Joseph was asked to step in. He began a kind of "shuttle diplomacy" to try and restore peace. It took several rounds of private conversations with each of the parties to finally get them to mend their differences.

So it was that Joseph constantly practiced his "little apostolate." Nearly all the recess periods were devoted to this cause. Some thought it excessive. They would watch from a distance and elbow one another when they saw him "on the prowl" for another apostolic "victim." To them it looked like someone trying to snare sparrows. "Look at Engling! He's catching one of his birds again," they used to remark. By now Joseph had reached a circle of boys. He smiled in his gentle, boyish way and gave everyone a friendly greeting. Then he would tug the sleeve of whoever he wanted to see or gave him a soft jab in the ribs. More was not necessary, and the two would walk a bit aside for a private conversation. There was occasional ridicule about how he went about it. Some thought his approach too awkward, that he was too abrupt. But the harder he tried to be polite, the more awkward it seemed.

No, it was not as bad as all that. Anyone scrutinizing his method more closely would have to admit he was prudent and courteous enough. He might have been too zealous at times, and Joseph himself knew that his style was awkward and unpolished. When he recalled his life's ideal—to be all things to all men—he felt compelled to improve his manners. He studied a book of etiquette quite often. But that only seemed to make matters worse. There were times at table, in a moment of public speaking, or in his deal-ings with superiors and fellow students when it was plain that he was trying to apply a rule he had learned. The effect was often comical. But for him the inner spirit was more important than the external rule. In his diary he wrote the resolution: "To see in my neighbors the image of God so that I can deal with them in the proper way." Even his critics admitted that, despite his external shortcomings, he was noble and candid of character.

As the weeks turned into months, his persistent, energetic work on behalf of souls was crowned with visible success. An enthusiastic striving for self-education and genuine love of Mary began to flourish in the sodality. One could see that the life of the community was focused more and more on a single aim. The Schoenstatt-Ingolstadt ideal entered more and more into public awareness. The story of Joseph's own spiritual life seemed to repeat itself in the community. He was clearly its spiritual leader. His great ideal in life, "to become all things to all men," began to take definite external form.

Effects of War

One day in March 1916, some of the junior sodalists had some surprising news. They had heard that the Senior Sodality was starting a magazine. The rumor was soon verified. One day Alex

Langner, prefect of the Senior Sodality, came by with a big smile to solicit subscriptions for it. They soon held the first issue in their hands. It was very good looking. It was typed and lithographed on professional paper. The masthead featured the picture and name of the Mother Thrice Admirable. The magazine's name, in bold letters, was: *Mater Ter Admirabilis*. It was the "Mother Thrice Admirable" magazine, soon known affectionately as the *"MTA"* magazine. "Where did the Senior Sodality get the money to publish such a respectable magazine?" the treasurer was asked. He just smiled and revealed that there was a grand total of fifty-seven cents in the treasury. *"Mater habeit curam*—Mother takes care." The magistrate had taken this slogan to heart. The others had never heard of such a strange way of bookkeeping before, but the future would show whether it would stand the test.

The new magazine caused general admiration and interest. Its contents appealed to the sodalists now fighting in the war. It was designed to keep the spirit of the sodality alive while some of its members were exposed, in the barracks or on the battlefields, to the dangers of an enticing and differently minded world. Subsequent issues featured articles written by the sodalists themselves. Excerpts of letters to the spiritual director or of correspondence to other sodalists were published. Such letters were special favorites; especially when they were not signed by name, but only with an 'X.' If that were the case, a fellow sodalist was describing an interior struggle he had to fight out in the world. The younger generation at home eagerly awaited these. If someone wanted to say that the last issue was especially interesting, he would say "There were lots of X's again this time!" Those who remained in Schoenstatt wrote articles too and told something about their work in the sodality. Many a student took special pride in seeing his name in print for the first time.

Indeed, the magazine proved to be a Godsend in the needs of the times. More and more members of the Senior Sodality had to interrupt their studies because of the war. Toward the end of 1915 the men born in 1896 were drafted into the army. Four of them were in Berlin for basic training. In order to help and encourage one another, they started a Schoenstatt group. The "97ers" followed in early 1916. How much longer until the "98ers," including Joseph Engling, would be called to arms? In Schoenstatt, the Senior Sodality was shrinking rapidly. Almost all of its leaders were in the war. The "97ers" soon had a Schoenstatt group in the army too. Little by little, an "external" sodality was being formed around the one at home. It was soon called the "External Organization." The *MTA* magazine tied the two together. Its expenses were paid for by the sodalists themselves. The sodalists in uniform considered it a matter of honor to contribute something, no matter how small, even if it had to be saved from their meager pay.

There were always mixed emotions when another class was called to arms. There was patriotism of course, but also the anxious question: Will all return from the war? The war took its toll with unrelenting fury. Just recently the first death notice had arrived: J. Heinrich, killed in action in Galicia. Many of the school's alumni from the major seminary were already buried in graves on the theater of war. How well they had known them! Every evening the school prefect read the war report from the Kaiser's chief of staff. Everyone listened anxiously. Since 1916 the reports of victory had become rarer and rarer. Now all the news was about the terrible war of attrition. Most in Schoenstatt had one or the other close relative in the war. For many it was a brother; for some even a father. Because of this, victories rarely brought any joy. A heavy cloud hung over the students when the war report was read.

One recent hike took them to the *Wandhof* [1]. At the crest of the hill they stood in silence for a long time, listening to the west. Since the end of February the battle of Verdun had been raging. Even at a distance of 130 miles, the thunder of the heavy artillery could be heard. It was a terrible sound. Every so often duller thuds were audible. Were those the famous 42-mm guns? Someone finally broke the silence. "My brother is there." "Mine, too," said another. They continued their hike in a sullen mood. Would bad news come with tonight's mail? There was always much military mail for Father Prefect to hand out each night. One night Hans received a letter and

[1]   The farm at the crest of Mount Schoenstatt beyond the present Adoration Church and House Marienland.

102

turned white as a ghost. Without speaking a word he retreated to the back corner of the study hall. He laid his head in his arms and started to cry. Before him lay a letter. It was one he had sent to his brother. A red pen had crossed out the name and written, "Return to sender! Honorably fallen in battle!" No one asked what had happened. They knew all too well. He was not the only one to receive such a letter. Joseph Engling had gotten one not long ago[2], and Hans Wormer, and Alfons Hoffmann, and many others. It was war.

Although such hardships may have temporarily set back the life of the sodality, the striving of the sodality never stopped completely in spite of the war. Of the Junior Sodality, at least, one could say it was steadily improving. Joseph's own enthusiasm seemed to grow with the difficulties. He got involved in the new magazine and the growing External Organization. Schoenstatt a second Ingolstadt! Did it not look like even the war was helping make these words come true? The sodalists, unexpectedly thrown into life's battles, now had a chance to promote their great ideal and pass it on to others. Many of them promoted it by lending the MTA magazine to like-minded comrades, especially to other students. Word came back from the front that it was well received. Was this a hint of Divine Providence to win over students to the influence of the Blessed Mother of Schoenstatt? This could be an important step on the way to their goal.

One day a former schoolmate returned to Schoenstatt and told about his work with other boys in a high school in Limburg[3]. He had been sent there by the superiors to earn his diploma in a public high school. Now he had started a religious-academic study group. It was similar to the Schoenstatt Sodality. Joseph was excited by this news. Schoenstatt's Mother of Grace evidentially wanted to extend her realm beyond the narrow confines of their local sodality to all

[2]   His oldest brother August was killed in action in Galicia on the Russian front on October 6, 1915.

[3]   Fernidand Kastner had to leave the Schoenstatt Minor Seminary in Spring 1915 for health reasons. On May 30, 1916, he was the first "external" member officially accepted to the Schoenstatt Sodality. Kastner later became a Pallottine Father and major Schoenstatt leader.

students. As Joseph Engling noted in his diary, the topic of the discussion at this meeting was how a spiritual renewal of Germany could go forth from Schoenstatt, beginning with students their age. This thought of expansion occupied him for a long time afterward. Some time later he wrote in his diary:

"The sodalists have set themselves to a noble task, or rather, the Sodality Queen has showed it to them. A spiritual renewal of our nation is to go forth from Schoenstatt... We want to gather students, enthuse them for our ideas, and establish our organization among them."

True to his nature, Joseph was not satisfied with merely making plans. He wanted to make an active contribution to their realization. He started to correspond with students he knew from his homeland in East Prussia. He encouraged other sodalists to do the same. Soon he could write in his diary, "The sodalists of the Junior Sodality, too, have worked to realize the idea that from here, the Shrine of the Mother Thrice Admirable, a spiritual renewal of our nation should go forth." He then gives the names of sodalists who have won over students from other high schools to subscribe to the MTA magazine. Considering this newest development of the sodality and its modest successes among outsiders, he saw the World War taking on new significance. In his diary he wrote:

"In these days the significance of the World War has become clear to me. Although moral conditions have worsened and, on the whole, no spiritual or religious improvement can be seen, the war has nonetheless led to positive gains in these areas. How many incentives have the present conditions given us sodalists! Because of the struggle, many of the sodalists have taken command of their own interior life and become spiritually strong. They are already working quietly in the background for a spiritual renewal and will one day do great things in public life.

"This is even more true of our sodalists in uniform. How much good has already been accomplished by the MTA magazine, established solely because of the war. As soon as the plan for the spiritual renewal of Germany is put into effect from Schoenstatt, the educated classes will defend their faith and morality, and will draw the ordinary people after them." (June 28, 1916).

The more that sodalists were drafted into the army, the bigger the

External Organization became, and the larger the circulation of the MTA, the more heavily Joseph felt his responsibility of sodality prefect. Now the sodality had to do its utmost to foster a strong life. Otherwise the growing work would lack firm foundations. He focused his efforts primarily on the magistrate, for they would have to be the main motivators. He met nearly every week with his officers to discuss their progress.

Magistrate Meeting

It was a holiday in Schoenstatt, giving Joseph a perfect opportunity for a magistrate meeting. He sent word to his co-workers that there would be a meeting in the spiritual director's room at four o'clock. Everyone was on time. Father Kentenich was at his desk writing letters. "You go ahead and start," he said. "I will be listening." Joseph started the meeting with a prayer. Then he opened the chronicle where the minutes were kept. He gave the secretary a reproachful look. The minutes of the last and second-to-last meeting had not been entered. The secretary blushed and mumbled something about not having had any time. He promised to make up for his failure. Joseph gave the chronicle to him and posed this question to the others: "How are things right now with the life and striving of the sodality?"

One reported: "Right now there is a lot of talk again about food and complaints about hunger. If we talk too often about such things, it is hard to awaken interest in the ideals of the sodality."

But another expressed the opinion that the hunger really was too hard. The amounts rationed were too little to live and too much to die. Sister Superior was supposed to have wept not long ago when she saw the faces of some of the younger students, empty dish in hand, eyes pleading for more food. She had nothing more to give.

"The night before last," reported a third, "Bergen is supposed to have broken out with some of his friends. Someone fooled him into thinking that the beet roots near the farm buildings would be edible and as tasty as apples. They were so hungry they began to think it was true. So Bergen and a few others slipped out at night, dug out a few roots, peeled them and ate them."

Another added, "A similar thing happened to the four who clean the house chapel. Last Saturday they went to the dishwashing area to get their mops and buckets. On the counter they found a dish with cold, watery rutabagas left over from dinner. The boys were so overcome by hunger that they started to eat them right then and there. Suddenly one began to panic: 'What if we're caught and reported to Father Prefect?' They beat a hasty retreat to the chapel, dish and all, and finished the food in the corner next to one of the side altars."

"The worst hunger," remarked another, "always plagues us during the last class period before dinner. Florin's hunger pangs tormented him so much a few days ago that he bit into the cover of his Greek Grammar. You can still see his teethmarks in it."

Members of the Magistrate During Joseph Engling's Term as Prefect, 1915-16

Prefect: Joseph Engling
Assistant Prefect: Hans Wormer
Second Assistant: Alfons Hoffmann (representative from the third-year class, starting February 1916)
Secretary: Wilhelm Girke
Treasurer: Valentine Rumpf
Leader of the Mission Section: Hans Wormer
Leader of the Eucharistic Section: Adolf Baldauf

This is where Joseph jumped in: "We have to promote more games and good humor. It banishes many gloomy thoughts. If people don't stand around during recess, they won't talk so much about food." Hans Wormer suggested that the various sections resolve not to talk about food and being hungry.

Some objected, "We won't be able to keep it." Hans replied, "A sodalist must be able to keep it," and pressed his lips together.

"And I suppose that will fill him up," Alex said dryly.

So the magistrate started to look for a different solution. They began to talk about the capital of grace. "Couldn't the sodalists be motivated to remain silent about their everyday troubles and bear them patiently out of love for our Blessed Mother? The month of May is just around the corner. We should get ready to make it a real month of sacrifice." Joseph, of course, gave such suggestions his

106

full support. As the discussion continued, the spiritual director looked up from his desk. He looked sympathetically at the pale, thin faces of his boys. Four of them were already infected with chronic disease because of their undernourishment. They were going to die while still in their teens. "It is really touching," thought the spiritual director to himself, "how the boys' hearts cling to Our Lady. They must go through such distressing times filled with bitter hunger, but they do not let it stop them from serving the Sodality Queen."

By now the conversation had moved to another subject. There was great consternation among the students over one of the teachers and a superior. It acted as a drag on the work of the sodality. The attitude toward the teacher in question was getting very bitter indeed. It came from the students' impression that he did not teach in the correct manner. He simply read the rules from his grammar book without any commentary. Then he gave incredible amounts of homework. If anyone pointed out a grammar error which he had made, he became furious and shamed his accuser. The relationship with one of the superiors was also turning from bad to worse. Its crisis came when he ordered that no more food packages could be sent to the boys from home. He felt that the law was the law, saying, "Either your parents have too much, and then the law says they must give it to the state. Or they only have what they need, in which case you have no right to it." The students considered such reasoning nonsense. His punishments also caused much resentment. He insisted that the house rules be oberved to the tiniest letter. For instance, it was against the rules to enter the big classroom in the Old House through the windows, even though these went all the way to the floor. One day the classroom door was locked and some boys went in through the windows. The superior saw them. Their punishment was to "kneel one out" at supper. Others stayed inside one day at recess to warm their freezing hands around the pot-bellied stove. The rules said they must be outside for recess and they, too, had to "kneel one out." The most dreadful part of this punishment was not getting anything to eat. The priest in question did not realize how badly this hurt the boys. He only saw the law and his obligation to uphold it in the name of discipline. When it happened, some table groups of four relished their "good fortune" of being reduced to three or even two to share the same dish of food. The boys being punished looked on in torment while their comrades ate their rations. In other table groups, however, solidarity and friendship were stronger than hunger. Friends would secretly let potatoes and sausage slide into their pockets, to be given to their starving comrade in an unnoticed moment after the meal.

Frequent eruptions of malcontent against the teacher and superior just mentioned gave the magistrate plenty of trouble. Joseph Engling and Hans Wormer argued for an unpopular approach. They were of the opinion that teachers and superiors must always be treated with courtesy. Under no circumstances did they consider it permissible to criticize their actions, even though the complaints might be true and justified. All the students owed them reverence, love and obedience. It was therefore the officers' task to encourage the sodalists to make their superiors happy by faithful fulfillment of their duties, thereby eliminating all cause for reproach. They should also defend their superiors' actions as well as they could. "We have been doing this for a long time already," remarked Alex Menningen excitedly, "and we were still publicly scolded by one of the superiors recently. He said that we talk big in the sodality, but fail to fulfill our duties. The fact of the matter is that a non-sodalist broke the house rules, not a sodalist. When we have a celebration, none of the teachers shows up, even though they are invited. And I know the reason. They are against the sodality. How many of us would have lost our enthusiasm for our vocation if it had not been for the sodality? I would have been one of them." He was visibly upset. When the discussions took such a turn the spiritual director intervened and tried to reconcile the opposing views. Finally, they agreed on a resolution for the coming weeks—to work especially on courtesy and good manners among the sodalists in order to keep the existing frictions from becoming even worse.

Joseph directed the attention of the magistrate to a new question. They had to expect that the "98ers" would be drafted soon, making it necessary to involve them in sodality work in a special way. By the time they were called to arms, they would have to be so firm of character that they could withstand the moral dangers of army life. The officers were asked to make suggestions as to what could be done, but the discussion was not very fruitful. Finally, someone thought that self-education should be specially stressed. Others suggested that they be introduced to the methods of quiet apostolate. The more active they would become in the sodality, the more support they would find in the community. The discussion did not come to anything concrete, so they moved on.

The leader of the Eucharistic Section now brought a complaint against Nick Angermaier, a member of his section. So far Angermaier had been in charge of the index file which contained material for talks and conferences. A few days ago he had returned the box, stating that he would no longer do the job. He had heard that a few sodalists said bad things about him, so he lost all interest in his section and would have nothing to do with the index file anymore. Here the prefect stepped in with a clear, brief decision: "We cannot let Angermaer's arbitrary action stand." Turning to the section leader he continued, "Inform him of the following: If he wishes to resign from his office for any reason, he should do so in the proper manner. As long as the resignation has not been formally accepted, he will have to do his duty. The reasons Angermaier has given are insufficient for resigning from office. Return the box to him and make it clear that he will have to take care of it if he wishes to remain in the sodality." A few days later it became clear that the prefect had made the right decision. Angermaier admitted his mistake and asked Joseph for forgiveness.

Now the magistrate had to discuss their "problem child." It was not for the first time. John Rausch, member of the fourth-year class and the Junior Sodality, was really getting out of control. There were many complaints about his rough and quarrelsome way of dealing with others. He would break any rule of the house as soon as nobody was watching. For quite some time he had been indifferent toward the sodality. With great sadness, Joseph told how Fritz Esser had informed him that Rausch had not visited the sodality chapel for 12 weeks. Some thought that they had been patient enough and wanted Rausch to be expelled. At this point the spiritual director intervened and asked the members of the magistrate a question of conscience: Had they really done everything in their power to lead him to better ways? Only if they had done so, could they think of expelling him.

But the officers of the fourth-year class knew that many sodalists had tried for weeks to influence Rausch in the right way. Especially Fritz Esser had tried everything to get him to change. But Rausch just laughed at the sodalists. Joseph himself could verify these statements. He had made similar efforts too.

"But if we expel him," one of the fourth-year men objected, "there will be a ruckus. He will instigate the whole class and build support among the lukewarm. He can talk big, and he will form a party to oppose the sodality. He will split the class."

"This cannot keep us from doing what is right," remarked Hans Wormer. Joseph agreed with him and added, "We will have to find ways to prevent a split in the class." Several suggestions were made. Rausch would have to be approached calmly and with sincere friendliness. Patience and kindness would take the weapons out of his hands. They would also have to keep in frequent touch with his friends to prevent them from segregating from the rest of the class. Perhaps the punishment would shake him up and bring about an inner conversion. The magistrate proceeded to vote on Rausch's expulsion. The motion passed by majority vote.

The matters for discussion were finished. At the end, the prefect summarized the results of the discussion: "In order to properly master the difficulties existing in the community, we have to make a good preparation for May and make it a real month of sacrifice for the capital of grace. At the same time we have to promote games and good humor to prevent a gloomy and irritable spirit. The magistrate must emphasize the quiet apostolate and give special attention to the 98ers.' At table and in conversation we want to cultivate politeness and good manners. The leaders of the magistrate must work more as a team." Joseph said the concluding prayer and the meeting adjourned.

At the end of June 1916, the third class took over the leadership of the Junior Sodality [4]. The fourth-year men prepared to move up to the Senior Sodality. This concluded Joseph's activity as a leader in the younger sodality. Looking back on the past half year, he could

---

[4]   Alfons Hoffmann was elected prefect and Alex Menningen his assistant.

summarize the fruits of his interior development and exterior activity with the words: "All things to all men, and Mary's very own!" This is how his personal ideal stood out in his mind. The thought had shaped his striving for sanctity and his activity as prefect of the Junior Sodality.

Summer Vacation At Home

Toward the end of July 1916 the Engling family was filled with excitement. In a few days Joseph would be coming home for his annual summer vacation. It would be his fourth visit home. His father, in the living room, was working on some item of clothing. Sewing was his time to think. How quiet it was getting at home! One child after another was moving away. The two oldest girls had been working for quite some time now. August, the oldest son—God rest his soul! Only nine months ago they buried him on one of the battlefields of Galicia. Eternal rest grant unto him, O Lord! He looked at August's picture on the wall. Again and again the father thought about his oldest boy. Valentine, too, had been enlisted not long ago. His father hoped that he himself would not have to go to war. Now he had only two of his seven children left —John and Lucy. So he was glad that Joseph was coming home for vacation. Last year they really appreciated his help during the harvest. The big, strong fellow always did his share. He hoped that the war would not last so long that Joseph, too, would have to be enlisted.

As always, his mother kept house with quiet, loving devotion. She was especially happy about Joseph's visit. His little room was already cleaned and ready. How fast the years had passed! Would she live to see her boy ascend to the altar as a priest? This would certainly be the happiest day of her life. During his first weeks and months in Schoenstatt she had been greatly worried. She was anxious about whether or not they could use him, about whether he was smart enough for the long studies. But then came Joseph's reassuring letters that had nothing but good news to tell.

Yes, his letters! Joseph described everything so beautifully that she felt practically a part of everything he did. This was why she saved all his letters. They formed quite a bundle in her dresser. Joseph wrote every month, sometimes twice a month. On a Sunday afternoon, after quietly praying the stations and the rosary in the village church, she felt like reading some of his letters. One after the other passed through her hands. They told about life in the Schoenstatt seminary, the celebration of the house's dedication, the fun they had on St. Nicholas Day, the play they had put on, and many other great and small events of everyday life. Among the letters was a long poem congratulating his brother Valentine on his nameday. Joseph could even write poetry! A very lengthy letter described his first visit to Cologne, the life and activity in a large city, and the wonderful things he had seen in its museums. How simply and intelligently her educated son could write about all these things! Then there were the many letters for birthdays and namedays! No member of the family was forgotten. The letters John and Lucy had received for their first Holy Communion were exceptionally good. Something would have been missing at these family celebrations if Joseph had not been represented by a letter. She especially loved to read the ones where Joseph assured her how beautiful the vocation to the priesthood was and how happy he was in Schoenstatt. And then came one that she could only read with tears in her eyes. It had been written when they heard about August's death on the front. Joseph wrote:

"Your letter confirmed my suspicions. When no cards or letters came from brother August and when you wrote me in your last card that he had been wounded, I felt somehow that he had fallen and I doubled my prayers for him. Certainly, it is a great sorrow for me, but how much greater for you, my dear parents! But be consoled! Your son died defending the fatherland. He died a hero. He gave his life for a worthy cause, the fatherland. But this should not be your only consolation.... He has surely reached his eternal goal.... Perhaps he will already celebrate tomorrow's feastday in heaven together with all the saints. After all, he viewed the war as a punishment from God and, as we can tell by his letters, he bore its hardships in that spirit; hence he shortened his suffering in purgatory. My dear brothers and sisters, this should be a consolation to you as well. I am sure you will not take this the wrong way. We must now love our parents all the more, console them, make up for the natural love taken from them by the death of our dear brother." (October 31, 1915).

112

His mother wiped the tears from her eyes. She had to think of her dear son buried somewhere on foreign soil. But she was also touched by how much Joseph had shared her heavy load of grief. What a good boy! Yes, from childhood on he had always been that way—always so faithful and genuine in his childlike love.

It was a happy moment when Joseph finally completed the long journey and arrived home. Everyone commented that he seemed a bit thin, but nothing mother's home cooking couldn't remedy. Twelve-year-old Lucy, the youngest, was quite impressed by her big brother. He had a brand new student cap and even wore glasses. In earlier years she had always viewed him as an authority, for he knew everything and did everything right. Now he looked even more learned. In spite of it all, he remained the same Joseph, just as unassuming and friendly as ever. That was clear just a few days later when, on Saturday, he helped her clean the house. She had to admit that for a boy he did a pretty good job!

Immediately after getting home, Joseph had a few important matters he wanted to take care of. First of all, he worked on his written spiritual daily order. As before, he wrote in big letters at the top of the sheet: "Contributions to the Capital of Grace of our Mother Thrice Admirable during Vacation 1916." The daily spiritual order was otherwise nearly identical to the one from the year before. He then added in his diary, "While at home, I want to rise at 5:30 am. After getting dressed and saying my morning prayers, I want to do my spiritual reading and then my calisthenics. At 7 o'clock I will go to Mass. I will occupy the time between calisthenics and Holy Mass with a short walk or reading a passage from (Schiller's) *Dreizehnlinden.*" After a few days he felt that the time between rising and Holy Mass was too long. So he changed his time of rising to 6 o'clock.

After completing the work on his spiritual daily order, he set out to make the customary visit to his pastor. He had a definite purpose in mind. He wanted to introduce frequent Holy Communion in his home parish. Up until now it was not common practice. During vacation Joseph was the only one at the communion rail. Of course, the pastor had to be won over first, which was not so easy. The pastor was a somewhat elderly, reserved man who adhered tenaciously to the old traditions and had little use for innovation. Joseph had already made efforts in the Eucharistic apostolate during his last summer vacation. At that time he visited the pastor several times and tried again and again to direct the conversation to the desired topic. A real conversation about the matter just never got off the ground. Afterwards he was upset with himself and called himself a dumb fellow. His efforts in the family were at least somewhat more successful. His mother let herself be talked into joining him at the communion rail. It broke the ice and other women followed their example.

In the first days of his vacation Joseph was happy to see that the women had faithfully continued the practice all year. Now he had to convince the pastor to expand the little beginnings into a full-fledged Eucharistic movement within the parish. Unfortunately, the pastor was out of town. Then on the following Sunday Joseph was treated to a pleasant surprise. His pastor preached on frequent Holy Communion! On his trip to several large cities he had seen great numbers of the faithful flocking to the table of the Lord. He was suddenly aware of his own rural foot-dragging. From then on he promoted frequent reception of Holy Communion in his parish. Joseph's other apostolic endeavors could now benefit from this step forward.

Joseph's vacation apostolate included a still more daring plan. It was nothing less than the spiritual conquest of Warmia[5] for the work of the Blessed Mother of Schoenstatt. Like all his apostolic plans, this one was inspired by enthusiasm for the "Ingolstadt-Schoenstatt" parallel. He was especially enthused by the idea of a movement of renewal reaching out from Schoenstatt to high school and college students. He had been thinking about this for weeks. While in Schoenstatt he had heard about the successes of the sodalists in uniform at winning over students their age for the sodality ideals and a subscription to the MTA magazine. Their example was a powerful impetus to him. Would it not be possible, he thought, to do the same

[5] The *Ermland*, Joseph's home district in East Prussia. Warmia was the only Catholic district in the otherwise Protestant East Prussia.

in Warmia? If he could get branches of the sodality started in a few high schools, from there all high school and college students could gradually be won over. Before vacation he and two classmates from Warmia, Gustav Rischewski and Otto Boenki, made a plan. They decided that all the Schoenstatt sodalists in Warmia would meet at Dietrichswalde, a local pilgrimage place, for a vacation meeting. They would also invite other befriended high school students—from Rössel and Allenstein. Otto thought he could win over a large number of students. Three talks would be given. Gustav would be the first speaker and talk about the moral condition of youth today, its struggles, and its responsibility for the future. Then Otto would speak about the need for youth to constantly work on self-education in order to be ready for its mission. Joseph wanted to talk about banding together to support one another in a mutual organization. Toward the end of his talk he would prove that the sodality, under the protection of the MTA of Schoenstatt, would be best suited and divinely called to fulfill this task. The conclusion would of course have to be the real hit, with everything else building up to it. With their plans in place, the three went home for vacation.

Already in the first weeks of vacation, Gustav and Otto sent their well-prepared talks to Joseph. He was to express his opinion about them and suggest improvements. Now everything was ready. A number of students promised to attend. As previously agreed upon they met at Dietrichswalde on August 13. Joseph made the great sacrifice of rising at 3:30 am and fasting till 12:00 noon. The speakers were ready, but the listeners failed to come! There were many different excuses. In the end only Otto's brother and one other non-sodalist showed up. For the three organizers this was, of course, a great disappointment. Three speakers and no audience! Measured by their first goal, the day had failed. But they didn't let it bother them. They held the meeting anyway, speeches and all. Gathered around a table, each one read his talk. At the end they noticed they had at least reignited each other's enthusiasm for Schoenstatt's ideals. Joseph was not discouraged in spite of the failure. Sooner or later the Blessed Mother's victory from Schoenstatt would come. What did it matter if they experienced a momentary setback? After a visit to the "holy spring" near the pilgrimage church, they all returned home.

This year his family experience was an especially profound one. The relationship with his mother was closer than usual. With her he could talk about religious things in a natural and unaffected way. In fact, his relationship to her seemed to be a reflection of his love for Mary. On the other hand, his love for Mary was deepened through the close relationship with his natural mother. The noble and pure motherliness he knew in his natural mother helped him picture the deep nobility of the Mother of God. At home the children often called their mother *Muttchen* ("Mommy" or "Little Mother"). No wonder that Joseph later began to speak to Our Lady this way, too, calling her *Mütterchen* or "Little Mother."

Broken Glasses

The family experience also had its harder moments. On the very first morning after his arrival, he dropped his glasses, breaking one of the lenses. A new pair had to be ordered. Now he could not do as much reading and writing as he would have liked. When the replacement pair came, his father was upset by the price. To a simple tailor it seemed an exorbitant sum. Joseph wrote in his diary:

"When I came home Saturday, my dad was angry at me for choosing such expensive glasses. (. . . .) I really could do nothing about the price. After all, they were very simple glasses. I almost cried. I gave him my whole allowance. Then my sister gave me 1 Mark of her own allowance. The good sister! Mother, reward her for it." (August 22, 1916)

At the end of vacation, Joseph wrote the following lines in his diary. They tell better than all else how deeply rooted he was in his home and family:

"The last days were days of hard work. But all of it was done out of love for my parents. Mother, I give you everything, my whole vacation. In this vacation I really experienced what love can do. How beautiful life is when it is filled with mutual love, when children try to please their parents, when parents experience joy in their children, when one hand helps the other and works to make the other's life more bearable. Then there is true joy in the home. How good it feels to have such parents, such brothers and sisters! Such love must also prevail in Schoenstatt. To bring this about will be my aim as a member of the Courtesy Group. *Volo omnibus omnia fieri, tibi, Maria specialiter mancipatus* (I want to be all things to all men for you and Mary's very own). Mother bless me."

6. The New Recruit

Boot Camp in Hagenau

Nearly a month had passed since the end of summer vacation. The leadership of the Junior Sodality was in the capable hands of the new fourth-year class. Joseph, now a fifth-year man, was less satisfied with the Senior Sodality. Things were very unsettled for the older students. A rumor was flying that the "98ers" would soon be drafted and none of them felt like studying. The teachers tried to enforce some concentration by assigning great amounts of homework. But then, at the end of October 1916, the word spread like wildfire: "On Friday and Saturday the 98ers have to report to Koblenz for their physical!" All 25 Schoenstatt "98ers" passed the examination. Eleven of them, including Joseph, were fifth-year men.

On November 16 they received the order to enlist. After three tense weeks the day was coming. School books were abandoned. Personal belongings were packed and sent home. Joseph had already made spiritual provision for the new situation. Knowing that he would not be able to make his regular weekly confession, he resolved to make a mini-recollection-day every Sunday. He would review and renew his resolutions and particular examination then and determine the state of his spiritual growth. When he kept this recollection day, he would make a note of it in his diary. It would also be the best opportunity to write to his spiritual director. He chose Sunday because he wanted to keep the Lord's Day holy, and he knew that on the front weekdays and Sundays would look very much alike. Just before he left for the army he added four special resolutions to his list from the year before. He would especially renew them every Sunday:

"1. I want to strive with still greater zeal for sanctity.

2. I want to be a physical guardian angel for my fellow sodalists in the army.

3. Never tell a lie!

4. I want to keep Sunday holy."

He made one further adjustment to his program. It was his practice to make Holy Mass and Holy Communion the center of each day. That was where his striving for his personal ideal had its deepest roots. But in the army he would not be able to attend Mass daily. He needed a different solution. Instead of being physically present at daily Mass he would have to be spiritually present. He would spiritually attend Mass every day and receive Communion in spirit. With these adjustments his spiritual daily order looked like this:

Morning prayer
Sodality prayers
Spiritual attendance at Holy Mass
Spiritual Communion
Good intention
Holy hour in the shrine
Decade of the rosary
Night prayer
Asking God's blessing
Act of perfect contrition.

He planned to check these points off in writing every night, and make a note as to whether he had kept his particular examination.

Sunday, November 19, 1916 brought the big good-bye. Father Prefect gave each of the recruits three bars of soap, three cans of shoe polish and a shoe brush. Given the privations of war it was a very practical and valuable gift. Joseph and ten other Schoenstatt seminarians had to report to the military office in Koblenz by 6 o'clock that evening. Before leaving Schoenstatt, the spiritual director gathered them in the Shrine one last time. He gave a short farewell. The Sodality Queen had brought them this far; she would continue to hold her protecting hand over them. Father Kentenich promised his priestly blessing every night to all sodalists outside Schoenstatt. Joseph wrote in his diary: "Child, do not forget your Mother!" These were the closing words of Father Kentenich's talk. "Then, with firm voices, we renewed our consecration to Mary." What did Joseph feel at that moment? He must have prayed words similar to those written in his diary a few days earlier: "Mother, *Mater ter admirabilis*, I offer to you all my actions, all good works, my entire striving for sanctity—for the purposes you, O Mother, have in mind for our sodality."

Of the eleven young men who left Schoenstatt that day, three would be killed in action. Three more would be crippled for life by the war. Only three would reach the goal of their lives—the priesthood.

The Schoenstatters hoped that they, like the "97ers" would have their basic training in Andernach, not far from Schoenstatt. But when they received their traveling orders, it was to go to Hagenau, a town near Strassbourg in the Alsace (present northeast France). Any hopes of spending their Sunday leaves in Schoenstatt were dashed. Hagenau brought many surprises. The "barracks" did not look like barracks at all. In fact, the first "barracks" they were sent to was a high school before the war. Here they waited until 3 o'clock in the afternoon, when they were divided into companies. Then they went across the street to the "barracks" which had been a restaurant called the "Crown Prince." Here, on what was once a dance floor, were bunk beds for 200 soldiers. Ten Schoenstatters were assigned to the "Crown Prince," including Joseph Engling. Seven other Schoenstatters arrived the next day and were assigned to the "barracks" in the old high school, making 17 in all.

Theday at Hagenau began at 5 o'clock in the morning. The recruits had to rise immediately. A moment's tardiness meant extra chores. Then the beds had to be made. And made and made again. "A civilian doesn't know how to make a bed, only a soldier!" Even if they did it right, the bed was messed up and they had to start over. The military principle was clear: Recruits knew absolutely nothing. Not how to walk. Not how to stand. Not even know how to lie down. Just like with marching—shoulders back and head erect—every single movement in life had to be relearned and drilled. It was hard work. Between drills, roll calls, fixing their uniforms and cleaning their rifles, there wasn't a moment's leisure for the recruits. When they came to their senses again at the end of the day, their arms and legs felt like lead. Even those who were used to hard work would drag themselves up the stairs and collapse, exhausted, into their bunks.

For someone trying to live up to high ideals, it was a hard test of character. A sergeant was drilling his unit one day on the grounds between the high school and the "Crown Prince." He knew what it took to make a sharp soldier. In just a few days he had whipped this group into shape. When he shouted, "Fall in! Straight line!" they obeyed at once. There was only one blemish in his perfect order. "Private Engling! Chest out! You're a mile out of line again!" The shout went out again and again. Again and again Private Engling tried to hold his shoulders erect. He always seemed to ruin the good sergeant's proud joy in soldierly order. The sergeant ranted and raged at Joseph, but it did no good. Mother Nature had made him this way and the Kaiser's Army could do nothing about it.

Now the sergeant called an inspection. Reproaches rained down on nearly everyone's head. This time Private Engling came out ahead. "Look at Private Engling! Why are all his things clean and orderly? Don't you idiots know how to do it?" More drills followed. The recruits had to practice the "march and salute." When Joseph came by, the sergeant winced as if he had been slapped in the face. The only words he could mutter were, "Go back, on the double!" He explained exactly how it had to be done. Joseph tried his utmost to comply. But his step was still heavy and clumsy. The sergeant reached his wits' end. "Listen, boy, how can we ever let you out of boot camp? A soldier who can't march and salute is a blemish on the whole German army!" But it was of no use. Private Engling would never be a parade soldier.

Fortunately, the unit's lieutenant was a sensible man. He was too old to serve on the front, but he knew his stuff with the recruits. He soon saw that what Joseph lacked to become a parade soldier he more than made up for with faithfulness to his duties, willingness to help others, reliability, and obedience. Because of this he cut Joseph some slack here and there and did not demand the impossible. The lieutenant was a Catholic and secretly admired the Schoenstatt seminarians.

A month into boot camp, the recruits earned their first Sunday leave if they could execute the "march and salute" with the required precision. Joseph had to stay in camp. His "march and salute" did not pass muster and leave was denied. He had to remain in the barracks while the other Schoenstatt sodalists went to Marienthal, a nearby pilgrimage place. It was December 17, 1916, and com-memorating the feast of the Immaculate Conception, they renewed their dedication to Mary. Joseph wanted very much to go, and was dis-appointed. But he made the best of it and saw his chance to have a day of recollection. At least he could write some letters without being disturbed.

He looked back over the last four weeks. How many new impressions and experiences! He really couldn't complain. Things had gone quite differently from his friend Karl Klement who was now in an artillery unit in Koblenz. Karl had had some very bad experiences and wrote to Joseph, "I'm sick and tired of the whole mess." Joseph did not feel the same way. The officers demanded much, but in his estimation they were men of character. It was hard, of course, to constantly be the drag on his sergeant's desire for order. His clumsiness had even cost him his furlough. "But tomorrow I will try again," he thought to himself and renewed his determination. Nor could he complain about his comrades. They were mostly Catholic farm boys from around Koblenz. Some had even shared their lunch with him on the train from Koblenz to Hagenau.

But now came the most important question. Was he making use of his life so far in boot camp as a real school of character formation? Had he really worked at living his personal ideal and given everything for the work of the MTA of Schoenstatt? Joseph pulled out the blue notebook he used to check off his spiritual daily order. First to be reviewed was his particular examination. In the last weeks it had been "At least once an hour I want to sanctify my work with an ejaculatory prayer." He had to admit it was not a very practical resolution. It had been practically lost in the flood of new impressions and countless drills. How easy it was to lose oneself in the ceaseless train of events and not to think of God! He was in danger of becoming a mass-man. Now he looked at the record of his "P.E." through the month. An upright tally mark meant he had kept his resolution for that hour. A minus sign meant he had not. There were not many minus signs. But he was not totally satisfied. Although he had offered everything to the MTA and her capital of grace at hourly intervals, he felt it could have been so much more loving and vigorous!

He now reviewed his spiritual daily order. Spiritual attendance at daily Mass and receiving spiritual Communion were the points that had worked best. He was having some trouble extending the Eucharist into the day. His "holy hours" were often forgotten or poorly done. In this column there were so many minus signs that he felt ashamed. In contrast, he was quite satisfied with his morning and night prayers. Not one minus sign there!

More of a struggle for him had been the decision whether to say night prayers kneeling by his bed or not, and whether he should make the sign of the cross when saying meal prayers. They were not strictly expected of him. And would they make him look too pious to the others? But then he thought: "Are you not a Sodalist of Mary, a knight of your Heavenly Queen? Do you let human respect tell you what to do? Wouldn't kneeling and a sign of the cross be a true sign of bravery?" This thought won out. From then on he said his night prayers kneeling beside his bed and made the sign of the cross before every meal.

The decade of the rosary had been fulfilled every day, but, oh, how hard it had been sometimes! At night his arms and legs were heavy as lead and he would fall asleep the moment his head hit the pillow. In order to make sure he said his decade before falling asleep, he hung his rosary around his neck. It helped him every time.

Looking over the first four weeks of spiritual life in the barracks Joseph had to conclude: Exteriorly life may have changed dramatically since leaving Schoenstatt, but his interior life had remained the same. This first thorough examination of conscience as a soldier reawakened in Joseph all his determination to reach for his ideals. Even army life could be used to become a modern saint! As his personal ideal demanded, each day's sacrifices had to be a contribution to the capital of grace of the Mother Thrice Admirable and her work.

Joseph put away his blue notebook and began to write a few letters. The first one was to his friend Karl Klement. He missed him in Hagenau. How much he longed for deeper discussions about the spiritual life! Of course he had many Schoenstatt friends here, and they talked. But their conversation rarely turned to deeper spiritual matters. Everyone was so tired. It made thinking hard and when they had a little time in the evening the conversation just never went the way Joseph longed for. He felt this pang so deeply that he mentioned it in his letter to Karl:

"Only one thing is missing—a friend with whom I can share

everything, everything I have, including my joys and sorrows, a friend for whom I would walk through fire and who would walk through fire for me. My heart has longed for such a friend here many times, but so far I have not found one. But one person always remains loyal to us if we only remain loyal to her: Our Mother" (December 17, 1916).

Unpleasant Company

An unexpected change came just before Christmas. All the recruits were reassigned to new units. Joseph suddenly found himself in the barracks known as "Depot 3" near the large infantry barracks. Of his Schoenstatt comrades only Clemens Meier was still in the same barracks.

While the first impression of their new comrades was anything but positive, not even Joseph could guess that they would make his next four weeks the most difficult in boot camp. As a good judge of character he immediately knew that the trade had not been a good one. In the coming days he found out just how bad it was. Most of the new comrades lacked any morals whatsoever. How did they ever come together in one place! Their language was filthy and suggestive. Their talk about women was so impure that it was best to cover one's ears. It was especially bad following Sundays. Their misdeeds on the Sabbath were unfathomable. Even if only half of what they said was true, they were living lives of vilest corruption. Joseph found it incomprehensible that anyone could live that way for weeks and months at a time. They repeated again and again the same filthy jokes, songs, and language.

It was a good thing that Father Kentenich had prepared the Schoenstatters for this in talks given just before going to the army. Their spiritual director found the right way to tell them what they needed to know. After he finished, the mystery of life and the sexes stood before them as something sacred and transfigured. Now they were repulsed by how these same holy things were degraded in idle conversation. But the dark background only made their Schoenstatt ideals shine more brightly.

Of course, the companions in "Depot 3" were equally quick at seeing that the two Schoenstatters were morally pure. And they didn't like it. That Engling and Meier so plainly avoided their shameless banter made them angry. In a short time life became nearly unbearable. Joseph was especially targeted as the butt of their mockery and crude jokes. He was given all the dirty jobs in the barracks. If the sergeant found anything dirty or messy, Joseph was the scapegoat. But it was especially his religious practices that drew down their unmitigated ire.

They soon found out about his night prayers kneeling next to the bunk. They also saw him wearing a rosary around his neck before going to bed—his reminder to pray before falling asleep. It prompted an attack. Barbs flew the moment Joseph knelt down to pray. First came rude comments and mean jokes. When this failed to get his attention, they pelted him with various objects. Then they resorted to tripping over his legs, hypocritically accusing him of blocking the aisle. Now Joseph's patience snapped. He angrily jumped up, fists flying left and right. The cowardly molesters immediately dispersed. Joseph was not bothered for quite a few days after that. For a while he struggled with the question of whether it would be better to drop the outwards signs of his prayer to keep from looking too "holier-than-thou." But in the end he decided against it. To give up the fight now would be cowardly, he thought, and amount to caving in to human respect. It would also just egg on the rest instead of keeping them in their place.

On December 21 Joseph had to write home that ugly boils on his hand, underarm, and right eye prevented him from participating in the outdoor drills. He would have much preferred to be outdoors than doing the indoor tasks now assigned to him. The outdoor activities at least kept one's mind off the gnawing hunger. In terms of food, things were scarcely better for the soldiers than they had been in Schoenstatt. Because he was indoors, though, his comrades accused him of being a "slacker."

The days after Christmas were especially hard. His boils were better, but on December 27 someone stole the muzzle guard for his rifle. The inspecting officer had no sympathy for missing muzzle guards and since Joseph did not feel it right to steal someone else's to cover his loss (as was commonly done), he had to pay for honesty with an extra hour of drills. The next day he was wrongfully accused of stealing bread and had to endure being publicly called a thief by the sergeant. The night after *that* he had to stand the night watch. Still, Joseph did not lose sight of his ideals and mission. In a letter to his spiritual director he wrote:

"It is a Christmas present from the Blessed Mother. She is demanding more of me now that I could receive Holy Communion on St. Stephen's Day. And to think that I couldn't even get to Mass on Sunday and Monday because of my bandages. This way I have a greater chance to increase her capital of grace. Father, give this to her in your Shrine." (December 27, 1916).

The four weeks at "Depot 3" were filled with exercises: marching, sharp shooting, practice with the bayonet. Joseph's new sergeant took a positively wicked delight in running his recruits ragged. His moral standing was deplorable, and when he saw in Joseph a man of untouched purity, it seems to have touched off a sinister rage. If Joseph failed to follow an order by even a split second, or wavered even slightly in how he held his rifle, the sergeant shouted, "Engling, up front!" and made him do exercises in front of the whole unit. Because Joseph was nearsighted and had eyes of uneven strength, his accuracy in sharp shooting was deplorable. The sergeant made him shoot even more rounds than the others, claiming he needed to shoot "by feel."

Joseph was also in the clinch with his Schoenstatt friend Clemens Meier. The latter had a somewhat delicate and reserved nature, and had trouble with the way Joseph sometimes did things. There were two other comrades, for instance, who were constantly being taken advantage of by the rest because of their simple nature. Joseph defended them, causing more arguments than Clemens thought was wise. Joseph noticed the growing alienation with Clemens, but felt he had to continue his chosen course of action.

The experience of the last weeks began to take a toll, however. Thoughts began to work in him which bordered on indignation: Was this any life worthy of his human dignity? Now his sense of justice began to boil over: Was I not good to others? But then they stole my muzzle guard! And I paid with extra drills! The more he thought about it, the more a foul and bitter mood overcame him. Before he knew it, it took command of his soul and changed the way he acted.

Clemens Meier took him to task one day for being cross all day. Even his old explosions of anger, which he thought were tamed so long ago, suddenly reappeared. On the last march a comrade had stepped on his heal. Thinking it another affront, rage suddenly got the better of him. He gave the offender a sharp blow with the butt of his rifle. Such incidents awakened him to his peril. The matter became totally clear to him at the next Sunday's examination of conscience. It helped him make up his mind: He would have to take strong countermeasures to overcome these moods using the particular examination.

Anger and Reconciliation

This did not prove easy. There were ups and downs. No sooner had he regained a certain interior equilibrium when another irritation knocked it over like a house of cards. At one point his irritation was so strong he did not even keep the written control of his particular examination. But Joseph could not stand such inactivity for long. "I want to become a saint"—Now his ideal became a warning to him. And Our Lady? Did she not expect that he prove to her that he really loved her? He wanted to give everything joyfully and willingly to her capital of grace.

His most tenacious enemy was, without any doubt, his sudden anger. It flared up once more in a way that made Joseph very ashamed. His pistol was stolen and a useless one left in its place. When he saw a companion with *his* pistol, he demanded it back. It not only came to blows, but to a full-blown brawl involving many from his bunk room. He felt very sorry about this afterwards. He certainly didn't have to just take an injustice like this, and he was right in demanding his pistol back, but did he really have to fly into such a rage? He was filled with remorse. His sense of guilt did not leave him until he approached the comrade and reconciled the wrong he had done.

On Sunday, January 14, 1917 Joseph could hold a thorough day of recollection. So far he had tried to sanctify the Sundays by making them a day of review and prayer. This time his review of the past weeks, the hardest of his life so far in the army, demanded particular scrutiny. He wrote in his diary, "Mother, today I want to make a thorough examination of conscience. I believe that I have failed in many ways. Help me, Mother, to find my weaknesses." The past weeks had put him sore to the test. He checked his spiritual daily order. It did not look bad. In spite of the many incidents and foul moods, he had kept it every day. The holy hours had even shown improvement. The "problem child" was his particular examination. At times he had not kept his written control at the end of the day because of anger and irritability. On another occasion he had forgotten. But around the first of the year it began to fall in place again.

What brought this victory? He wrote it in big letters in his diary at the first of the year:

"[All] For Mary! Forwards! Upwards! Never backwards! Mother, lead me. At your hand I want to strive for our high, exalted ideals. Bless me, Mary!" (January 2, 1917).

And about a week later he wrote:

"I want to struggle and fight with the help of my Mother. *Volo!* (I will!) I want to become a saint!" (January 7, 1917).

Apathy and Spiritual Dryness

On January 22, 1917, the recruits in Hagenau were assigned to new units again. For Joseph it was a great relief. He was assigned to the 1st Company and was now stationed in the old St. George School. It was only a few yards away from St. George's Church, which was both the parish church and the military chapel for the Catholic soldiers. Joseph stayed here until May 24. These months would be the most important for his spiritual life in Hagenau.

Both his new officers and comrades were decent people. Most of them fulfilled their Sunday obligation and did not swear. He even made three friends. Although there were many improvements, he faced a major problem. He could not find a taste for the now monotonous Hagenau routine. Every day they went through the same exercises. They were learning nothing new. Not even the tirades of an officer could break the rut. It was all old hat.

The monotony of the drill and the feeling of boredom posed a new kind of problem. Just weeks ago he had been in a tense spiritual battle. His wrestling with his bouts of anger and foul moods gave his spiritual life some powerful impulses. But now he was like a sailing

128

ship calmed at sea. The dull routine threatened to put him to sleep spiritually. He was surrounded by decent enough people, but they did not share his high ideals. They tried to be friendly with one another and went out for a beer here and there or to the movies on Sunday night. They read books—nothing serious or strenuous, but entertaining. Should Joseph choose the same diversions? He had already learned the soldier's vice of smoking (and would later have to work hard to quit); now he acquired a taste for playing cards. He only went to the movies once—to see "Quo Vadis." In that case his motivation had not been entertainment, however, but learning.

The danger was creeping up on him that his previous striving for religious excellence would be replaced by the desire to fit in and lead a comfortable life. He spied a new adversary for the first time on the battlefield of his heart: indifference and dryness. His heartfelt enthusiasm for ideals now became dry and unfeeling. It was plain to him at the next Sunday's examination of conscience. He described it this way in a report to his spiritual director:

"I already wanted to write to you on Saturday, but I didn't get around to it until today. In the military one is often so indifferent to everything, more indifferent and unfeeling than I have ever been. It seems to me that I am getting more and more weak of will and afraid of making sacrifices. I didn't make my weekly examination of conscience until today, even though I should have done it on Sunday and firmly resolved to do it yesterday. The same thing happened two Sundays ago. I notice the same carelessness in doing my particular examination, even in finding a resolution and saying my daily prayers, in fact in all my religious exercises including the sodality prayers. The last issue of the *"MTA"* came quite a few days ago and I still haven't read it. I am constantly resisting, but so weakly and unthinkingly that it almost seems I haven't mustered the energy yet. I hope I can now manage to come up with the needed will-power. I want to! I owe it to my Mother and my fellow sodalists..." (February 13, 1917).

Two weeks later he wrote to his spiritual director:

"...[A]rmy life makes me so apathetic. I don't even know how to express it. And if I am so cold, how can I warm up others? This apathy is found in all the sodalists here. It is really hard to lead a spiritual life. There are no impulses, unless you read, absolutely none. Many read, but just novels, nothing which could stir one to spiritual striving. But it takes real self-denial. I have a hard time too. (...) If I now look back over my interior life in the army, I first see a time of great enthusiasm, then a gradual ebbing away and indifference which lasted a long time, then a battle which is still ongoing. I hope I can win the victory. At the moment the noble image of our Mother is again more vivid in my mind." (February 25, 1917).

A Letter from Father Kentenich

Although Joseph wrote frequently to his spiritual director, for a long time Father Kentenich only wrote back with a postscript here or there on a letter to one of the other Schoenstatters. Finally, after almost four months in the army, Joseph received a letter directly from his spiritual director:

"Schoenstatt, March 2, 1917

"My dear young friend!

"Your letter of February 25 arrived yesterday. Thank you for the letter and for all the other news about your interior life which you have sent since your departure. Your loyalty and childlike openness may have been sorely tested, for I did not answer your letters on purpose. But now you have a better overview of the difficulties around you and the changes and doubts within you. You have also grown appreciably in the longing for an energetic offensive [in the spiritual life]. The time should now be right for translating these experiences into a new striving for the heights.

"Some advice towards this end: Now more than ever you recognize your own weakness and failings. That is the best imaginable foundation for an undying childlike devotion to our heavenly Mother: Mother, here you look upon your poor, weak child. He cannot do anything on his own. Take me completely into your warm, motherly arms; tell Our Lord for me that I am sorry... and then give me your hand. With you I want to live, suffer, die, fight, and work... You, my Mother—and I, your child.'

"If you resolutely continue to educate yourself in this direction—and it will certainly not be hard for you, since Our heavenly Mother has stolen your heart so completely—then the

> advantages of your development will significantly outweigh the disadvantages. (....)
>
> "For now, heartfelt greetings and my priestly blessing in sincere love,
>
> J. Kentenich

Joseph now faced a whole new task in his self-education. How should he tackle his dryness and indifference? How should he counteract the numbing effect of his outward existence? Under no circumstances could he just capitulate and "wash his hands" by blaming his environment. He would have to maintain his striving for his ideals by resolute action and an iron will. In a letter to his friend Karl he confided:

"As you could see in my last letter, I have been stricken by inner apathy. Before this was a time of hard battles, but now I face total, complete dryness. Spiritual reading can shake me free of it for a moment, but then I am overcome by the same coldness. But I don't stop working and striving. Work done without enjoyment or reward builds character. Our dear Mother is now giving us 'war bread' after feeding us 'sweet bread'..." (April 1, 1917)

As he wrote, he lived. The particular examination, spiritual daily order, and Sunday examination of conscience remained an unbending part of his persistent battle for the ideal. Prayer, spiritual reading, and the examination of conscience and its written control often cost him a gigantic effort. So great was the dryness! But how long could he stand the shear exertion of will-power? A new thought came to him. Perhaps his old vigor would return if he put his heart into it more, if he would take a less defensive stance toward his surroundings and go more on the offensive. So he tried being an apostle of friendship among his comrades. He did little services for them. He shared his bread. Instead of withdrawing from them in order to read as he had done before, he sat with them and struck up a conversation.

These were successes, to be sure, but they did not bring the interior change he sought. Was it perhaps his old desire to learn that needed a boost? But when Joseph thought about it, he had to admit that he was reading sound books. He had read works by Weber (*Goliath* and *Dreizehnlinden*) and Dante (*The Divine Comedy*),

131

and Gillet's *Character Formation*. These had temporarily rekindled his idealism, but they did not lift him out of the doldrums.

Now his thoughts returned to his personal ideal—"All things to all men and Mary's very own." Had he not written just recently to one of his former teachers, Father Kaufmann: "It is exactly as you write, Father: Unless a man has a high idea which constantly shines before him, he will be enmeshed by the mundaneness of everyday life. In this regard I find the greatest support in the sodality, its Queen, and the increase of her capital of grace" (April 17, 1917)? More and more the part of his ideal about Mary came to the foreground. He saw her as the Mother of the little Sodality Family who had established her throne of grace in the Schoenstatt Shrine. From there she wanted to initiate a movement of renewal. It was his life's task to help her do that with ceaseless contributions to the capital of grace. Now he wrote the following resolution in his diary: "My daily work must be still more permeated by the thought: All for Mary, the Mother Thrice Admirable of Schoenstatt and Sodality Queen."

This resolution was no mere lip service. Soon there was not a single event which he did not raise in his heart to the Mother of God. When he experienced success, he thanked her. When he was struggling with the burdens of the day, he turned to Mary for courage and patience. If he was guilty of faults or imperfections, his humbled heart sought her out to ask forgiveness. In his diary we find it expressed in one short sentence again and again: "Mother, all for you!"

In the meantime May was coming, the favorite month of every child of Mary. In Joseph the anticipation was growing for some time already. He was experiencing a time of tender and sacrificial Marian love and its intensity was greater than at any other time in his life. In the foreground of his thoughts was a tender wish. If only his furlough would fall in May—then he could visit Schoenstatt! "How I look forward to soon being in the Shrine of our dear Mother," he wrote to his spiritual director. His wish came true; his leave began in early May. He went from Hagenau directly to Prossitten to visit his family. Then on the way back he visited Schoenstatt for one precious day before reporting to duty in Hagenau again on May 16. His stay in Schoenstatt brought him unforgettable hours of quiet prayer and spiritual renewal. A few days later he wrote from Hagenau:

"Schoenstatt and the homey confines of our sodality chapel attract me now twice as much. My memories of earlier times and of my day in Schoenstatt are so beautiful. I have returned to the world with vibrant love for our Heavenly Mother and a better knowledge and renewed love and enthusiasm for our sodality goals and ideals. Our aim is the whole world, and we must take it" (May 21, 1917). This time his May striving had a simple and straightforward motto:

"May blossoms for the increase
of the capital of grace of our
Mother Thrice Admirable from a
Soldier-Sodalist in Hagenau"

In addition to the faithful fulfillment of his regular spiritual daily order, he wanted to use every chance he had to prepare little joys for the Mother of God. He took this resolution quite seriously. The many mysterious lines and dashes on his sheet of "May blossoms" testify to countless little sacrifices in everyday life. His May striving helped raise his love for Mary to ardent heights. At last, in the final weeks of May, his interior life attained the victory he longed for. The time of interior apathy and foul moods finally passed. He became master of the monotony of army life. His spiritual life regained its original freshness and vigor.

Nor would he ever forget that he passed this test by fire with Mary's help.

Fostering Schoenstatt Spirit

The new springtime of Marian love gave Joseph the impetus he needed to overcome his apathy and foul moods. At the same time, his old sense of responsibility for the sodality and his fellow sodalists reawakened, too. His time as prefect in the Junior Sodality had been a veritable school of leadership. When he came to boot camp, he took it as self-understood that he would work in the same way together with the other sodalists. The older birth years already had a working "external organization" for quite some time, and worked closely with the home sodality in Schoenstatt. They kept a fair amount of correspondence even while scattered throughout the

German army. Their desire was to continue the life of the sodality and to help one another as they strived for their ideals. The sodalists in Hagenau went to boot camp determined to do the same. Did they succeed?

During the first few weeks of army life the sodalists were much too occupied with the many new impressions and physical exhaustion. Joseph tried to do what he could, but managed little more than a few informal visits and short walks with some of the others. They had greater hopes for Christmas. After all they had been through in the last weeks, they sincerely looked forward to having a little time in a different atmosphere and with peers who honored the same ideals. The Mother Superior at the local hospital was related to one of the sodalists and gladly offered a place for their meeting. But when they got together, they found another young man had come in and made himself at home. He apparently felt these soldiers needed a good laugh, so he started to tell funny stories and drew all the attention to himself. This was not what the sodalists wanted at all! They were thinking of something more religious and to themselves. The conversation fell flat and the whole gathering became a bore. Everyone was relieved—but disappointed too—when it came time to go. It was a poor beginning.

It was followed by Joseph's long struggle with dryness and bad moods. He needed all his strength just to keep his own religious fervor above water. Should he be the support for the others, too? Nor should it be overlooked that not all the sodalists agreed with Joseph about the degree of self-sanctification in the army. They agreed, without a doubt, that one must be solidly Catholic and courageously stand up for their vocation to the priesthood, must regularly go to the sacraments and say their daily prayers. It was also only right that they occasionally visit the Blessed Sacrament in the local church or make a pilgrimage to the nearby pilgrimage place in Marienthal. But otherwise, they said, we are soldiers and soldier life doesn't leave time or energy for more. Some of the Schoenstatt sodalists took pride in being sharp-looking soldiers. Some had passed an exam and cherished the hope they might even become officers.

Many of the sodalists just couldn't understand Joseph. In

134

Schoenstatt they were one or two grades ahead of Joseph and were unfamiliar with his flavor of devotion and the hidden strengths of his character. To them he seemed just plain too "pious." In addition, he was not a "parade" soldier—even his uniform was older and more wrinkled than theirs—and this was an obstacle to those who were so proud of their soldierly appearance.

Joseph did not let such things stop him. He set about the task of organizing the sodalists. First they had to be divided into groups. Johannes Blümer, Hans Wormer, and Joseph would each lead one group. A fourth group consisted of those already transferred to the boot camp in Elsenborn. But group meetings didn't happen. Schedules were impossible to work around: When some were off duty, others were on duty. When they finally found an open slot in everyone's schedule, a sudden change of orders ruined their plans. Some of the sodalists were so tired from the daily drill that they wanted to be left alone during their free time. Then the monotony of life began to wear them down. "If we get together, what would we talk about?"

Joseph viewed the situation with growing concern. Where would the spiritual energy come from to inspire their groups? He looked to the sodality at home. Was it not at the immediate source of life? Did they not have regular meetings and conferences? But the news from Schoenstatt was not encouraging. After the 98ers had left, the sodality lost its steam. The magistrate was weak. Many of the sodalists were lukewarm. Striving for ideals was in a downward spiral.

Counteracting Lethargy at Home

Joseph saw that, for now, he could expect no help from this quarter. On the contrary, he had to get to work and help them get through their crisis with letters of admonition and encouragement. He took up his pen. He first wrote to Fritz Esser, whom he had worked with to good effect in the past:

"As I hear from [Karl] Klement, things are not going very well with the sodality. This is the reason I am writing to you today. You are my greatest hope in this matter. You and [Paul] Rüber have to get things going again, if the others and the magistrate are unable or unwilling. It is not only [important] for the others, for us outside of Schoenstatt, but for our Mother, the Mother Thrice Admirable, who is so close to you in the shrine. (....)

"If the magistrate is not doing its job, it must be replaced. But then others must try to get things going again; they in turn will be recognized as being the most qualified and be elected. You must not forget the capital of grace of the Mother Thrice Admirable. Schoenstatt, a second Ingolstadt what a great, ideal thought!" (January 1, 1917).

Fritz Esser wrote back in very discouraged tones:

"If only you were here, then things would be different in our section... I just want to give up..."

Joseph would hear nothing of it:

"Pester the leaders if they are not doing their duty. Go to them again and again and shake them out of their lethargy. Above all, they need to excel in the spirit of sacrifice. If they don't, though, the zealous sodalists will have to work all the more zealously and try to win over the others. You want to see to it that at least your group works well. Do so! But also see to it that your group's life carries into the other groups. Go with them hand in hand. I can well imagine that the work in the sections is hard..."

After some weeks, the crisis in Schoenstatt passed. And in Hagenau help seemed to come from a totally different quarter. There turned out to be a recruit in Hagenau who was a Pallottine seminarian. He took the sodalists under his wing and tried to help them. But he did not understand the Schoenstatt approach. He only thought they wanted a big reunion. Joseph's interest, on the other hand, was in the quiet educational work of his "little apostolate." The seminarian managed to arrange a meeting with Father Wernert, the pastor of St. Nicholas Parish. When Joseph and his three comrades came to the rectory on the evening of January 28, they expected a room for their sodality meeting. Instead they got a talk on the spiritual life given by the pastor in his office. At first Joseph was enthusiastic. It reminded him of Father Kentenich's talks. But while the pastor gave many practical tips, he never gave the sodalists a chance to share their own experiences and discuss what initiatives they could take. A second meeting with the pastor on February 13 went the same way. Although the priest meant well, these meetings

136

were not in the spirit of the Schoenstatt sodality. Joseph was not sad when further meetings with the pastor did not take place.

Joseph Engling and his Schoenstatt group in the war. Back row: Dekarski, Engling, Rath, Blath. Front row: Eckhard, Friedrich, Blümer, Steinert, Wormer.

But how to get a Schoenstatt group going? He evaluated the division of the Hagenau sodalists into their groups. Had they made an organizational error? Father Kentenich had already pointed one out to him. The groups had been formed too quickly; they were created by a few hasty decisions. One could see that they were constructed artificially. A whole different approach was needed. The best first step would be to win over a few individuals for a greater educational striving. At the same time, those who got along especially well should combine forces. Surely, this would create a viable group. With whom should he start? Hans Wormer was the first to come to mind. Joseph felt the closest to him and he was the most supportive of starting groups. It was similar with Walter Steinert. He met with them during a walk. He told Father Kentenich about what happened:

"I just returned from a walk with Steinert and Wormer and want to write a few lines to you, Father. It was a real heart-to-heart

137

conversation. We shared openly about our spiritual life and experiences. We came to the conclusion that the sodality work will have to be a work that each of us does on his own... (....) We ended our walk with a short visit to the Blessed Sacrament. Then we met with Dekarski, Meier, and Reinhold. We commented on the lack of news from Schoenstatt and put ourselves into the situation of the Schoenstatters and saw that we were asking a lot of them..." (March 11, 1917).

Joseph was full of hope about this new start. But a new disappointment followed. He used every opportunity to win over his fellow sodalists to a group. Hans Wormer and Walter Steinert did their part, too. But given the circumstances, it was incredibly difficult for the others to keep a constant striving for ideals. The dryness Joseph had battled was even more intense in the others. He sadly observed how their desire to stay in touch with each other declined. Many found good Catholic comrades in their units and were satisfied with this friendship. They felt less of a need to reach out to their Schoenstatt comrades. Joseph stubbornly worked on. He managed to get a larger meeting together. "Last Sunday," he wrote in a letter, "with some arranging and luck I got together a larger meeting. Because of bad weather we could not go for a walk. We stayed indoors" (April 1, 1917). The meeting did not bear much fruit, at least in Joseph's estimation. They read the latest letters from Schoenstatt and other sodalists in the army. When they didn't know anything else to say, they played cards. When a few sparks for new groups finally began to catch, several were suddenly ordered to report for duty. The goal of creating a coherent group of 98ers now seemed more distant than ever.

Joseph almost lost hope. Here again his trust in Mary came to his aid. And it was a consolation that the sodalists could often go to the Marian Shrine in Marienthal. Joseph was there a total of three times; the first time was on February 4, 1917.

May offered a new ray of hope. A meeting of all the 98ers was held on April 29. This time Joseph was happy with the results. On the same day he could write back to Schoenstatt with visible satisfaction:

"The approach of May has finally shook us from our sleep and reminded us of our solemn surrender to Mary. We have closed ranks to support one another and want to foster more letter-writing with the other sodalists. Each of us must have something to do. We arranged that in today's meeting. The following suggestions were made and accepted for May:

1. Say our daily prayers more devoutly.
2. Make the good intention before each act: 'Mother, all for you.'
3. Make a daily visit to the Blessed Sacrament.
4. Go to the sacraments each Sunday.
5. Make a pilgrimage to Marienthal on the first and last Sunday.
6. Do something for the Sodality treasury.
7. Do better with the particular examination, or begin to use it."
(April 29, 1917).

What became of these resolutions? The newly enkindled enthusiasm was no straw fire, though it did suffer somewhat from the fact that many went on leave during May. Joseph himself left Hagenau on furlough on May 2, returning May 16. Still, a pilgrimage to Marienthal took place on May 20, complete with the renewal of their consecration to Mary.

May came and went, and Joseph still did not manage to form a group as he had set out to do. In spite of nearly six months of work the 98ers still lacked a viable "external organization." Still, his tireless efforts paid off in one regard: At least the sodalists had met as a larger group or on pilgrimage nearly half a dozen times. It would not be until reaching the Eastern Front that Joseph succeeded in organizing a Schoenstatt group to his satisfaction.

Joseph was hoping the order to leave boot camp would come soon. After six months it was time to move on. On May 24 new orders were issued, but only to regroup. Joseph was transferred to the 2nd Company and had to move to a different barracks. But at long last, on June 6, 1917, the day came to leave Hagenau. The order was given to move out!

7. The Eastern Front

Tests of Strength in Jablonna

The first days of June were filled with activity in the Hagenau barracks. The troops were being sent to the front. Field uniforms and a full outfitting of gear had to be issued. Soon each soldier stood before a mountain of clothing and equipment: underwear, uniform jacket, pants, boots, shoes, neckband, cap, helmet, belt, haversack, ammunition pouch, gas mask, knapsack, blankets, tent canvas, tent poles, trowel, rifle, bayonet, canteen, cup, etc. When the recruit finally had his gear together and carried it off wrapped in the tent canvas, he felt like a furniture van. Before carrying it off, the quartermaster made it clear that each of them was now worth 500 Marks more than before. Back in the barracks, the young soldiers sized each other up in their new uniforms:

"It looks good on you," said one. "You're dressed to die a hero's death."

"I'm just happy," said the second, "to get rid of those shabby blue uniforms. They were practically falling apart!"

"It is probably our funeral gown," added the third, somewhat melancholically," and the tent canvas might be the shroud."

Once equipped, the recruits were suddenly given a taste of the first weeks of boot camp again. There was one drill after another. The sergeants barked at every misstep—even the smallest. The soldiers were soon sick and tired of this nitpicking and ceaseless drill. Then came a big party on the last day in camp, with the alcohol flowing freely. On the morning of their departure, Joseph Engling rose early to write a letter to Father Kentenich:

"I just got up after four hours of sleep and want to quickly write you a few lines, Father. I have never been filled with such rage—I think one must call it that—at the Prussians[1] as on Monday morning and especially yesterday. I wanted to make this discontent and

---

[1]   The drill sergeants and military perfectionists.

The Eastern Front

dissatisfaction with the officers, etc. the object of my particular examination, but didn't think there would be much opportunity to complain during the transport. But I should have done it anyway. That would have been a real particular examination and taken self-denial. I now want to patiently bear the faults of my comrades. For the most part, these faults probably lie in my own over-sensitivity.

141

"Father, I am also sending you my May blossoms and the written control of my particular examination. Please take them to our dear Little Mother in the Shrine. I trust in her protection, even in little things. She has always helped. I still get to receive communion today. Must go! Adieu! Until we meet again!" (June 6, 1917).

The corporal gave the order to move out. Flowers were tied to the gun barrels. "My home, my home, until we meet again," sang two hundred young men as they passed through the streets of Hagenau. Joseph was moved. But unlike many of his comrades, he was not moved by a "gallows humor" or too much liquor. He and his fellow sodalists had been able to receive Holy Communion that morning. The joy was so great that he even mentioned it ten days later in a letter to Karl Klement. He was happy to have been able to receive Our Lord. Now his opportunities would be less and less frequent. Already last Sunday he was not able to go to Holy Mass.

The transport rolled east. The train passed through the whole length of Germany to occupied Warsaw. Outside, God's nature was radiant with the loveliness of spring. Warm sunshine poured in the windows of the cars packed with so many young men and military gear. On June 8 they reached Jablonna, just north of Warsaw. It was a former Russian army barracks. Their new quarters were hardly inviting. The nights were the worst, when the bedbugs, fleas, and lice appeared. Boot camp may have been hard, but this new camp was worse.

These camps for recruits were by no means places of rest and recreation. The soldiers were given intense training and final preparation for duty on the front. Hagenau may have been bad at times, but what the soldiers experienced in Jablonna surpassed all previous hardships. It would not have been so bad if there had been enough to eat, but they were practically living off a starvation diet. Rations were meager and dished out much too sparingly. No wonder that their faces grew gaunt and their morale declined by the day. It made some of the recruits irritable and unbearable; others it made sullen and numb.

Joseph did not feel the hunger any less than his comrades. He had just finished scraping out his mess kit one day, so as not to lose a single crumb of a meager meal. It had only reminded him of how really hungry he was. He went to the canteen, but the food there was outrageously expensive. A pound of butter would have cost him ten days' pay. Why didn't the war administration confiscate these provisions when there was so little to go around? His sense of justice was offended by the private marketeers who made money off the war.

The Honey Incident

A long line had formed in front of the mess tent. Artificial honey was being handed out. Someone said that everyone was getting half a pound. Joseph got in line. Almost an hour later he was issued his honey. But when he left, he noticed some of his comrades getting in line again. There were ways to get around the identification checks. Shouldn't he do the same thing? He was tormented with hunger. But wasn't that fraud, wasn't that cheating the army? He had no right to receive a second package. Fraud? Who was committing fraud! He felt bitterness to think about the war-profiteers in the canteen. He got in line a second time.

A long time passed again. Half a dozen soldiers were still in front of him. One of the cooks handing out the honey took down the name of a soldier. He suddenly paused and gave the soldier a hard look. "Show me your identification," he said gruffly. The soldier's face blanched; he began to stammer. The cook took him by the breast and tore the identification out of his hand. "You lied about your name! You were in line already! Your company will hear about this and you'll spend a few days in the brig." A few of the soldiers behind Joseph fell out of line, mumbling something about it taking too long today. They "would come back later." Joseph broke out in a cold sweat. Now it was his turn. He said his real name. Would the cook turn back his register a few pages and see he had been there before? He did not and Joseph got a second package. But now his "booty" burned his fingers like hot coals. Was it not stolen? His comrades would have laughed at him if he had told them of his pangs of remorse. At this very moment, Nicholas Gilgenbach of the Eifel area near Schoenstatt came by. "Here, Comrade," said Joseph, "Here's a package of honey." Nicholas didn't need to be asked a second

> time and walked away quite pleased with his prize. "Yes, that Engling," he thought to himself, "He's always been a good comrade. Now he even pilfers honey for the others."

Bitterness and irritability were surfacing in Joseph's soul again. Like his friend Karl Klement half a year earlier, he was "sick and tired of the whole mess." What would he have done without the Blessed Mother! He wrote in his diary:

"Little Mother, if I had no support from you, I would have been very discouraged today and impatient. Today, when the others had time off, I had guard duty and I have it again tomorrow. Hunger gnawed me, I didn't receive any mail, and I had to bear harsh words from my comrades. Love for you helped me bear all this to some extent. After all, I want to become a saint, a religious. Must I not then bear these trifles patiently, no, even cheerfully?" (June 16, 1917).

The thought of Our Lady gave him courage to do battle against his faults again. He began with his particular examination. "I will not get impatient with duties, orders, and regulations; nor will I murmur and grumble about superiors, even when treated unjustly. I will gladly carry out every command." This was to become a real test under the conditions he now faced. He was not successful on the first try. As the days passed, he had to put a minus sign in his written control more than once. Then came his daily spiritual order. He did not have any trouble keeping his spiritual exercises so far, and he had kept his written control every day. But he saw that to master the new and difficult situation, he would have to increase his life of prayer. He resolved, therefore, to insert little moments of religious recollection throughout the day. Every one or two hours he wanted to recollect himself, renew the good intention, and offer everything to Our Lady's capital of grace. In the midst of all this he kept his regular weekly day of recollection and examination of conscience. He judged his spiritual life as strictly as if he were living in normal circumstances and wrote to Father Kentenich:

"It is just past 1:00 a.m. and I am sitting barefoot in shirt and pants all alone at the table. I was sleeping, but at one o'clock I had to report to the quarter master, and since I am up anyway, I am going

144

to continue the report on my spiritual life. I had no time yesterday or the day before, except during the noon break, when I took a three-hour nap. On Sunday I wrote 16 pages to others. In the last three days I have really begun to see what self-denial means. On Saturday I had just read, in *The Marian Conferences*, how as a postulant Father Rem went without food and drink for three days due to the forgetfulness of one of his confreres, but uttered no word of complaint. This incident was often in my mind during these three hard days and showed me my pride and selfishness. It started already on Saturday. I was ordered on guard duty and had to stand guard for three hours while the others had free time. I started to boil inside. On Sunday, at one o'clock, a week started unlike any I've ever seen. The corporal was constantly criticizing. I grumbled behind his back several times. On Monday we had just returned from guard duty, tired and worn out and having scarcely eaten, when we were ordered to get ready for target practice. After I packed my knapsack—out of anger I did not pack it according to regulation—we started out, the sun beating down on us. It must have been 95° F. in the shade. Then I was assailed by one temptation after another: 'Let yourself go; give up your striving for perfection; it is enough to live like any ordinary Christian and to refrain from committing mortal sin; cheat whenever it is to your advantage.' It was a hard struggle. Only the thought of our dear Little Mother gave me strength to overcome these temptations, in fact, I was already giving in to them. And even with the thought of our Blessed Mother to help me, I did not succeed at once. A letter from [Nicholas] Wilwers helped move me to the victory for a time. When we reached the rifle range, we started to practice shooting with our gas masks on. I missed the mark every time and had to stay to the end.

"I was passively resigned to my fate and threw myself on the ground, not caring about anything. When we arrived home, we had coffee, that was all. I had already eaten my bread on guard duty. Afterwards we had to surrender our field uniform. It was nearly nine o'clock when this was done. Later others came to our room and started to cook. It became so hot and noisy that one could hardly bear it. I would have liked to write to you, Father, at least a few lines, but it was not possible. I waited for mail in vain. Sullen, but perhaps with a little goodwill, I fell asleep after I said my usual prayers. The next day was not better. The whole unit was reprimanded. In the evening I had to water plants in the garden. I finished at a quarter past nine. In spite of it all, I made the resolution to use everything in a heroic spirit of sacrifice for my self-sanctification. It is a wonderful preparation for the religious life. I want to [be a great saint]! Mary will help me. She has often rewarded my confidence in the past. One more thing: On guard duty, I failed to salute a lieutenant because I did not recognize him. He rebuked my harshly. My corporal heard about it, took my name down and remarked that he would report me. I thought about begging the corporal not to report me. But my pride got the better of me. I would rather have an extra hour of drill than to ask a favor of this corporal and give him occasion to poke fun at me. No, I did not do it. Oh, how imperfect and selfish I still am.

"I am not as considerate as I used to be toward my comrades just because they do not give me any recognition or consideration. No, they fight and quarrel. They'll cheat you whenever they can and then ask one favor after another. I have become outright inconsiderate and stingy. I cannot bring myself to do anything for them. It is perhaps not unjust, but it is certainly not perfect.

"This week I have kept the resolution for my particular examination pretty well. It was not definite enough though and so I could not check it accurately.

"Because of the change of address, correspondence with [Karl] Klement has been interrupted. I have not heard from him for a long time. [Adolf] Baldauf, too, has not written. For some time I have not met my fellow sodalists. We have not helped one another spiritually. Father, commend me to the Mother Thrice Admirable. I need it. If you, Father, consider it necessary, you may always write as my confessor" (June 20, 1917).

Just as formerly the thought of the Blessed Mother brought decisive changes in these critical situations, so too in this one. To Eduard Struth, a trusted fellow sodalist he confided the following:

"I have just experienced some trying days, more trying than in boot camp. But it is still possible to bear them. Everything becomes easy when one thinks of the dear Mother Thrice Admirable, our dear Little Mother. I could make this experience during three trying days at the beginning of the week. It all became too difficult for me. I grumbled and muttered like the rest. But as soon as I thought of our heavenly Mother, of her kindness and love, of my fellow sodalists,

146

and the capital of grace I accepted the trials contentedly" (June 23, 1917).

Joseph may have had many crosses to carry, but he always remained faithful. The bitterness and resentment that he sometimes felt over disappointments and injustice never became permanent, either. This was because he cultivated his spiritual life. Tests of inner strength could bend him, but never break him.

The Coal Mines of Upper Silesia

The hot July sun was beating down on Jablonna. It was time to receive the day's orders. The recruits feared another day of marches in the pothole-filled roads around their camp. But instead they heard that a red-alert had been issued. Were there new developments on the front? Were the Russians attacking? Was a new German offensive in the making? The officers knew as little as the soldiers. Days passed. Finally, one morning the men were awakened earlier than usual. Soon they were heading south on the train. They did not know where they were going. To their left and right they saw the damage done to fields and forests, farms and factories by the battles of 1915. The train kept rolling, farther and farther south.

Then one morning they were suddenly told to disembark. By dawn's early light they could make out a town. "Bendzin" was the name written on the train station. The people spoke mostly Polish. But they soon knew they were near to Kattowitz. But this meant they were close to the German border. Why had they been sent here? They soon knew. The coal miners had begun to strike in Upper Silesia and the soldiers had been sent to protect the mines. Their new quarters were some 200 yards from the train station. It was another barracks formerly used by the Russian Cossacks and even more primitive than the one in Jablonna. No tables, benches, or beds! The two-hundred-man company would have to make itself at home in the one-room barracks with straw on the floor. The German soldiers soon called it the "stable."

Joseph was not even there for half a day when he and twenty others were ordered to move to nearby Lagisza. There they had to guard a mine. Their day went from guard duty to walking the

Joseph Engling during the war.

grounds to time off. It was quite bearable, especially considering what their comrades had to do in Bendzin. Joseph put his time to good use. In Jablonna he had begun to learn some Polish. Here he continued his studies. If only he could find someone to talk to in Polish—he always learned a language best when he could use it! A seventeen-year-old boy came by. Joseph tried his Polish: "Hello, young man, how are you?" The boy answered in pretty good German. But his accent was noticeable. Joseph and he were soon friends and the young man helped him learn Polish. His new "teacher" even brought a German-Polish dictionary one day.

A Dangerous Swim

But his lessons soon ended. On July 18 he was transferred back to Bendzin. A few days later came a real scare. After a strenuous day of duty in the muggy summer weather, many of the soldiers went to the river for a swim. While swimming, Joseph saw one of his comrades lose his footing and go under. With a few powerful strokes, he got within reach. The comrade was thrashing in the water. Joseph took him in tow, but the drowning man panicked and latched onto Joseph, making it extremely difficult for him to swim. Now he had to fight both the strong current and the panicking comrade. They slowly approached the shore. There others waited to bring them in. The current slackened. Would Joseph make it all the way? His strength was beginning to fail. Only a few more strokes and he would make it. But now his comrade suddenly loosened his grip and was swept away. He couldn't hang on any longer. Joseph was also at the end of his strength. With his last ounce of energy he reached the shore. There he lay, gasping for air. It took quite a while for him to catch his breath. In the meantime the other soldier had been saved. "I thank Our Lady for her protection," he wrote with emotion to his fellow sodalists.

In Bendzin, Joseph busied himself with an important question. How were things going with his new Schoenstatt group? Since leaving Hagenau he had given up on the plan to form an organization uniting the 98er-sodalists. His plan now was to gather an active group of sodalists around himself. Perhaps the others would do the same. The magistrate in Schoenstatt helped him greatly by proposing Hans Wormer, Karl Klement, and Joseph to the army sodalists as group leaders they could join according to their free choice. Seven sodalists chose to join Joseph's group. Three of them belonged to the birth year 1899, which had been drafted into the army just recently. The rest were of his own age group.

To Joseph, seven members seemed somewhat large for one group. But he would not turn anyone away. In Schoenstatt a "point

149

man" was chosen to represent each external group. It was his job to keep the group in touch with what was going on at home in Schoenstatt. Above all, it was the point man's job to remember the scattered confreres in prayer in the Shrine of the Blessed Mother. Joseph's point man was Alfons Hoffmann, who had been his successor as prefect of the Junior Sodality.

The fledgling group demanded a lot of letter-writing. No sooner did Joseph come off duty when he turned his energy to this task. Equipped with pencil and paper, he walked over to the "serviceman's club." There he hoped to find a quiet corner to sit and write. He was badly disappointed. The house was full of smoking and beer-drinking soldiers and there wasn't a single place to sit. The noise was so great that it was impossible to even hear himself think. After waiting half an hour for a place to sit, he left and returned to the "stable." He lay flat on his bunk and began to write. But this position was soon too uncomfortable. He needed something to write on. After looking around, he found an unclaimed piece of cardboard. It was just what he needed. If he propped it on his knees, it was as good as a desk. From then on Joseph could be seen every day in his free time writing at his "desk" and sending letters to his fellow sodalists. From then on the image of Engling writing letters became an indelible part of his comrades' memories.

On July 25 Joseph was ordered to Grodziec, a town just a few miles west of Bendzin. He was there for three days. The soldiers were then stricken by an outbreak of dysentery. Joseph had a fever and splitting headache. About one-quarter of his company was affected. When Joseph returned to duty, a whole pile of mail was waiting for him. It was always a happy moment when he received letters from the other sodalists. And today there was even one with the familiar handwriting of their spiritual director. His letters were rare. He usually only wrote a postscript on the letters written by the sodalists. "It must be something important," Joseph thought. Indeed it was. But Joseph could not fathom what he read. On July 15, Hans Wormer had been killed in action on the Western Front. He immediately set out to find his Schoenstatt comrades. They stood in a circle. They had serious faces. No one could say much. The news of this death hit them hard. Hans Wormer dead! They had just been with him not long ago in Hagenau. "Let's put together what we can from our allowance to have a Mass said for Hans in Schoenstatt," said one. Then they dispersed bearing the weight of grief. The older age groups had already lost many, but Hans was the first of the 98ers. How many more of them would follow?

Into the Trenches

On August 6, the company left Bendzin to return to Jablonna. On August 9 they were on the train again, traveling southeast to Galicia[2]. Here they could well imagine what was waiting for them. For more than a month a great Russian counteroffensive had been raging between Lemberg and Brzezany. The Germans had held their own and even gained some ground. At eleven o'clock in the night the train pulled into a larger city. The signs said Lemberg. They knew they were close to the front. The train continued to Brzezany. After three days' train ride, they reached Brzezany at midday. "All out! Prepare to march!" The city was filled with the destruction of war. Hardly a house was intact. Their march brought them to some old trenches. For the first time they spent a night in the trenches.

The front was still a good distance away. They had to march nearly a week—south and east—to reach their position. It was a torturous march, first through sweltering heat on rough, dusty roads, then through mud and pouring rain. Covered with a thick layer of dust or drenched to the skin, they staggered under the weight of their packs, hour after hour. On August 20, 1917 they reached their assigned position in Probudzna. It was some 10 miles from the front. Now they learned that they had been assigned to the Reserve Infantry Regiment (R.I.R.) No. 25. It was part of the 15th Reserve Division. The core of the division was in Husiatyn, near the little Zbrucz River. For now, the new company was in standby readiness preparing for the front.

The day after the Birthday of Our Lady, Joseph looked back on

---

[2]   Presently part of the western Ukraine; until 1918 the northeastern corner of Austria-Hungary. Lemberg is the German name for the city of L'vov.

the past four weeks. For the first time since joining the army, he had to paint a truly unfavorable picture of his striving for sanctity. Why? The cause was soon clear enough. During the past few weeks his interior life had suffered a subtle decline. Was it perhaps the unusual conditions of life on a train or in endless marches?

His particular examination was the first to be omitted. Then his spiritual schedule suffered. The daily written control was omitted, in like manner his entries in the spiritual diary. His group work gradually ceased, too; for weeks he carried letters from his group brothers in his knapsack without answering them. His spiritual life began to lose its fervor, especially because he dropped the day of recollection on Sundays. The ideals of his former days which had so gripped his soul seemed lost in a fog. His inner self became empty. Formerly, Holy Mass with spiritual Communion and its continuation in the two holy hours had been an important part of his daily life. In place of the former high ideals, the ideas of the average man began to gain the upper hand. The average man's only thought was: How can I get through the day with the least amount of trouble? It took an eye for one's own advantage, for getting out of things and foisting them onto others. Naturally one has to know how to help oneself in a pinch and not be too scrupulous about the truth. You don't have to be a bad man by any means; on the contrary, you can still adhere to your Christian duties. But a man of ideals? In such conditions it was asking too much!

Without really noticing it, Joseph had gradually reverted to "the average man." Of course his conscience occasionally protested and reminded him of his former zeal. But soon some excitement, some new experience intervened and turned his attention away from the reprimands of his conscience. Once the tedium of the three days in the train and the endless marches wore off, however, he began to reflect again. And in such moments his present condition made him feel totally miserable. True, he had not committed a serious fault, but his standards were higher than that! He had given up striving for sanctity. Could he not excuse his actions, though, on the basis of the irregular lifestyle of the past weeks? Everything had been so topsy-turvy. No, that would not be right. He demanded of himself that his striving for ideal holiness be kept under all circumstances. There would be no excuses. He had to return with a penitent heart to his former ideals. He pulled out his long-neglected diary and made the follow-ing entry:

"Little Mother, you are my hope. You must obtain forgiveness for me from your beloved Son, *Mater ter admirabilis!* Ora pro me! [Mother Thrice Admirable! Pray for me!]" (September 9, 1917). This marked a start of a new phase of progress in his spiritual life. The weeks of carelessness taught him some valuable lessons. He noticed that his inner life suffered as soon as he did not keep a particular examination or the moments of quiet prayer prescribed by his spiritual daily order. To give up these things meant taking the first step toward becoming like his surroundings—a mass man!

Meanwhile, in Probudzna the troops heard more about the progress at the front. The active war had become a stagnant one. The Russians were dug in on the high ground on the other side of the Zbrucz River. On the low ground near the river, the Germans were easy prey for enemy machine guns. A slight retreat was planned to a new position on higher ground. Soon Joseph's company would see fighting for the first time. There were 11 Schoenstatters scattered throughout the regiment. Two days before the move to the front, Joseph gathered three members of his group—Clement Meier, Paul Reinhold and Johannes Dekarski—for a group meeting. Their discussion centered on Joseph's most recent letter to the group. In it he talked about daily prayer as a soldier. Now they began to discuss how to best keep a spiritual daily order. It was clear that they wanted to seriously try to keep it in the trenches. At the next group meeting they would talk about how it went. Before adjourning, Paul suggested that they send part of their next paycheck to the sodality in Schoenstatt to help pay for some of the printing expenses of the MTA magazine.

There was a field Mass before going to the front. Joseph had never experienced an afternoon Mass before, or one with the dispen-sation to receive communion without the usual midnight fast. The Catholics of the regiment gathered around the altar. The chaplain was wearing Russian-style vestments. There was no confession, only general absolution. Almost all the soldiers went to Holy Com-munion. Each stood before the judgment seat of God, not knowing what fate lay ahead on the front. When would they be able to go to Mass again? As it turned out, for Joseph it would be four full months.

That evening the troops were brought to the new German position on the heights west of the river. They found themselves in three-foot foxholes dug into the ground at certain intervals. In the grey light before dawn on the morning of September 18 they were ordered to begin digging. Dawn and dusk were dedicated to extending and connecting the foxholes into a full network of trenches. The foxholes were wet and cold. With all the autumn rain, the soldiers' pants legs never seemed to get dry. At night their legs felt like blocks of ice. During the day the Russian positions could be seen at some distance on the opposing eastern heights of the river. Here and there the Russian artillery made itself known, and the newcomers got their first taste of enemy fire. At least the food was plentiful. The newcomers had not had such good food in months. And they could get what they wanted of potatoes, beans, and corn from the unharvested fields around them.

In spite of the many new experiences in the trenches, Joseph often thought about the last group meeting. Should he not share the discussion and resolutions of that meeting with the members who had not been able to attend? However, it was not so easy to write letters in the trenches. During the day, he had to lie under his strip of tent canvas to keep from being seen by the enemy. In addition, his cold, loam-encrusted fingers could barely hold a pencil. But with some difficulty it could be done, although the writing was not too clear and smudges could not be avoided. He used the next round-robin letter to prepare the group for the month of October. As the month of Mary and the Holy Rosary it ought to be properly commemorated by the sodalists. He took up Paul's suggestion to make a contribution from their pay to support the sodality finances. It really ought be a contribution to the capital of grace as well. Hence the money could best be saved by cutting down on smoking. Moreover, he passed on Alfons Hoffmann's suggestion that each sodalist pray at least a decade of the rosary daily during the month of October.

Joseph himself took the proposed resolutions very seriously. To

154

keep the spiritual daily order and to record if and how it was kept did not give him any noticeable difficulty. At this time his schedule comprised thirteen religious exercises distributed throughout the day. He had difficulties keeping his spiritual reading though; it was not so easy to do this in the present conditions. His particular examination was to be absolutely sincere and truthful. He meant to eliminate any remnant of his lukewarmness of the last four weeks. He needed to be especially alert about keeping his accustomed day of recollection each Sunday. The monotony of the trenches was such that every day seemed like all the others. One had to check the calendar to see if it were really Sunday! Taking his group resolution seriously, he gave up smoking entirely during the month of October.

After some weeks, Joseph was assigned to the "field watch." Those who had this duty were stationed in positions about 300 yards apart all along the front. They were about halfway between the entrenched position on the heights and the river. This put them in a place of increased danger. Their job was to warn the main line of any surprise attack. The night hours passed slowly and were dreadfully monotonous. The beads of Joseph's rosary slipped through his fingers while he prayed. Sometimes he was filled with thoughts of God and eternity. At times he thought of his friends in Schoenstatt, and of the sodality meetings, and of the shrine.

One night there was a special mission. A German reconnaissance patrol was sent out to try and capture Russians in the forward position. Joseph and the rest of the field watch were responsible for backing them up. A skirmish developed. The Russians became uneasy and began to shoot wildly. Even their artillery came to life. Joseph and his comrades were being shot at! For the first time he heard bullets whistle by. Some came very close to him. A grenade exploded and shrapnel whizzed dangerously close to his head. One piece, as long as a finger, landed right next to him. It hadn't missed by much. He felt the closeness of death. In his heart he prayed an act of perfect contrition and commended himself to the Blessed Mother. Suddenly before his mind's eye he saw the Schoenstatt Shrine. Why did the distant, simple Shrine of his Sodality Queen come to his mind just then? He didn't know. But it suddenly filled him with a deep sense of shelter and calm. His captain looked in

Joseph's direction and was somewhat surprised. He thought, "This man acts like a front line veteran. I must remember him for later." It no longer mattered if one were a sharp-looking "parade soldier." What counted in the trenches was bravery and faithfulness to one's comrade. Joseph, once scorned for his lacks as a "parade soldier," was beginning to gain esteem in the eyes of his comrades.

Not long after this, Joseph was assigned a new post. An officer of the Infantry Observation Outpost (I.B.O.) was teaching him the ropes. Joseph was soon observing the Russian lines through a field periscope. He was amazed at how well he could observe the enemy. It was the job of the I.B.O. to make exact notes about every movement and change of position that took place during the day. This information was relayed daily to the higher authorities. Joseph immediately noticed the advantages that this change of commando meant. The I.B.O. dugout was quite pleasant compared to other places in the trenches. He even had a bunk! It may have only been a few bare boards, but it made sleeping much easier than on the cold, damp trench bottoms. In addition, observation was strictly a day job and he did not have to do field watch duty. Best of all, there was a little oven which he could use to warm his hands. This made reading and writing letters much easier. He could make much better use of his supply of stationary that he kept in his knapsack.

Lately, his group had given him much joy. They had all agreed to forward all their group letters to Joseph as group leader. That way he could better monitor the life of the group. As a result, Joseph received a lot of mail. Most were presently about the group work in October and reviewed how they had kept their resolutions. How was it going with daily prayer? Almost all of them reported that this resolution had fared the best. Joseph could say the same thing. He noticed, however, that his meal prayers were being neglected. This was because of the irregular eating patterns on the front lines. There simply were no regular meals. They ate whenever they had something. He had not been very attentive during his prayers either. In the future he wanted to impose heavy penances on himself for these faults. The second resolution, to say a decade of the rosary each day, proved to be more difficult for the group. One letter reported: "I have not done so well with the rosary. On some days I did not succeed in praying it, but on most days I did; often I finished a whole rosary." Another wrote: "I prayed the decade as often as I could. Some days I forgot it or it just wasn't possible. It is rather hard to keep something like that." The other exercises fared quite well. It was clear that the third resolution was the most difficult of all—to refrain from smoking. Clement Meier wrote from the very beginning that he could not do it. How else could one while away the hours in the trenches without any reading material? In a later letter, however, he said that he had occasionally refrained from smoking and had even saved a little money in the process. When Joseph counted the money saved up by all the members of his group from giving up smoking it amounted to 24 marks. This meant quite a help for the sodality treasury.

Joseph's Schoenstatt Group
Joseph Engling (born 1898, infantry, group leader)
Alfons Hoffmann (born 1900, point man in Schoenstatt)
   Paul Reinhold (born 1898, infantry)
   Johannes Dekarski (born 1898, infantry)
   Clemens Meier (born 1898, infantry)
   Eduard Struth (born 1898, infantry)
   Florin Rüber (born 1899, radio operator)
   Gustav Rischewski (born 1899, pilot)
   Karl Klement (born 1898)

Joseph was very satisfied with the group work during October. In the meantime a new plan had come to his mind. Alfons Hoffmann recently suggested to the group that each make a written report of their particular examination and send it to the spiritual director as a kind of spiritual accounting. Joseph liked the idea and wanted to win over the whole group. This would have to be done through a general discussion carried on through the mail. It meant clarifying the importance and methodology of the particular examination. He would have to write a group letter and a letter to each individually. The particular examination was one of his favorite subjects, for he had much experience with it.

Winter Roads

By the end of November the region around the Zbrucz River was in the midst of winter. A thick layer of snow covered the whole area. The ground was frozen solid and the north wind whistled through the trenches. But good news came. The Russians were ready for an armistice.

On December 6, 1917, the regiment was told that a general cease-fire around Husiatyn had been reached. The regiment was to be in readiness to remove from this position at any time. The soldiers were overjoyed. Peace was another step closer. When would an armistice be reached in the other theaters of war? On December 8 the company moved out. On the first day they had orders to reach Tudorow, a twenty-mile march. Now they noticed how "rusty" their marching legs had become. It was a hard march over icy and snow-blown roads. Joseph was lost in his thoughts, but not about sore legs or feet. Today was the feast of the Immaculate Conception. How lovely this feastday always was in Schoenstatt! On this day all the sodalists renewed their consecration to Mary. In spirit he joined them in the shrine and renewed his consecration. He quietly prayed his covenant prayer. What should he offer Mary with today's renewal? The hardships of this march back from the trenches? Surely! But he wanted to offer something even greater. How had it been three months ago when he had marched out to the front? He had stopped keeping his spiritual daily order and particular examination. Yes, it was then that lukewarmness had overpowered him. He now faced the same conditions. It would be a real sacrifice for the Blessed Mother if he could be faithful this time. He renewed his pledge to live up to the ideals of sanctity.

The company spent the next days in Tudorow. It was a time of basic drills and cleaning and mending. Joseph's sergeant was not well-liked. Many of his orders were totally unreasonable. Joseph had to apply his particular examination to keep his anger from getting the best of him. His corporal was entirely different! He even anticipated that the next march would be during Christmas and declared a Christmas celebration on December 16. Presents were given to the soldiers. They were simple, but enough to remind the men of Christmas joy.

Joseph wrote letters to his group brothers in every spare minute. He had to hurry. It was normal procedure that as long as the company was on the march or in transport, there was no mail. His weekly day of recollection showed that he kept his spiritual daily order practically without interruption. He felt that his striving and interior life possessed their old vigor. Still, he found shortcomings that needed work. The primitive conditions of life in the trenches had left some marks. He ate quickly and without any form or attention to good manners. If he wanted to be a modern saint, he would have to have more manners in everyday things. He also noticed that he was becoming a pack rat. He lugged around pieces of string, half blank sheets of paper, etc. because he couldn't decide to throw anything away. It was becoming obsessive. Something would have to be done. A modern saint cannot be a strange saint. He did not want his life to be a witness of odd habits but of Our Lady.

Around Christmas 1917 the company was on the march again. They followed the Sereth River to reach Tarnopol. The weather worsened. The temperature fell and icy winds blew over the snow-covered roads. Bread and butter froze in the soldiers' knapsacks, becoming as hard as rock. A sharp northeastern wind cut into the face of the marching column and slowed down its progress. It swept some stretches of the road clear of snow, laying bare the icy ground. On these stretches marching was even more difficult and one after the other fell on the glare ice on the road. Now word came from the rear that the field kitchen was not keeping up. Some good, strong men were needed to fall back and help. Joseph and some of his comrades were sent. They had to push, pull, or help turn the spokes. The horses became restless and stubborn. Whenever they reached a particularly dangerous place, Joseph prayed an ejaculation to the Blessed Mother. One time the wagon slid totally out of control towards a cliff. The whole kitchen with its horses would have been lost if it had not been caught by a tree.

An Act of Self-Denial

Late one afternoon, Joseph was doing his daily spiritual reading by the flickering light of a candle. His name was called. He had orders to join the advance team to prepare the battalion's

---

quarters for next night. Joseph left part of his equipment with the company baggage. The little advance team had to leave at six that evening. It was already dark. Around midnight they reached a village where they camped before marching two more hours in the morning. When they reached the designated site, they had to make arrangements. Then they went back a ways to meet the battalion and direct them to their quarters. It was strenuous work until everyone was in their place. By night Joseph's whole body ached with exhaustion. Finally it was done and he could look forward to a much-deserved rest.

He went to the baggage car to retrieve his knapsack. His two blankets were gone! And a pair of shoes, his shoebrush and polish were missing. Even his sewing kit was gone. They had been stolen. Joseph's wrath began to build. What a mean trick! He wore himself to the bone for his comrades and this was the thanks he got! What was he going to do without blankets on such a bitterly cold night? When he arrived at his lodging, he wrapped himself in his overcoat and prepared to sleep. His eyes were about to close when he remembered that he had to say his night prayers and record his spiritual schedule.

He examined the thirteen points of his daily order. Morning prayers and sodality prayers had been said. The good intention was made. His spiritual participation in the Mass and act of spiritual Communion? Also good. How about his holy hour? He was sure about the one in the morning. So he marked it kept. The one in the afternoon? In the midst of so much work he had not thought of it. So he made a question mark behind it. Rosary, night prayers, examination of conscience, perfect contrition and request for the priestly blessing in the evening had all been made. The last point was an act of self-denial. It expressed his desire to contribute something daily to Our Lady's capital of grace. In his heart he was still resentful toward those shameless thieves. Should he continue to be a good comrade or become as shamelessly selfish as they? "Today's sacrifice for the capital of grace," said an inner voice. So he marked this down as his act of self-denial.

So it went day after brutal day until the end of the long march. Joseph had to continue the exhausting pace of the advance team. On

Christmas Eve he could not turn in for the night until 11 pm. On Christmas morning he had to be up early for the next day's work. At least the day after Christmas was free. He wrote the following in his diary:

"Second Christmas Day! I am sitting in the parlor with some civilians in distant Galicia. Christmas—I think of home, think of Schoenstatt. They have celebrated the Holy Night and Christmas and thought of us and we of them. (....) Today we had a complete rest. I prayed, read, and did my spiritual examination of conscience and placed my ideal before me again. Yes, man is just too human and easily distracted from the goal. Christmas! Christ is born; Christ became a tiny, helpless baby for me. I must therefore become another Christ" (December 26, 1917).

Joseph chose as his particular examination to make at least three acts of self-denial each day. Three hard days' marches were still ahead of the battalion before they reached Tarnopol and the train. The last stretch was even a night march. Joseph kept his particular examination and daily spiritual schedule faithfully day after day. He had to use every available free minute to make the exercises, but he succeeded in doing it. Just before entering the city of Tarnopol the exhausted soldiers were permitted a rest of thirty minutes. Despite the cold weather the perspiration ran down their faces from sheer exertion. Instead of resting, Joseph made use of this time to write letters.

For Joseph the march to the front had been a spiritual defeat, but his return from the front was a victory. Conditions had not permitted Joseph to go to Mass for four months, but his interior life had not suffered. His spiritual daily order and the daily written control had carried the day.

8. The Front Near Verdun

Dun and Rémonville

In the final days of 1917, the train rolled out of Tarnopol carrying Joseph's regiment (R.I.R. 25) westward. The soldiers already guessed that their next stop would be the western front. With the Russians out of the war and the Americans newly into it, the Germans would have to play a bold hand in the west. The trip by train would take a whole week. Each boxcar held thirty-eight men. To battle boredom, someone broke out the cards. Wagers were mandatory, 20 cents a game. Soon many were out of money.

"I'm broke," said one, "but Engling here has some loose change." "Join in, Engling!" encouraged the others. Joseph hesitated and wanted to get out of it. "Don't be a spoil sport, Engling," insisted the others impatiently. "If we don't have a game, we'll die of boredom." Joseph did not want to be a bad comrade, so he joined in. He played until quite late and had a fair amount of luck. When he counted his nickels, he had over 13 Marks.

The money did not make Joseph happy. He considered giving it back. The next day his comrades insisted that he play again. After all, he had been the previous day's big winner. As the cards were being dealt, Joseph could feel the itch in his fingers. On New Year's Day 1918, Joseph didn't need to be asked. The cards already exerted a secret power over him. He played cards until 10 o'clock that night. But Joseph's conscience began to bother him. The troops had to get off the train at Kalisch for delousing. This gave Joseph time to think. Was a passion for cards and gambling taking command of his life? How much time he had wasted which could have been put to more profitable use! What the long march back from the front had not accomplished, his passion for cards now did. His spiritual daily order was crumbling. It was already several days since he had done his spiritual reading and prayed the rosary. He had not written in his diary. He spent practically the whole day doing nothing but playing cards. No wonder there was no time left for his interior life. Was this really a good way to begin the new year? His conscience gave him no peace. When he boarded the train again he managed to get on a different car from the "card sharks." For now it allowed him to escape the temptation, but this new adversary on the battlefield of his soul was not yet vanquished.

The train rolled through the heart of Germany. They passed through Leipzig, Eisenach, Bebra, Hanau. They crossed the Rhine and on January 6 the signs in the train stations were already in French: Montmédy, Sedan, Stenay. Around four in the afternoon the wheels of the train screeched to a halt. The sign said "Dun." They were some 20 miles north of the front at Verdun, on the Meuse River. Joseph and the Fourth Company were quartered in comfortable barracks in nearby Doulcon. The arrival in Dun meant that for the first time in weeks Joseph's regiment could receive and send mail. Joseph sent out letters to let his group brothers know he was ready to continue at once. His goal, to win over the group to the particular examination and its written control, stood vividly before his mind. But first he had to regain his spiritual equilibrium. For three days during the trip he had given in to excessive card playing, a weakness which had paralyzed his spiritual striving. To be sure, on New Year's Day he had immediately taken up his spiritual schedule again. A few days after that his particular examination returned to normal. He even used the last day of the trip, a Sunday, for spiritual recollection and a thorough examination of conscience. But he could only gradually overcome the effects of this defeat. No sooner did he make some progress when the passion for cards triumphed again and sent him back to square one.

Some of his comrades found a barn in nearby Rémonville. It was not far from Joseph's barracks and was a good place to play cards away from the prying eyes of the officers. Besides, the soldiers had some time on their hands. One day some of them met Joseph and pressed him to join them. Joseph resisted. "You only have to play *one* game," they insisted as they took him in tow. "All right, to do my comrades a favor I will play a short game," thought Joseph. One game turned into a second and then a third. Every time Joseph wanted to leave, the others said, "Just one more game—then we'll quit." But they never did quit. It was already late. The card players hardly noticed. Joseph's conscience bothered him. This was no longer camaraderie but compulsion. What about his night prayer?

He still had to do his spiritual reading and rosary. But every time he started to think, someone said, "It's your turn!" and the fire of his passion took command. They played and played. Suddenly, at the first gray of dawn, Joseph Friedrich, a fellow Schoenstatter, opened the door and cried with surprise, "Engling, you too?" Joseph got up without a word. On the improvised card table flickered a few candle stubs.

As the new day broke an intensely sobering feeling overcame Joseph. All day long he was oppressed by a sense of guilt. As soon as he came off duty he reached for a pencil and paper and started to write. The pressure on his soul was too great; he could stand it no longer. He had to make an honest report to his distant confessor, admitting all the faults and weaknesses of the past two weeks, and that the cause for it all had been cards.

The "Poor Sinner" Letter
He wrote to Father Kentenich with the following words:
NcppbvM[1]   Doulcon, January 9, 1918
Reverend Father Kentenich,

I am finally getting around to sending you my confession of sins. I would have had enough time yesterday between 5 pm and 8 pm, but I was talked into or—I must be honest—I succumbed to the temptation to play cards. During the last three weeks I was very negligent. (....)

On December 31 and on New Year's Day I had good thoughts. I ignored them. I let myself be talked into playing cards, wagering 20-cent stakes, which is forbidden. I won 13 Marks. But I was not happy. The loser was sore. I almost returned the money. I made the resolution not to play again. But because I had won, I could not refuse the invitation the next day. We gambled from morning till 10 pm. After we were deloused in the town of Kalisch, I got away from the gamblers. At least I did my spiritual reading again. On January 3, I began to keep the PE again. On Sunday, January 6, I kept the weekly recollection. I had not kept

---

[1]   Nos cum prole pia benedicat virgo Maria (Mother with your Blessed Son, bless us each and every one).

it the previous Sunday. On Monday, January 7, I wrote to all the group members. But yesterday I let myself be talked into gambling again. As a result I did not do my spiritual reading and rosary. I thought of it when I started playing, but I even forgot the *MTA* [Magazine] which I received yesterday with the first mail.

Reverend Father, you see how many graces I have forfeited. I am twice as sorry now that I write it down. Please intercede for me to our dear Little Mother. Tell her in the shrine that I want to be more diligent in her service again. (....)

(Continuation of letter on January 10)

Since I used the opportunity to go to the movies last night, I did not finish the letter.

Our group work was also affected by the transfer. Most of our mail was kept back since December 7. The written control of the PE is not practiced by everyone. Rischewski did not begin with it yet. Dekarski started again; I do not know how it is with Reinhold. (....)

Reverend Father, you see that I have been weak again and have seriously failed. Please, intercede forgiveness for me and give me a penance. I humbly accept the punishment. In humility, but also in confidence in our Mother I want to strive again towards the goal. (....)

Your penitent,

Joseph

Now it was necessary for Joseph to decide what he wanted to do about card playing in the future. He thought about it. Playing cards to bridge monotony and enforced idleness was certainly not a fault. To find a certain pleasure in cards was no fault either. Playing to show charity towards his comrades would even be a virtue. But he could not let cards become a passion and run his life. An ill-ordered passion for cards took away his inner freedom. As soon as he had lost dominion over himself, his religious life and striving for sanctity grew cold. It caused him to neglect his spiritual exercises and waste time only playing cards. After the experience of the past weeks, Joseph made the resolution to play only out of good motives in the future. Furthermore, he wanted to play only as long as he had time at his disposal. What was the principle he had learned in Schoen-statt? First comes the necessary, then the useful and only then the pleasant. This principle applied to the case at hand.

He soon noticed that this resolution did not work. When his passion for cards took over it clouded his judgment. He talked himself into believing he was playing for only noble reasons, even when this was clearly not the case. At the same time he lost track of how much time he really had to play cards. Every time he played, he felt totally dissatisfied. After he had considered the matter well he knew exactly what he had to do. First of all, he had to break the influence of the passion for playing cards in order to gain inner freedom and dominion over himself. This, however, was possible only by temporarily adopting radical measures. He promptly entered in his spiritual diary:

"Dear Mother, forgive me. I want to [become a saint]! From now on I want to record here if I had the necessary strictness with myself. Moreover, dear Little Mother, I promise you not to touch cards till March 1. Help me!" (January 24, 1918).

He had made the same experience with smoking. For the month of October he had decided to quit smoking altogether. From that time on he had given up the habit. He did not feel dependent on it any more and now only smoked on rare occasions.

For four weeks he faithfully kept his resolution not to play cards. Consistently he declined the invitation of his comrades even though it annoyed them, but one day he gave in. He immediately imposed severe measures against himself. As a penance for breaking his resolution he deprived himself of supper one day. Considering the meager fare the soldiers were getting during the war, this was a very severe penance indeed. Furthermore, he extended his resolution not to play cards to include the entire month of March. These strict penances brought about a change. From that time on he remained loyal to his resolution.

In the meantime, he faced another test of his moral strength to face. Through all of January, units of troops drilled back and forth over the fields around Dun and Rémonville. The weather was dismal. Night frosts were followed by thaws; snow showers followed icy rains. Everywhere the ground was soft. The fields were strewn with puddles of slushy mud. Here and there one could see dirty patches of snow. Biting winter winds blew over the open fields. No boots could keep out the frigid slush, no uniform keep out the cold rain. The companies marched out in the morning in most miserable weather. The inevitable "army crawl" put them right in the mud. When they returned, it was with wet clothes and stiff limbs, looking like they had rolled in the mud all day.

In camp one inspection followed another. The uniform was put in order only to be dragged through the wet clay again and again. This was the routine for day after grueling day. They cleaned, patched and polished more than at any other time in army life. The unreasonable severity at the exercises, the senseless drills, the chicanery of some of the noncommissioned officers, all worked together to bring about a turbulent state in the soldiers' minds. Anger and bitterness stirred in their hearts. War weariness, the hardships of the campaign, undernourishment, the anxiety over dying in battle had broken the strength of some. They were no longer able or ready to accept greater hardships. A newly arrived unit of relief troops compounded the problem by spreading dark words against the "Prussian military" and even the fatherland. For the first time Joseph's regiment had cases of open insubordination and even desertion.

Joseph stood in the midst of these events and was fully aware. He, too, felt the turmoil in his soul. The world didn't make sense any more. There were things he saw and heard in the army which he felt were wrong. And he had to take care that his anger did not get the best of him when he felt that he or his comrades were treated unjustly. Now hearing agitators speak angrily against military, war, and fatherland, he knew he was facing questions that would one day demand a serious answer from him. For now, however, he felt he must steer a course which did not question why he was in the army. If others did so in his presence, he would not condemn them; he knew their dilemma. But he would not support them. He would keep silent. A feeling that he would sin kept him from any other course. He must remain true to himself and to his past. But something had changed inside. Just a year ago he was still filled with youthful enthusiasm. Today his love of country was not kept going by the vitality of youth. He kept going because of the eternal things instead. Here he had to honestly admit: If it were not for his faith in God and eternity, his thoughts would resemble those of the hot-headed comrades claiming to want nothing better than plant to a bullet in the head of a hated sergeant.

When he penetrated more deeply into his soul he found a firm standpoint amid the swirl of emotion and events. It was his religious life's ideal. To him the great hardships of the war seemed to be a mighty school of education determined by God to help him reach his personal ideal. By means of it, he was to become a saint. How could he then complain? The daily difficulties and trials were given to him that they might become contributions to Our Lady's capital of grace in Schoenstatt. There a movement would one day take hold which would bring religious and moral rebirth to his fatherland. This gave deep meaning to all the privations and sufferings of his army life. Loyalty to his military oath resonated with his religious ideal. In it he found the strength to keep his soul in balance and to achieve his objective in spite of the discouragement of his environment.

While reflecting on such matters, he knew how he must respond to one of his group members bothered by the same problems. He picked up his pencil and wrote:

"Yes, the world needs religion. Without it the state is a shaky edifice. How much dissatisfaction and how many rebellious thoughts are rampant in our company! I personally could keep myself free only by thinking of God. We are sodalists, apostles. Our sodality, in particular, has taken for its purpose the spiritual renewal of Germany, or rather our Mother has given it to us. Let us direct our attention to it. Little occasions always present themselves. For example, I succeeded in getting one of my comrades to go to Mass on Sunday by saying: 'Well, Max, do you want to come along?' " (February 9, 1918).

When Joseph surveyed his situation he could draw only one simple conclusion: Do not become sad and discouraged! Believe in your ideals! Courageously live the demands this means—in your own heart and in the presence of those around you!

How did his interior life fare during the storms of the past few weeks? It was almost like a peaceful island in a stormy sea.

Gradually he experienced a deep solitude which the noise of the daily occurrences could not dispel. Here he was alone with God. This was the reason why his spiritual schedule, his particular examination and the weekly day of recollection remained unaffected by the raging storms. He felt very much fortified when, at the end of January, he could attend Mass every Sunday. It occurred for the first time on January 20. His last holy Mass had been four months ago on September 14 in Galicia. A feeling of unspeakable happiness filled his heart at Holy Communion.

In January 1918 his particular examination was: "I will not shirk any work or let others do it all. Three times a day of my own free will I will do work which concerns all of us." He succeeded rather well in keeping his resolution. He thought he needed to be more strict with himself. For some time he checked whether he had used the necessary severity toward himself. Even though the exterior conditions of his life were so severe he asked his confessor: "Father, by all means treat me with severity. Treat me with an iron hand."

There was another conclusion which Joseph drew from his present condition. Instead of permitting himself to be affected by the general dissatisfaction or to take part in rebellious talk, he thought it was more important to devote his strength to the work of his group and to participate in building up the external organization of the sodality. His letters to the various group members brought many responses. When he scanned their letters to him, he found much sincere striving to arrive at a clearer understanding of the particular examination and its difficulties. Paul Reinhold wrote:

"To stick to the written control of the particular examination is difficult. If only one had a regular routine and a room with a lamp. But here, a few days in a foxhole, ten days in the forward position, then a few days in a village barn without light. It could be done in the trenches, but then you need energy and perseverance. I will discuss the matter with Engling once more, but if it is introduced in the group, I'll go along."

In another letter Reinhold wrote:

"I agreed with the resolution and my recordings went as far as December 7. On the 8th we were unexpectedly relieved. But after marching through foot-high snow I was so tired that it was impossible to make my written control in the evening. Our Mother Thrice Admirable will, I hope, forgive me. I do not know if the others made it. As soon as we have settled down, I will start keeping a record again. So far, I was together with Joseph Engling in the same group, but today I am attached to a machine gun unit. Hope, however that we can get together from time to time."

Clemens Meier also seemed to have his difficulties. In his report to Joseph he wrote:

"With regard to our resolution to record our particular examination, I must present myself as a sinner. Fatigue and the cold on the march and the transport led me to omit the written control. I ask you, therefore, for a severe penance. To this petition I want to add the promise that I want to do much better with regard to my group work. I know that in spiritual things I have failed grievously from the middle to the end of last month. I did not care for anything. On some days everything went against me. The principle cause for all this was our move from the eastern to the western front with all the privations that went along with it. But from now on it must be different. I will not permit myself to be influenced by my whims or fancies anymore. Beseech our MTA sincerely that I may not fall back into this condition again."

A third group member reported:

"I have made a firm resolution concerning the particular examination. It costs much effort. Sometimes I feel like giving up altogether. Slowly, however, it is getting better."

Almost all the letters were written in this vein. The group was seriously striving to make good use of the particular examination.

Operation February

On January 29, Joseph's regiment was transferred to better quarters in the vicinity of the front. It was called "Camp Cecilia" in the woods around Brieulles. The wooden barracks were well-built, and there was a canteen and a special training area. Once there, Joseph was given a new task. He was assigned to the shock troop which the regiment had to form. It was a dangerous job—going on scouting raids over the no-man's-land to the French front line. But after some days Joseph could report that he really liked the shock troop. The company spirit was better than in the regiment as a

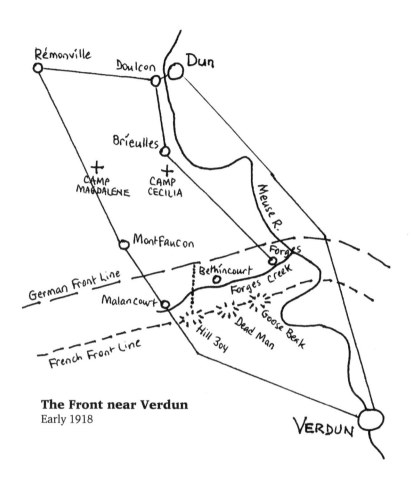

The Front near Verdun
Early 1918

whole. There was hardly any complaining and things were done with a lot of enthusiasm. The lieutenant and his sergeants knew their stuff. Joseph could hardly believe it. In just a few days and with hardly a curse they trained their charges into an exemplary group. Here one saw what good leaders can do, he thought.

He also liked his new comrades. They hit it off right away. And what did he feel about the dangers he would soon face? He had already confronted himself quite honestly with what was ahead. He knew that any mission with the shock troop would be a matter of life and death. Joseph took some quiet time to reflect on the possibility of death. He shared some of this thoughts with his friend Karl:

"We are stationed behind the front and will only be sent forward if a scouting patrol is needed. I am not afraid of danger. To me personally it is totally immaterial whether I am sent to a sector of heavy fighting or to a place of calm. I am resolved to accept even death from the hands of our Mother."

On February 10, 1918, Engling's regiment (R.I.R. 25) was moved to the line of fire on the front near Verdun. Their trenches ran parallel to Forges Creek in front of the infamous "Hill 304." It was a hill bathed with the blood of thousands. R.I.R. 25 had been sending out two patrols on nearly a daily basis. An attempt by the shock troop of R.I.R. 69 to penetrate the French lines had been repulsed. The major in command made the following decisions: "The next forced penetration of the enemy line will be undertaken by the shock troop of R.I.R. 25 and attack at the fortified position 'Bear Paw.' The code name in all communications is to be 'Operation February.' The operation is to be kept top secret."

In Camp Cecilia the shock troop was briefed about the lay of the land around the 'Bear Paw.' "Here in the south," the captain said while pointing to the lower edge of a map, "is Verdun. Here is the Meuse River as it flows north. We are on its west bank. Along this ridge—Goose Beak, Dead Man, Hill 304—runs the main line of French resistence. Just behind it is the French artillery. It could give us the most trouble in our operation. Just to the north of Hill 304 is a slight rise, the so-called Bear Paw. The French have set up a well-manned fortified position there. North of the Bear Paw the land slopes gently down to Forges Creek.

"On the northern side of Forges Creek is a bluff. At its foot are the villages of Forges, Bethíncourt, Malancourt. Above it is the present German line. This was also the German line when we started the 1916 offensive. Much German blood was spilled in this valley in 1916. Between our lines and Hill 304—passing through the Bear Paw—is a connecting trench dug in 1916 when the Germans briefly held Hill 304. We have to follow this trench. The creek has been shot out of its bed, leaving pools of water all over. They make a treacherous obstacle for a night raid. The few passable ways are near the trench. On the other side of the creek at the foot of the Bear Paw is barbed wire up to about 70 cm (2 feet) high. Right at the front of the Bear Paw are two protruding French machine gun nests. The Bear Paw is protected by three lines of trenches with well-built dugouts." The captain continued on with similar descriptions. The shock troop knew they had hard work ahead.

The next days were filled with practice runs involving every detail of the operation. The shock troop had to learn how to act under heavy fire, how to remove the opposing wire entanglements and clear the enemy trenches, how to throw hand grenades and how to fasten charges. Everything depended on quick action and keeping a clear head. The operation was excitedly talked about by the members of the shock troop. The veterans of the battles of Champagne, of the Aisne and of Galicia had much to tell about their own experiences.

Joseph remained conspicuously silent during these days. Whenever he could, he went off by himself. Was it perhaps the thought of the imminent danger of death which affected him so deeply? No, it was something else. He had agreed with his group members to devote the days preceding Ash Wednesday to a thorough recollection. He considered it something of a retreat. It was to be a time of meditation and prayer. He took this resolution seriously. On the first day his mind was occupied with the eternal truths of God, the destination of man, final judgment, heaven and hell—all thoughts which he had been thinking about in recent weeks. On the second day he reflected on the way he had spent the two months just ended. He recalled God's mercies and ackowledged his own unfaithfulness in so many faults and weaknesses. He spent this day in the spirit of true contrition and humility.

On the third day he ordered his future life. In trying to do so, he went back to his retreat of 1915. In those days so long ago he had first laid down the fundamental principles of his plan of life. They were still in force for him in the struggle for his great ideal. He had copied them into the front page of his current spiritual diary. This diary was now filled, so he took a new volume and wrote his ideals again on the very first pages. He then added the four special resolutions of his military life—to keep up his striving for perfection, to be a guardian angel to his fellow sodalists, to keep Sundays holy, and to never tell a lie. These were still valid, of course. It also seemed advisable to him to write down what had given him such great support in recent weeks: his regular examination of conscience, the report to his spiritual director; the ideal of the sodality—especially the thought that Schoenstatt must become a second Ingolstadt; finally, the brief moments of prayer inserted into his spiritual schedule. From these experiences he formulated four additional resolutions:

1) I want to become a saint through my spiritual director
2) I want to become a total sodalist and adhere to the sodality with body and soul.
3) I want to keep my particular examination with still greater zeal.
4) I will not shy from any sacrifice to make my daily spiritual reading and say a decade of the rosary every day.

To these resolutions he added a little prayer offering up his daily work for Our Lady's capital of grace. At the end he reiterated the resolution to read these entries every Sunday at his weekly examination of conscience. The three-day retreat gave his spiritual life new fervor and determination to strive for his special aim. It affected him more deeply than the impending operation in which he was about to play a part.

In Camp Cecilia the shock troop was informed that the operation would soon take place. Twenty-four volunteers—about a third of the shock troop—were needed to do the actual raid on the Bear Paw. The rest would back them up. "Who volunteers?" came the question. Joseph wrestled with himself. Should he volunteer? Could he submit his parents to the suffering it would mean if he were killed after volunteering? And if an early death kept him from becoming a priest, could he bear this responsibility? He would have preferred that the commander just pick the raid party. By now the lieutenant was counting, "...twenty-three, twenty four. Enough!"

The shock troop moved up to the front lines by night. Then after a night of feeling out the terrain, the operation began. It was 2:20 am on Feburary 24.

The drama began with German artillery opening fire on the French lines. The French responded in kind. Soon mortars and granades were flying. The fire of machine guns was heard. There was a great deal of commotion and shooting along the whole sector. All of Forges Creek Valley fell under heavy fire. It was a deadly and nerve-wracking affair for all involved in the operation. Towards dawn, when things quieted down again, the shock troop returned. The break into the French lines was successful. Parts of the French trenches had been cleared and dugouts blown up; nine French soldiers were taken prisoner. But the shock troop had suffered casualities, too—four wounded and one dead. One of the Germans on the regular field watch was also found dead in the morning. The following day the shock troop stood in uniform at the cemetery in Brieulles to bury the dead.

That evening Joseph sat in the canteen and wrote to his spiritual director in Schoenstatt. He wrote so intently that one would have thought he was writing about the operation. In fact, he did not devote a single word to describing the military endeavor. Instead, from beginning to end, he wrote about his spiritual striving and the progress of the group.

In the early hours of March 10 the shock troop of R.I.R. 25 was called on again to strike at Forges Creek. Operation February was to be repeated. This time Joseph was not one of the reserves, but part of the raiding party. He had volunteered this time, in spite of his resolution to never do so. Was it to "prove" himself in front of comrades? No. It was to support Bruno Karthäuser, a high school student he had befriended and with whom he had several quite good conversations. Bruno had been assigned to the raiding party. Joseph did not want to let his friend go alone. In a letter to Father Kentenich he wrote simply,

"I volunteered because Karthäuser was there" (March 11, 1918).

This time the raid failed. The French were ready for the attack. Joseph's job was to man the breach they had made in the enemy's barbed wire. At the end of the raid, he would have to help his comrades find the breach again and direct them back to the German lines. He would also have to take care of any wounded. As he lay on the cold ground with shells exploding overhead, he was sorry he

175

had volunteered. Only afterward did he hear how the French had pretended to retreat, setting a trap that very nearly led to the capture of the raiders. One soldier was killed and ten were wounded, with nothing to show for their effort. On the way back to camp Joseph prayed his morning prayer. He thanked God that he was still alive. He made the good intention for the day and prayed his sodality prayers. Then he spiritually went to Mass and Communion. Somewhere where there was no war, it was Sunday.

In the Cloister of His Heart

For some time Joseph had been experiencing a strange discontent. He was, of course, always in some way dissatisfied when he reviewed the progress of his life and striving. But this time his discontent was mixed with odd feelings of sadness and melancholy. When he wrote about them in his diary, he often used the expression "melancholy moods." He often found himself thinking about death. How transitory were the things of this world! What bothered him most was not that he might die, but that his life might pass without making proper use of it. Often he became especially uneasy when he thought about his great mission in life. As he had once put it, he wanted "to become a learned and saintly priest." Yes, this had to be realized; otherwise, his earthly existence would have no real value for eternity. The spring offensive, so he hoped, would bring the war to a close. Then he could fully resume his studies and continue his preparation for the priesthood. However, he did not want to wait that long with his spiritual work. Here he could throw himself into doing things right away. Once again the old thirst for knowledge took hold of him and he felt the urge to read and study more.

About this time at Camp Cecilia, Joseph heard some news which greatly interested him and his comrades. It was said that a lending library had been started in the camp where one could borrow books free of charge. After some investigation he found that the books were in the care of Medical Sergeant Winter. Sergeant Winter explained that one of the chaplains, Father von Köth, was responsible for starting the library. The sergeant sang the praises of the chaplain's sincere kindness. He mentioned that the priest, ever alert to his comrades' needs, had long been thinking about how he could

176

alleviate the monotony of the long leisure hours brought about by stabilized wafare. So many bad books and magazines poisoned the good morals and souls of the soldiers. This had prompted the "padre" to start a library for the division, which he did at his own expense. It cost him several thousand marks. The books came from the St. Charles Borromeo Society in Bonn. Any soldier, regardless of creed, could borrow the books free of charge. And, the sergeant added with some pride, "the books are very much in demand."

Here Joseph could quench the recently reawakened thirst for knowledge. He also bought a few small books in the nearby town of Brieulles. He had a comprehensive educational plan he wanted to work on. Since most of the books available in the library were lighter reading, only a few fit his purpose. Though he felt handicapped in the selection of books, he was nonetheless determined to study regularly. In a little notebook he jotted down the title of every book he read, sometimes adding a few glosses about their contents. The titles included *Parcival* by Wagner; *The Trumpeter of Saeckingen* by Scheffel; biographies of Gottfried Keller and Michelangelo; the Goethe epic *Reineke Fuchs*; and *Willing—A Kingly Art* by Fassbender.

His comrades wondered why he was so set on reading and studying. The company tailor passed him by and thought, "This fellow Engling with the big spectacles seems to be an odd fellow. He spends every free moment reading and writing. I must talk with him one day and see what kind of a fellow he really is." Many of his comrades could not understand why he lugged around books in his knapsack. When they went on a march or moved to the front they left behind any and every unnecessary thing, heavy books in particular. But Joseph carried them without the least hesitation. He could no longer stand to be mentally idle.

The books made him think of a subject which had once been his favorite—the German language. In Schoenstatt he had plunged deeply into the study of his mother tongue. Since then he had been taken up with the goal of gaining total mastery of German style and grammar. His future vocation urged him on. In the next letter to his parents he asked them to send his German grammar from Schoenstatt. Now he could better follow his inclination and enjoy the wonderful riches of the German language! From then on the German grammar went with him wherever he went.

If Joseph thought that mental work would banish all his melancholy moods and his interior unrest though, he was mistaken. He enjoyed the reading and studying, but his melancholy moods did not go away. On the contrary, at times he was so overwhelmed by restlessness that he could not even stand to read. An inexplicable roving and restless spirit would come over him. He would go from conversation to letter writing and from letter writing to reading. So it went back and forth. He had felt like this just a few days ago. At first he was writing a letter to his brother, Valentine. Then he went to the canteen in search of conversation with a comrade he had befriended. But he cut it short and read *The Trumpeter of Saeckingen*. While reading, the urge to exchange thoughts with a friend came over him again. He did not understand what was happening inside of him and how he should interpret this puzzling unrest. It did not yet dawn on him yet that God was calling him. It was a call to a deeper solitude of prayer. Before eye and ear could open themselves to the mysteries of the interior life, he first had to become discontent with all externals.

For the time being Joseph knew nothing better than to adhere steadfastly to the resolutions he had made during his private retreat. They mainly dealt with the faithful observance of his spiritual schedule. He sensed more and more how important this faithfulness was. The more unsettled his exterior life, the more necessary it was to have a place of calm in his heart. The more that paralyzing influences rushed in on him from the outside, the more he had to find solitude from the world. He did not want his surroundings to dictate his life. He wanted to live wholly under the mandate of his personal ideal. In these efforts the spiritual schedule was like a cloister wall. Within its protective walls was the tranquil island of deep solitude. Only God was admitted there. The religious exercises of his schedule were the soul's opportunity to breathe in this solitude, filled with God's presence. No danger or event of the day was allowed to steal into the inner sanctum of his heart and hold it captive. That is why he took such pains to keep his spiritual schedule in all situations of life. In the course of the past years he had succeeded in keeping it even during strenuous drills, on long marches, and amid the stupefying idleness of "stabilized" warfare. His prayer life could not be adversely affected by provocations of the men in his environment or by the violent outbursts of their passions. Indeed, he remained essentially unchanged throughout the nerve-wracking trials of the front. Although he did not succeed at once and he made mistakes, no setback could deprive him of his courage.

Joseph (second from right) with comrades in a dugout on the Front.

The following Holy Week was a school of prayer. On March 20th Joseph's regiment was moved to "Camp Magdalene" near Cunel. Here the chaplain conducted devotions every evening; the soldiers were offered Holy Communion. Joseph attended and received Our Lord as often as possible. The chaplain praised the men of the 25th for their regular attendance. Joseph, too, joyfully noted how well the services were attended. Whenever he approached comrades, they gladly accepted his invitation to come along. Through his influence quite a few others joined him. The provisional altar stood under a cluster of trees which protected them from aerial reconnaissance. Behind the altar the men had even built a confessional for their "padre." On either side of it the soldiers stood in long lines waiting to make their Easter confession. One day Joseph observed to his great joy that even the company commander was standing in line.

This did not surprise him. In fact he had taken it for granted that his commander would, without fear of human respect, fall in line with the rest. More of Joseph's comrades lined up only after he had encouraged them to do so.

Now that he could go to Communion every day, Holy Week became a week of prayer. This helped deepen the experience of grace brought to him by the Eucharist. Spiritual attendance at Holy Mass every morning and his two holy hours had long been a regular part of his spiritual schedule. Joseph had gradually developed a definite way of keeping his holy hours. He spiritually placed himself in the little shrine at Schoenstatt. There he saluted his Savior in the Blessed Sacrament and renewed his spiritual Communion. Then he gave himself, together with Christ dwelling in him, as an offering to the heavenly Father by presenting the precious blood of His Divine Son. After that he would say ejaculatory prayers to help keep the hour a time of interior recollection. This way he could connect his whole day's work with his Divine Master. For a long time he had felt the longing to sanctify the Lord's Day and to make it a day of prayer. Oh, how little one noticed it was Sunday on the battlefield! During the past, major actions at the front had taken place precisely on Sundays. Nonetheless, Joseph's diary tells us that he kept, almost without exception, his weekly day of recollection on Sundays as resolved. Of late he had a new-found interest in the mysteries and events of the liturgical year. These, too, he wanted to live more consciously in the future.

As Joseph continued to wonder about his "melancholy moods," he was struck by a thought which he wrote in his diary:

"Why is it that I have made so little progress lately? Probably because I pray too little in spite of having much time. My melancholy has reared its head again. I will and must become a saint!" (March 21, 1918).

In the end the key which led him out of the labyrinth of his melancholy was prayer. He was being forced to listen more intently to the voice within and hear the call of grace. There God was speaking to him. Close to God, all his unrest would turn to silence. A few days later this truth seemed to be even clearer to him, for he jotted down in his diary:

180

"How many graces did I recently leave unused, dear little Mother! You prompt me time and time again to practice the three kinds of prayer and you reproach me for not thinking of my patron saint. And how often did I fail to respond to your call of grace! From now on I must be determined to quickly follow the inspirations which have their source in divine grace and to make great strides forward on the road of virtue. I do not want to overhear any inspiration of grace, and you, little Mother, must help me" (March 27, 1918).

Joseph reflected. How could he best become receptive to God's call? How could he best learn to readily follow the promptings of grace? Soon he felt he had the answer. He wrote down the resolution: "I will devote fifteen minutes a day to prayer using one of the kinds illustrated in the booklet *The Idea of Ascetical Theology*." What kind of prayer was this? Meditative prayer! He had actually been doing it here and there without thinking much about it. But now that wasn't enough any more. He wanted to make it a conscious part of his prayer life. When Joseph made a thorough day of recollection on Easter Sunday, he found the clear direction he wanted to follow in his striving for holiness. His efforts would be directed at becoming more recollected in prayer, more intent on listening to the voice of God, and more willing to obey him. This would doubtlessly be the simplest way out of his spiritual restlessness and melancholy moods. In order not to forget this insight he wrote in his diary:

"Holy is the one who habitually and consistently acts in conformity with God. God is infinitely perfect. Therefore my actions must always be perfect in deed and in attitude. I will always do what I consider right" (March 31, 1918).

On Easter Monday services were scheduled for Camp Magdalene at 3 o'clock in the afternoon. Around noon, Joseph went to check the field altar to see if all was ready. Much to his surprise, he found the company tailor there ahead of him. He had never thought of this otherwise frivolous Rhinelander as being devout. The tailor had even made some banners for decoration—two large banners and three smaller ones. Now all that was missing were some flowers and a little greenery. Joseph went in search of flowers. There was not much around. He arranged some pussy willows and cowslips in a few old bottles and ration tins.

He and the chaplain's orderly were the servers at the Mass. Radiant Easter joy pulsed through his soul and he wrote in his diary: "Christ is risen. I, too, have awakened and risen for a new struggle with myself, to new and real life. *Ora pro nobis, Mater!* [Pray for us, Mother!]" (March 31, 1918).

Life in His Group

The more Joseph followed the voice of his heart to join God in the solitude of prayer, the more he shook his restlessness and melancholy. He also noticed something else. His relationship with his comrades not only did not suffer, it was greatly helped! Before, he had been upset by their brazen ways and bad habits. Now he began to look deeper. He could see the goodness they had deep inside. They, for their part, could also sense Joseph's benevolence toward them. They liked to be around him, especially in times of danger. They didn't know why. More than once it happened that a comrade gave Joseph a warm handshake after getting through a life-threatening situation. Joseph didn't know what to make of it, but it seemed that they wanted to thank him without being overly indebted to him.

As much as Joseph had focused recently on his life of prayer, his particular examination concerned itself almost exclusively with the relationship with his comrades. At one time his resolution was, "I will not withdraw from any conversation." At another time—"I want to join in all permissible fun...." Or again—"I want to pay attention to small apostolic opportunities." At another time he wanted to fight against being too dependent on human respect, so he chose as his resolution: "I will strive to have my own convictions about things." His written control indicates that he hardly had any problem keeping these resolutions. The night before Easter he even managed to get his comrades to sing together many of the old familiar songs from home.

More important was Joseph's concern for his fellow sodalists, especially his group brothers. In the last weeks he had focused his efforts on encouraging regular but heartfelt correspondence among the members of the group. He was especially concerned that the individual members grow closer together in a truly human and brotherly way. He was not entirely satisfied when the letters sounded too much like an essay from German class. The letters he liked most were those with a personal touch. They would bring some personal thought or suggestion into the group discussion.

For the next phase of group work Joseph had a clear aim: He wanted to introduce the spiritual daily order, or "SDO" for short. The particular examination with written control had become general practice in the group during the past three months. Now was the time to take a step forward. From personal experience he knew how important the spiritual schedule was for striving toward holiness, particularly under the conditions of military life. To get a discussion started on this subject, he wrote letters about it to his group as he had done in the past. This was not an easy task. He had to be very economical with the time left free from his duties. His task was made all the more inconvenient when his company had to move from the regular barracks to a corrugated hut. To write letters in such cramped quarters amid the loud conversations of his comrades, with a candle as the only available light, was truly difficult. No wonder that some of his comrades got the idea that Engling, with all his constant writing, must be an odd fellow.

He thought that the discussion about the spiritual daily order would get off the ground most quickly if he asked a question about its meaning and purpose. First he asked himself why he kept a spiritual schedule. The answer to that was easy. He needed it to live up to his personal ideal. Upon closer examination, he found three reasons. The first was: *it helped his interior spiritual life.* In this vein he wrote to one of his fellow sodalists:

A Letter from Joseph

NcppbvM   March 25, 1918

Dear Dekarski!

Heartfelt greetings and Easter wishes. (....) I want to ask you to use your days in the trenches to pay special attention to your daily spiritual exercises, to see how you can best do them, and to make a first draft of an SDO for yourself in the spirit of the group. We must take into consideration every possible situation that military life may send our way. I would advise against putting too many points into your first draft; the golden mean is

---

the better way to go. In making your first draft, keep in mind the following things:

1. Deepening and making your spiritual exercises your own,
2. Self-monitoring [of your spiritual growth],
3. Reporting to your spiritual director about your spiritual life. After all, these are the goals of our written SDO, even if no one has said these reasons in so many words.

First of all, I want to stress the deepening and internalizing of the spiritual exercises. Our whole day's work must be penetrated by God and our dear Little Mother, and by our striving to serve God. Our comrades must be able to sense our vocation through our whole being. Every action must bear the stamp of belonging to God. In the idea of the capital of grace of our MTA we have a means to give all our actions supernatural value. How would it be if we would include a daily act of self-denial and the daily general examination of conscience? Every exercise kept is best marked with a vertical line. One not kept out of negligence or laziness with an *n*. One not kept because of impossibility with a *u* (unable). (....)

Your fellow sodalist

Joseph

Joseph's second reason for the work with the SDO was *the capital of grace of the MTA of Schoenstatt*. As we saw above, he said that "In the idea of the capital of grace of our MTA we have a means to give all our actions supernatural value." This was his own experience. He wanted to dedicate himself heart and soul to the service of his neighbor. The best way to do so was by making the whole day one great contribution to Our Lady's capital of grace.

The third reason could be called *ordering of life* or *accountability*. He personally needed a carefully arranged daily order and a regular rendering of accounts to his spiritual director. Oh, what confusion he often found in his soul! Enthusiasm would change into melancholy, the planning of many deeds and fiery zeal would change into spiritual lethargy. And then came the irregular external conditions with their paralyzing and unnerving influence. He could not think of a better remedy than to faithfully keep a spiritual schedule and report on it to his spiritual director. His fellow sodalists in like circumstances certainly faced the same difficulties. From his own experience he advised them, therefore, to use this proven method—the spiritual daily order. It was in this spirit that he wrote letters to all the members of his group.

Joseph would have liked to talk about this topic with the members of his group who were nearby in the same regiment. The next days seemed to offer the chance. On April 6 the First Battalion was relieved and sent to rest camp. This gave him a chance to meet Paul Reinhold and Johannes Dekarski at Camp Magdalene. But at the noon roll call his hopes were dashed. "The shock troop must go up front tonight to put up barbed wire entrapments," came the newest order. Shortly before leaving, Joseph managed to find the other two. But more than a few words and a heartfelt handshake were not possible.

This newest visit to the front followed a rather unusual schedule. Depending on the weather and visibility, the shock troop had to work six hours before or after midnight on the barbed wire entanglements. On the first day the French gave them a strong "welcome." They peppered the division with 7,000-8,000 grenades. Thirteen were killed and 20 wounded.

Laden with screw-posts and rolls of barbed wire, the shock troop set out into the dark night to do their duty. They spoke in whispers and only when absolutely necessary. There was hardly a shot all night. One man twisted in the rods while two unrolled the barbed wire and two others tied it fast. Around morning the shock troop returned to the trench. The dugouts were rather narrow and not very comfortable. Since they were near the bottom of the Forges Creek valley, ground water trickled in. There were boards on the ground and the damp air smelled stale and mixed with tobacco smoke. Now that it was spring, there was the further plague of rain and melting snow. The water dripped incessantly in the dugouts. Ration cans were used to catch the water. Anyone who was lying idly on the hammocks could hear the whole musical scale as the water dripped into the different cans. The sound started quite low in the empty cans and gradually became a high pitch in the full ones. This was the sign that the can had to be emptied. One could sleep fairly well on the hammocks, though here and there a rat would scurry over a sleeping soldier, waking him from restless dreams.

The shock troop could rest until about noon. Then after lunch they had to repair their uniforms. There were usually many holes to darn from where the barbed wire had caught the fabric the night before. Then came trench duty until later afternoon. Joseph used his free time to pray and to write, especially to his group brothers. He was not quite satisfied with the echo he received to his last letters. But he knew that some of his fellow sodalists were caught in the German offensive. Some wrote back but did not dwell much on the systematic discussion of the spiritual schedule. They made practical suggestions instead as to what kind of exercises to make. He did not object to that, so he started immediately with the discussion of suggestions. If only he would have been able to write decently in his dugout! Things were so cramped that everyone bumped into each other. At times the conversation was so loud that it was impossible to concentrate on what one was thinking. Or it could happen that someone would bump into his knapsack, knocking over the candle and spilling the wax on his writing paper. Then the thought struck him: Not far away was group brother Clemens Meier. He was in a quieter trench in charge of weather observation. So Joseph took his writing paper and moved over to the meteorologist. There he could write without being disturbed and discuss the group work with Clemens. Both did so very thoroughly. As a fruit of their discussions Joseph sent the following letter to be circulated within the group:

"Dear Fellow Sodalists!

"After reading your letters and consulting with Meier I have compiled a list of exercises for our common spiritual daily order. These are the most necessary ones. I think we have to express our love of Mary by an act of surrender and love. Meier thought we should not omit the good intention because by it our actions become more meritorious and spiritual Communion should be a substitute for the real one we have to forego. As to spiritual reading and rosary we decided in favor of them sometime ago. The exercises are not easy, it is true, but they are rarely impossible. Although the general examination of conscience and an act of contrition are parts of our night prayers, I still expressly mention them because of their great importance for our spiritual progress and our eternal salvation. To

186

indicate when we go to confession and receive Holy Communion will give our spiritual director a better insight into our spiritual life. To these exercises everyone may add others which his personal needs require. Furthermore, we may jot down those we resolve to practice at certain times of the Church year. Every month I will give an intention for the rosary, if all agree to it, and I ask you to suggest intentions for May.

"On the reverse side of the sheet is a sample tally for the particular examination. The number of squares will depend upon the personal need of the individual. In the space provided, enter your resolution, let it take a very concrete form, at least this is what, in my humble opinion, is advisable. Every 14 days we will send in our SDO just as we did with the PE—provided you agree to it. So far no one has expressed his opinion about that. The suggestion comes from me. We want to begin with the written control on Monday, the 29th of this month; I kindly ask everyone of you to let me know if he has done so. For the purpose of deepening our religious exercises, I propose that you explain to one another how and when you say your morning prayers, make the general examination of conscience, the particular examination and the holy hour. Each one of us has his own experience and by sharing about it with the others we can make these exercises more fruitful. In this regard it would be advantageous if each one maintains a lively contact with one other [group brother], as is recommended by Point No. 1 of our new regulations. It should not be too hard to find two who understand each other well" (April 9, 1918).

The two sodalists were already thinking of Mary's month of May and preparing for it. They thought that keeping the SDO with its written control was a task suitable for May. But, was it opportune to make any additional proposals? They agreed to consult Johannes Dekarski and Paul Reinhold while at rest camp. An opportunity soon presented itself. After ten days in the trenches, Joseph's shock troop unit was transferred back to Camp Magdalene. Here he met the other two. He communicated the results to the rest of the group with the following words:

"During May we want to say the rosary to implore our Blessed Mother for an early, victorious peace, so that we can devote ourselves entirely to our vocation. Johannes, Paul and I want to refrain from smoking during the month of May and make a little material sacrifice in favor of our sodality. The latter was suggested by Johannes and Paul for all, whereas the formal proposal does not bind all since I have no answer from you as yet. Furthermore, as a practice for May, we want to begin with the written SDO which you have already kept for quite some time. In addition everyone should make special sacrifices for our beloved Mother. She certainly deserves it. We want to offer ourselves as instruments and to prove ourselves as such for the salvation of immortal souls" (April 27, 1918).

His activity as group leader was guided by the same principles as he had once used as prefect of the Junior Sodality. He lived the ideals he preached and spoke from personal experience.

Even as Joseph wrote these letters, new orders had reached his division. They were being transferred to another, more deadly, theater of war.

9. Flanders and the Gift of Self

Into the Fire

It was the end of April 1918. Company after company of German troops were passing through the little village of Rémonville. The 15th Reserve Division was coming back from the trenches facing "Hill 304" and marching back to base camp. Within the next few days they were to be transferred to another sector. They were considered rested and had to be ready for heavy fighting in the days to come. The first battalion of R.I.R. 25 took up quarters in Rémonville. The soldiers were abuzz in the houses and barns as to what would happen. The long-awaited offensive was already underway. "Operation Michael" had raged between Arras and La Fère starting in late March. The Germans had advanced nearly to Amiens. Now a second part of the offensive was unfolding on the fields of Flanders, south of Ypres. The enemy front was falling back. The German army suddenly felt a new surge of energy. For years they had been the anvil, forced to take the enemy's blows. Now they could be the hammer. General Hindenburg would surely crush the entire Western Front. The men were confident of victory. For this last strike they would give their all. Then there would be peace at last, the peace for which they so ardently longed.

By pushing back the British, the German offensive in Flanders had formed a wedge in the Western Front. Its forwardmost position was Calonne on the Lys River. But pressure was building on the other side as the Allies rushed in troops to the defense. R.I.R. 25 was assigned to the most sensitive point in the new configuration. As of May 2 the regiment would relieve the 68th Infantry Regiment and defend the two miles of front at Calonne. Their task was to maintain the advances and make the new position firm enough to continue the offensive. Batallions would rotate weeks: one week in the foxholes up front, one week of readiness duty, one week of rest camp. It was clear that the nerves and courage of the troops would be put more to the test than even in an attack. Their movements were easily visible to the enemy and they would face artillery fire from three sides—north, south, and west.

189

Joseph's battalion was briefed while in quarters at Emmerin, south of Lille. The officers instructed, "On May 2 the battalion will take up the readiness position at Lêstrême, about 2½ miles behind the front line. The enemy has a significant air force at his command. Therefore troops will have to take special precautions to conceal and camoflague their activities. Any duty requiring open-field movement will be entrusted only to the most reliable. On May 8 our battalion will take up front line positions. This movement must be

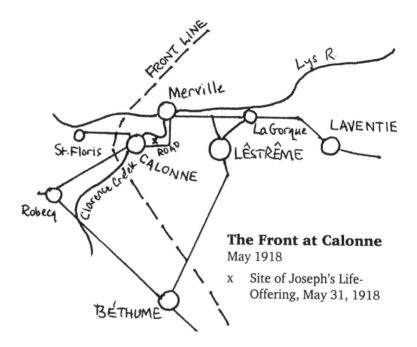

The Front at Calonne
May 1918

x   Site of Joseph's Life-Offering, May 31, 1918

made with the utmost caution, since the enemy is listening and will answer with heavy artillery. There are not yet any trenches or dugouts. These must be made as soon as possible. At the moment the front line consists of only a few foxholes."

On April 29 at about 3 pm, Joseph's battalion left Emmerin for the front. At Maisnil they crossed the old front lines. The next day brought them to the little town of Laventie, about 7 to 10 miles behind the front. There was an indescribable hustle and bustle along the artillery-pocked roads. A battery unit galloped ahead to reach its artillery position. Infirmary autos loaded with the wounded gingerly picked their way through the grenade holes in the road. English prisoners were being marched away from the front. The horses sensed danger, too. They could sense when dead bodies lay ahead or when the front was near. Their coats would turn stiff and rough; the hairs would be literally standing on end. They would suddenly rear up, front hoofs pawing the air, refusing to go forward until forced by the driver's whip. A few hundred yards later the driver himself would catch the poignant smell of decaying flesh; the horses had sensed it long minutes before and resisted.

The first night in Laventie was not a quiet one. Around midnight the battalion was ripped out of its sleep by the blast of a heavy artillery shell. It was followed by another, and another. When the shelling ended an hour later, there were two dead and three wounded. The next day the dead were laid to rest in the new military cemetery on the outskirts of town while the regiment band played a funeral dirge. More than 50 German crosses were already there from the 68th regiment. Now the men of the 25th stood in heavy thought before the open graves. "How many crosses will there be when we leave?" they asked themselves. The answer would eventually be 120.

It did not seem advisable to battalion command to remain longer in Laventie. They ordered the companies to move that evening to the village of Lêstrême, about an hour's march away. They would camp near the outskirts of town. To avoid detection from the air, the soldiers pitched their tents under a grove of trees. Joseph Engling was squatting in front of his little shelter, writing in his diary. His review of the last days of April was bothering his conscience. While moving from one sector to another he had lost the control sheet for his SDO. Partly out of carelessness he had failed to make a new one right away. His religious exercises had not suffered, but to have failed to keep his written control made him none too happy. The previous day had been the start of Mary's month of May. At home May devotions had begun. And what was he doing? Should he not be ashamed to have begun the month of the Queen of Heaven with so little zeal? He put his knapsack on his knees and spread a sheet of paper over it; then he began to draw lines on it for his spiritual schedule.

No sooner had he finished when he looked up and saw a little wayside chapel at the corner of the road near the entrance of the village. Not far away stood a large building visibly pockmarked by the fighting. A vague sense that he should ask Mary's forgiveness for his lack of zeal urged him to visit the chapel. A sudden inspiration began to take shape in his heart. Could he not hold a May devotion here with his comrades? Unfortunately, the little chapel, dedicated to Our Lord of the Scourging at the Pillar, had been damaged by the shellings. Moreover, the intersection nearby seemed to be a favorite artillery target. But the chapel's statues were still intact. Might there not be someplace else he could hold May devotions?

May Devotions in the Shadow of War

He read on the facade of the large building nearby: *Hospice du Sacre Coeur*—Nursing Home of the Sacred Heart. That meant it was a Catholic facility and should have a chapel. In the garden he met Medical Sergeant Winter. He and his men had pitched their tents in the grove of trees, too. He could talk openly with him about his idea of holding a May devotion. The sergeant had the reputation of being a close friend and faithful helper of the regiment's chaplain. He immediately showed Joseph a suitable room in the basement of the hospital and gladly made it available for the intended purpose.

Joseph hurried back to his camp site and looked for his Schoenstatt comrades. They were won over to his plan at once and promptly went to work. They thoroughly cleaned the basement room. An old dresser became an altar. They brought down statues and flower vases from the chapel. There were plenty of flowers in the garden. Now they could have real May devotions. Every evening at 9 o'clock they assembled there. They interested their Catholic friends and succeeded in getting a good crowd together every time. Joseph substituted for the priest and led the rosary. The makeshift chapel was filled with the murmuring of praying men, followed by the beautiful melodies of Marian hymns sung by rough soldiers' voices. Some four miles away the heavy guns were pounding out a different melody.

On Saturday, May 4, the corporal of the Fourth Company took roll-call. He announced that the battalion would be moving to the front line the following Tuesday. The next day, Sunday, would be an opportunity to go to Mass. Then he distributed the various duties for their stay in the forward position. Lieutenant Thalhofer was put in charge of the carrier troop. Its duty was to carry the food from the field kitchen to the trenches and dugouts. The lieutenant shuddered. It was the most dreaded task of all. This meant, however, that he could demand from the corporal a sufficient number of reliable men to help him. He approached the corporal immediately after roll-call and mentioned the names of several soldiers he would like to have help him. Among them was the name of Private Engling. The corporal consented to this list.

In the meantime, Joseph was with his Schoenstatt comrades deliberating on how they could beautify the divine services the next day. First they looked for a place sheltered from the view of enemy aircraft. Then they assembled a number of British ammunition boxes to serve as an altar. They used the fresh green branches of blossoming trees to decorate the altar. The following day a large crowd of soldiers gathered around the officiating priest. Anyone who could, attended the services. Everyone knew what they would be up against in the days to come. They made ready to face eternity.

The company made the treacherous march to Calonne in the wee hours of the morning. The British artillery pounded on all sides. By some miracle they arrived with only two wounded. As dawn broke, they got their first look at Calonne. The front line was no more than a string of fox holes. A few fence posts had been planted and fixed with barbed wire, but otherwise the "firming up" of the new front line had made no progress. They wondered what their comrades had been doing for a whole week, but found out soon enough. Day and night, the British showered down short, intense barrages of artillery fire at irregular intervals. No hour could be deemed safe. A "steel thunderstorm" of 50 to 100 shells could fall in a short time on a single sector. Regiment command estimated that their battalion was exposed to up to 6000 shells a day!

Joseph's unit cowered in their foxholes during such "thunderstorms." Fountains of dirt would shoot up in the air as high as houses as the line of fire would slowly meander toward their position. The blood would run cold in their veins when these dirt "geysers" fountained up before them, their eardrums deafened by the explosions. The scene repeated itself again and again, day and night. Because of the enemy's air superiority, the Germans had to spend most of the day crouched motionless in foxholes beneath tent canvas or in flimsy, makeshift quarters. When night came there was at least the relief of being able to move about and the prospect of a warm meal again.

But here was where Lieutenant Thalhofer had to rack his brain. The men in his carrier detail had done more than could be asked of them. After the harrowing days crouched in the foxholes they had to work nights carrying the food. The round trip to the field kitchen, always subject to the unexpected strafing of enemy artillery, was a race with death. Every food run took a bloody toll. "No," the lieutenant concluded, "I cannot order anyone to go today; I must see to it that I find volunteers." He asked in the first fox hole. No answer. Then he went to the second foxhole. Here too, he met with silence. Then a voice came out of the dark: "I'll go." It was Joseph Engling. A few others took courage and decided to go with him.

Loaded down with the big food-carrying canisters, the little group left the front lines for the field kitchen. It was about half an hour's march back from the front. They passed through Calonne. The most dangerous spot was the big intersection near the church. It was constantly under fire. They themselves didn't know how they got through. Meanwhile, Joseph had been watching the explosions in front of them. "Stay left," he waved to his comrades and raced ahead. Poof! Poof! A few unusual shells crashed ahead of them. In his gums he could sense a familiar sweetness. "Gas!" he cried to the others and quickly pulled on his gas mask. His sweat fogged up the mask and he could hardly see. Sometimes he stepped into empty space and fell hard into a grenade crater, banging himself on the big mess canisters. Finally they were out of the range of fire. They took off their gas masks and breathed deeply. It was as if they had been suffocating. Hurry! They had to reach the kitchen by midnight at the latest. They saw men gathered under a few willows. Thank God! The kitchen. But now they found it was not the kitchen for their

194

division. They had lost their way. One of the cooks sent them off in the right direction.

Once they reached the field kitchen, their mess canisters were filled. Joseph and the others got something to eat before heading back. They had to be back in position by dawn at the latest! They had to pass through the gas zone again. This time the gas mask made walking impossible. Joseph stumbled from crater to crater and fell into one. One of the precious mess canisters fell over and its irreplaceable food was lost. Now "Tommy" (the British) saw them and began to shoot machine guns. Joseph threw himself behind a furrow. He felt the warm contents of a second canister spilling out. When the gun stopped, he moved ahead. Rat-ta-tat-tat! He dropped into a hole again and a third canister was lost. By some miracle the whole group made it back to their comrades on the front line. In the darkness the comrades did not notice the carriers' wounds and what they had suffered. They only complained about the lost food.

In the meantime, Joseph had a plan. From his frequent passages through the village, he knew there were many knapsacks lying abandoned in the streets. They belonged to comrades killed in action. They would certainly still hold bread and condiments. He guessed that the British must have left stores of food behind too. It was risky to go into the village, but Joseph felt he could do it. At dawn he spirited into the village before the British might see him. He came back with quite a hefty supplement to what the soldiers had been eating. To the astonishment of all he had found three of the big standard issue loaves of bread, a big tin of flour, some bacon and quite a few cans of British corned beef. No wonder that Lieutenant Thalhofer said twenty years later, "He was the best man in my carrier detail."

A Line in the Diary

Once again heavy gunfire filled the air. Joseph sat in one of the foxholes and was reviewing his spiritual diary. Yesterday, a Sunday, should have been his weekly day of recollection. But there were too many distractions, and he chose to postpone it a day. Now he slowly read his retreat resolutions, the resolutions for his military life and, lastly, the results of his private retreat in February. He did that every week, and it still kept his interest. This time, too, the resolutions and retreat thoughts made an impression on him. Then he prayed the dedication prayer to the Mother Thrice Admirable he had composed and written in his diary. This prayer affected him more deeply with every reading. It contained his personal ideal and reflected the story of his whole life. When he looked at his spiritual daily order, however, he felt shame and sadness. Five days ago, upon transfer to the front line, he had lost his SDO sheet for a second time, along with his rosary and book for spiritual reading. He made a new schedule right away, but had to record that in the last days he had kept only a third of the points. As to the others, he was not sure whether he had kept or neglected them. And this was to be a special gift in honor of the Blessed Mother? A deep sense of guilt crept over him.

With his pencil he drew a heavy line after the day just passed—May 13. It marked an end and, he vowed, a new beginning. From that day on he wanted to perform all the exercises of his spiritual daily order with unswerving faithfulness. Nothing must distract him, neither heavy shellings nor trench-digging, not even his dangerous duties with the carrier troop. After this examination of conscience he wrote a letter to his spiritual director, giving him a report about the state of his inner life. Then he jotted down a few lines in his diary. In the weeks that followed, his SDO was quite satisfactory. He kept almost all its exercises perfectly. Peace returned to his soul. Around him the bloody war continued to rage with unabated ferocity.

Barely any progress was being made in digging the trenches. The ground was not good for it. The soldiers ran into ground water only 3 to 5 feet below the surface. And still, they needed the earth's protection from the shrapnel of the British artillery and the strafings of the British machine-guns. In addition, they needed a good foothold to withstand the enemy in case of an unexpected attack. The battalion had orders to keep constant tabs on enemy movements with night patrols. Almost every night a spy patrol was sent forward to slip as close to the enemy lines as possible. They were to track any suspicious noises or changes and bring back their findings. The British were just as stealthy and interested in intelligence. As a result, the two sides would often meet, leading to wild nighttime shoot-outs.

196

"Stay, Comrade, I'll Go for You"

Late one afternoon, a courier from company headquarters jumped into the fox hole where Joseph and his comrades were spending the idle daylight hours. "Kofel," he said, "you have been assigned to tonight's spy patrol. Report to the captain's bunker at eight o'clock." Then he jumped out and ran off again. Private Kofel heard this without speaking a word. He was one of the older soldiers in the company. He was married and had several children. The patrol could mean his death. He sat there, lost in thought. He brushed back a tear from his eye. He was probably thinking of his loved ones at home and bidding them spiritual farewell.

Joseph observed him and felt the heavy sorrow in this man's heart. In silence he made his decision. When Private Kofel got up to get ready for the patrol, Joseph stood up next to him and simply said, "Stay, comrade, I'll go for you." He went on the patrol in the man's place. The patrol took place without incident. But the fury of war seemed to have had it in for Private Kofel all the same. Two weeks later he was killed by a stray shell close to the rest camp. A tiny piece of shrapnel penetrated his heart and he was killed at once.

During these days Joseph was transferred from the carrier troop to the newly created courier and signal corps. It was a dangerous job responsible for keeping the front lines in communication with the artillery farther back. This had become necessary because of communications problems which had nearly led to the German artillery firing on its own line.

At last, the interminable eight days in the front lines neared their end. On the evening of the last day the order came: Prepare to return to readiness position! This would at least take them away from the front line. Various duties had to be taken care of. "The company's dead must be carried to the first aid station," came one order. Joseph volunteered and helped carry the bodies of his dead comrades. No sooner did he finish this task when Joseph and his companions heard that the two company leaders responsible for guiding the replacement battalion to the front line had been wounded. Without a guide the replacement troops would not find their position. Joseph knew the way and volunteered to lead them forward, placing his own life at risk again. The maneuver was accompanied by heavy enemy fire. It turned into a full-fledged firestorm. The troops had to scatter for twenty minutes and take cover as shells fell thickly on all sides. When a break finally came, Joseph forged ahead as fast as he dared. The others followed.

When Joseph was finally reunited with his company, another unexpected event took place. Two comrades were buried alive by the explosion of a heavy British shell. A few men had stayed to try digging them out. Again, Joseph volunteered. The rest of the company now left the front line. The volunteers dug hastily at the site of the explosion. Fortunately, a few beams had fallen together to form a little airspace for the men trapped below. After an hour of hard work, the men were freed and taken to the first aid station. Finally, Joseph was able to rejoin his company in readiness position. The first day away from the front line was beginning to dawn. Their move back had been at a cost of 13 deaths and 19 wounded.

The Fourth Company went to readiness position hoping for a reprieve. They were badly disap-pointed. The British fired on the reserve positions nearly as often as they did the front lines. In the courier and signal corps, Joseph and his two companions were exposed to more dangers than ever. They could not just take cover during artillery fire. They had to keep constant watch for signals from the front lines in case the German artillery needed to stop. Here and there they had to run messages to the front lines. This meant playing the dreaded game of cat-and-mouse with enemy fire that Joseph already knew all too well.

The duties of these last fourteen days were strenuous enough to wear down even the toughest men. Eight days under heavy shelling in the front line, carrier detail almost every night, the dangers of moving back into readiness position, all day long working as courier and signal man. Joseph felt a heaviness and exhaustion in his limbs. One day he wrote in his diary:

"I am finished—not torn to pieces but overtired. I worked all night again and now am on duty. Oh, if only I could lie down first; I can't keep my eyes open" (May 17, 1918).

But he could not think of his tiredness. The lives of countless comrades depended on accurate communication between the front lines and the artillery.

In spite of all this he did not give in to the demands of his overworked body. He pulled himself together energetically, performed his duty, mortified himself and prayed. At the time of his examination of conscience in the evening, he could record that, without exception, he had kept the many exercises of his spiritual schedule.

"May Blossoms" Amid Drum Fire

In his assigned foxhole as part of the signal corps, Private Grosse observed his comrade Joseph Engling with increasing wonderment. What an unusual man this Engling was! Almost every free minute he was either reading, writing or studying. Just now he was sitting on the rim of a shell crater with a notebook in his hand. Although shell fragments were almost constantly whizzed by, he remained calm and acted as if he did not see or hear them. This fellow was calm to the point of being cold-blooded. He executed the most difficult commands without batting an eye. He ran through the heaviest artillery fire without showing the least sign of excitement or fear of death. And how he practiced the spirit of comradery! It was matched by no one else in the company. He also seemed quite devout. One could tell from some of the remarks he made. Among his books were many religious writings. At times he seemed to pray quietly to himself. All in all, this comrade was a puzzle that gave Grosse no peace. It fascinated him to such an extent that he wanted to get behind the secret of this remarkable man.

Private Constantine Grosse was an art student. He had attended a school for painters before being drafted into the army. Behind him lay a frivolous life. Though well-educated in his Catholic religion, he had not gone to the sacraments for two years. The horrors of modern warfare affected him deeply, it is true, but not deeply enough to bring about a decided change in his life. The reason for this was not ill-will, but rather a fickle temperament. Deep in his heart he felt the call of a better self, longing again for the ideals of his youth. So far it had not been strong enough to carry the day. Since starting to live so close to Joseph Engling, however, his conscience was beginning to bother him. Finally, something happened that he would never have considered possible: He told his whole life story to Joseph. It was practically a confession! As if he were the closest of friends, he told him the errors of his youth. It did not take long before he was even praying the rosary with Joseph.

Grosse's observations were on the mark. Beneath the plain exterior of his comrade lay a hidden secret. Yet he could hardly have guessed that he was dealing with a man belonging to two worlds. The one world was the daily events and experiences which Grosse also knew. The other was more or less unknown to him. Grosse could only feel its mysterious presence. Joseph referred to it as his interior life. It was truly a world in itself. He was so filled with and dominated by it that the world around him influenced him very little. On the contrary, exterior happenings seemed to take their significance and meaning from their connection to his interior world.

What was going on in Joseph's soul during these weeks when the fury of war raged over the fields of Flanders? On May 13, Joseph had drawn the important line in his SDO. He did it to mark an end and a new beginning. In earlier years the month of May made his heart blossom in fervent devotion to Mary. Every year he gathered the little sacrifices of his everyday life into a beautiful bouquet of flowers, and offered them to his heavenly Queen. This year was no different. Even on the battlefield, in the midst of the heaviest shelling, he wanted to offer this bouquet. Even the grayest of all his workdays was formed and sanctified by the strength coming from his interior life. He therefore focused his attention once more on his spiritual schedule. His PE resolution for the days to come was to faithfully keep his SDO. In his mind there was no better means to transform his whole day's work into a May gift for his "Little Mother." What concerned him was not just rattling off a round of pious devotions during the day and recording them in the evening. No, he intended to make the exercises into creative pauses for the soul, a kind of "breathing in" of the spirit of God's solitude. Being alone with God was not to cease even in the midst of battle. To keep it more effectively alive, he made use of the exercises listed in his spiritual daily order. He had expressed this in a group letter explaining the meaning of the spiritual schedule: "Our day's work

200

must be a divine service; all actions must be stamped, as it were, with the sign of God." The idea behind this came from his personal ideal with its accent on modern everyday sanctity. This is why he chose this resolution for the month of May.

The day began with his morning prayer, the first raising of mind and heart to God. As a rule the dawning day found Joseph lying in a foxhole on the front line. At times the new morning surprised him while on duty in the carrier troop or carrying the wounded or just finishing the nightly trench-digging or returning from a patrol. Wherever he was, the first lifting of his heart at daybreak was a prayer of thanksgiving and self-offering. This day, too, would be dedicated to Him. His personal ideal stood before him: To become all things to all men and Mary's very own. Herein he saw the will of God. His personal ideal was primarily a call to be a saint, to sanctify the workday, and to make it a real divine service. In response he renewed the good intention. For him this practice had a special meaning, for it was then that he said his sodality prayers. These consisted of three Hail Marys and the prayer, "My Queen, my Mother." In this way he renewed his covenant with Mary as a sodalist, the consecration by which he had given himself forever to her service.

His aim was to become a saint under the protection and in the service of his beloved Mother. Not only his person, but his whole workday was dedicated to her. For this purpose he composed a prayer in the spirit of the good intention. He used it to offer up the whole day to the capital of grace of the Mother Thrice Admirable of Schoenstatt, placing all his strength at the disposal of her call for a movement of religious and moral world renewal originating from her little shrine. The day ahead might bring strenuous sacrifices, paralyzing fatigue, gnawing hunger, cowering in foxholes, the attrition of bombardment, the wearing labor of digging trenches. Yes, that is what today would probably be like again. In the good intention he offered all of this up in advance as a contribution to the great idea of the capital of grace.

Then he attended Holy Mass in spirit, thinking of Schoenstatt and of the many other altars where the Holy Sacrifice was being offered. He made an act of spiritual Communion in order to be united as closely as possible with the celebration of the holy mysteries, and to renew the indwelling of Christ in the soul. In Christ's unbloody sacrifice on the altar he found the example for his own personal ideal: To be all things to all men. Nowhere was this expressed more impressively than in Christ's sacrifice on the cross. Already as a student he had worked to make Holy Communion the main focus of the day. This close union with his Eucharistic Savior was renewed and deepened by the two holy hours. While in boot camp he had kept them during the periods of drill and marches. Even on the front he kept them despite sudden and unexpected turns of events. During these hours he would place himself spiritually in the little Schoenstatt chapel, making a spiritual pilgrimage to Mary's shrine.

Joseph spent the whole day conversing with his Divine Master. This prayerful union gave Joseph his inner peace in all dangers, that "cold-bloodedness" which so astonished his comrades. Because he knew he was united with Christ in sacrifice, he also had the courage and strength to give himself for others. For that reason, he did not hesitate to come to the aid of his comrades in danger. In order to keep this spirit of sacrifice alive he resolved to perform an explicit act of mortification every day, one that was extremely hard for him. This, too, was one of the exercises of his spiritual schedule.

In the course of the afternoon he had spiritual reading to help him recollect himself and to increase his knowledge of the spiritual life. For many weeks he was faithful to his spiritual reading in spite of exploding shells and fragments whizzing by him. While on guard duty the beads of the rosary passed through his fingers. At times he said it while carrying food to his comrades or on his way to a command post to deliver a message. He always succeeded in saying at least one decade. When alone, he prayed the whole rosary. For the past weeks his comrade Grosse joined him in this prayer.

The day ended with the examination of conscience and night prayer. First he finished the written control of his spiritual schedule. It took the place of an examination of conscience. Experience had taught him that it proved more fruitful if he did it in writing. Then it was made thoroughly and did not remain general or vague, for he had to decide if he had done it or not and remember the details. In judging his actions of the day and in preparing himself for confession he was guided by his personal ideal. Because of this, his first question was not: "Have I broken one of God's commandments?" but rather, "How have I followed God's call for heroism?" Of course, the former question was implied by the latter. It kept his life free from exaggerated fear of sin, fault-finding, and unhealthy feelings of inferiority. Still, no fault escaped his notice because his examination was guided by the clear light of an ideal. In connection with the examination of conscience he made an act of contrition for all faults and infidelities. At the close of the day his thoughts turned once more to Schoenstatt, and at this point he spiritually asked for his spiritual director's blessing. Under his priestly guidance he had found his personal ideal and gradually grown into it. His guidance was helping him on the road to sanctity. He therefore wanted to ask for his blessing at day's end. It was like a guarantee of the blessing of the Mother Thrice Admirable of Schoenstatt. With this last exercise his spiritual schedule was complete. Another day's bouquet of May blossoms in honor of Our Lady was finished.

In order to be able to live such a comprehensive daily schedule amid the distractions of everyday life, a soul needs a solitude and recollection comparable to that of a monk in a cloistered cell. If Joseph Engling succeeded in being alone with God to this degree, it was not just because he had the will-power. It was primarily the fruit of his richly cultivated interior life. What his comrade Grosse and so many others had sensed was this: In the depths of his soul he harbored a secret.

One day while on one of his daily courier runs Joseph met Joseph Rath, a friend from Schoenstatt. He brought the bad news that two Schoenstatters, Clemens Meier and Johannes Dekarski had been seriously wounded. Their company was currently on the front line. Clemens, caught in the fire of a British machine-gun, had been hit several times in the lungs. A shell fragment had shattered Johannes' foot. It was bad news. He hoped that they would not be crippled for life. In the days to come, he waited in vain for news about how they were doing. It was clear that the battlefields along the Lys River were consuming a great deal of German blood. For fourteen days his own company had been on the front. Even without a direct confrontation with the enemy, one quarter of the men had been killed or wounded by the long-range British guns. And the survivors? Their clothes were clay-encrusted and infested by vermin. Sallow cheeks with rough beard-stubble witnessed to the horrors of days gone by, to sleepless nights with too little to eat. It was high time that they be relieved and sent to rest camp.

Pentecost

One day in May the morning dawned radiant over the pock-marked battlefield. Exhausted from their trench-digging, the men of the Fourth Company were sleeping in foxholes in the reserve position. Joseph welcomed the spring morning in a happy mood all his own. It was Pentecost in places not touched by the war. It seemed almost a little strange to him that for the past half year the seasons of the Church year with their solemnities had especially appealed to him. It was no different today as he pondered the mystery of Pentecost.

For him the Sunday about to begin was to be a day of recollection and spiritual renewal. The longing to be present at the Holy Sacrifice and united with his Eucharistic Savior burned in his soul with great intensity. As usual on days of this kind, he read through the first pages of his spiritual diary. These lines rekindled the enthusiasm for his ideal to become a saint. This was necessary for, as he had learned, he had to take up the struggle for this ideal each day anew. He could not wait for times of peace; he could not put it off for better times. No, it had to be done now, in the midst of the unpleasant conditions of life at the front. He wrote in his diary:

"Pentecost. *Volo fieri sanctus magnus* [I want to become a great saint]. I want to strive with still greater zeal for holiness. Ah, if only I would always want the good readily, quickly, and joyfully! The opportunities to strive for holiness in the military are never lacking. If you really want to, you can advance on the way to perfection quickly, but it is difficult. Oh little Mother, intercede to the Holy Spirit for me so that he will grant me the seven gifts that I might always want and do good" (May 19, 1918).

The battalion finally moved to rest quarters. The very same day

Joseph went in search of the chaplain. At the camp he learned that the "padre," Father von Köth, was with the 17th Regiment in the neighboring sector. He sought him out and asked him to come soon to hold religious services for the 25th Regiment. Unfortunately, the chaplain was already scheduled to hold services that afternoon elsewhere, more than two hour's walk from the rest quarters of the 25th.

"Good," said Joseph, "we'll see you there."

Once back among his comrades, he set out to win his Catholic buddies over to attending the services. "Oh, Engling," they said, "We just got back from the front today. We are almost a total wreck and have to get some sleep. Two hours' walk is too much for our tired bones." But, Joseph did not give up. In fact he succeeded in getting a small group of church-goers together—eight in all, including two Schoenstatt comrades as well as Nicholas Gilgenbach and Constantine Grosse. He asked and obtained leave from his lieutenant. On the way to the service he quietly took them to the side, one after the other. "You're going to Holy Communion, aren't you?" he asked. Some were hesitant to receive without going to confession first, but Joseph knew how to dispel their doubts. He assured them that general absolution would be given on account of the large number wanting to go to confession. He advised Constantine, however, to make a private confession at a suitable occasion. Constantine answered that he would have to think about it. Joseph was happy that he himself could go to Communion again. This time he received with a devotion and fervor hardly experienced before. After Holy Mass he looked for the "padre" and asked him to come soon to the 25th to have Mass. "This coming Sunday," replied the chaplain, "I'll be with you to conduct the services you requested." Satisfied with this answer, Joseph returned to his quarters.

The following Sunday, Father von Köth heard confessions for a long time before Mass. Joseph was in line. Behind him was Constantine Grosse. He had really plucked up the courage and decided to change his life completely. Before the confession Joseph had to help and encourage him, but afterwards Constantine was overjoyed and felt like a new man. As always, Holy Mass was well attended. Joseph served at the altar.

During Mass the air was filled with a strange sound. British long range artillery was shelling the German position. Shells whizzed high over the heads of the worshipers. The silence of the service was suddenly interrupted by a nervous shout: "Watch out! Take cover!" In the next moment the crowd surrounding the altar seemed to vanish. A shell crashed about forty yards from the altar. It exploded and threw up a fountain of dirt. Shortly thereafter, the scattered congregation returned. The chaplain was still standing at the altar, and next to him knelt his faithful server. Neither had been disturbed, but had continued Holy Mass serenely. The priest had just reached the prayer before communion.

The day he returned from the front line, Joseph changed his particular examination. May was drawing to a close. The last week of this month had to be a time of faithfulness and heroic sacrifice. He was convinced that the spiritual schedule was not causing him any serious trouble. He therefore focused his PE on a practice that had caused him some difficulty in early May. While near Verdun, he had made the resolution to devote some moments every day to mental prayer. These were meant to be prayerful pauses in the course of the day. He took up this exercise again. Mental prayer now seemed easy to him when he connected it to the Blessed Mother. A personal practice was beginning to take shape.

He performed this exercise in the following manner. Several times a day he recollected himself. He pictured the Blessed Mother standing before him and watching his everyday actions, taking a lively, motherly interest in whatever he was doing. It was a thought born of his childlike love for Mary. From his catechism he knew that, in God, she can see all those entrusted to her care, can hear their petitions and intercede for them. In order to become more aware of this truth, he thought of Mary's presence and interest in his life. At times he proceeded from this image to a mental vision of her inner being and meditated on the qualities of her person. These thoughts and ideas were followed by a lifting up of his heart just as his simple childlike love suggested. Often it was an act of thanks for the protection afforded in the dangers just past, at other times it was a word of sorrow asking pardon for some carelessness of which he was guilty, or it was an act of confidence in the awareness of his own human frailty, or a prayer of surrender offering himself and his life before a dangerous situation, or an expression of reverence inspired by her nobility of soul and by her immaculate purity. He spoke these things to Our Lady just the way the moment and the language of his heart put them on his lips. The third part of this spiritual exercise consisted of a decision of the will concerning the activities ahead. This was an offering to the Mother of God and had to be done in a way that contributed to her honor and joy. This was true only if it was done with conscientiousness and purity of intention. A day's work was worthy of offering only when it bore the stamp of zeal, effort, and love.

For the object of his particular examination he took the resolution to insert three such prayer pauses with the Blessed Mother in the morning and three in the afternoon. Thus he walked hand in hand with her throughout the day. He sought and found her during the daily drill exercises, in his dealings with comrades, in moments of danger with death, during the fatiguing assault exercises in the evening. He lived in her presence in moments of joy and sadness. In this union with Mary he discovered the most beautiful kind of May blossoms. It was to bear unique fruit in his soul in the weeks to come.

Life-Offering

The offensive in Flanders came to a standstill in May of 1918. The nerve-wracking business of stationary warfare returned, with the artillery on both sides locked in a murderous duel. The price for this bitter struggle was paid for by the infantry in the front lines. Again Joseph Engling and his comrades had moved to the front. This time the location of the courier and signal post was a dugout very close to the Lys River, immediately behind the front line. There they were busy, uninterruptedly, day and night. Signal shots had to be fired and messages carried between the front line and the command posts.

The front around Calonne was a real firestorm again. In those days the signal posts constantly flirted with death. Rocket pistol in hand, Joseph was sitting in his dugout scanning the enemy's front line. It was a fearful sight, as if it were the end of the world! His company could expect to lose another quarter of its ranks in the days ahead.

Joseph thought about the day just past. He had kept his SDO without any problem. His new particular examination had been right on the mark. Four times in the morning and four times in the afternoon he had kept his spiritual dialogue with the Blessed Mother. Each time this practice of mental prayer made a lasting impression on him. Now his "May blossoms" were really filled with meaning. Today was the last day of May. A deep feeling of gratitude filled his soul. He recalled his years in Schoenstatt and the ideals he learned there. He recalled the persons he was close to in this large, spiritual family. He thought of the great work to which he felt called. In everything he saw the hand of Divine Providence at work through the Blessed Mother. Oh, there were so many things he owed her! Everything great and beautiful was a gift of her maternal kindness. If only he knew how to prove his attachment and devotion to her!

The 20-year-old Joseph was now at a critical juncture in his way of sanctity. On the fields of Flanders his interior life reached an extraordinary maturity. The fruit was an offering of self which has come to be known in Schoenstatt as the "Joseph Engling Act."

He wanted to work with all his might for the idea of the sodality, giving himself for it entirely, including his very life if it would serve God's plans. In fact he would not object if a British gunner were, at that very moment, loading the shell that would take his life. He wanted to offer everything for the cause of the Blessed Mother! He thought of the dead comrades he had carried away from the front. He thought of those, gruesomely mutilated, whom he had brought to the first-aid station. He was willing to suffer death or mutilation if, with the offering of his life, he could serve the Mediatrix of Grace in Schoenstatt. He raised his heart to her and with self-sacrificial love prayed: "If it can be reconciled with your plans, let me be a sacrifice for the aims which you have assigned to our sodality." It was a prayer to which heaven spoke: "Amen."

Since increased activity had been ordered by the German command, the enemy, too, was becoming more restless. Like the Germans, the British sent out their nightly spy patrols. The opposing forces clashed in no-man's-land and fought each other with hand grenades. Looking out over the front line from his post, Joseph could see the telltale signs of a skirmish just beginning between two patrols. Any moment he expected to get the signal for an artillery barrage in that sector. The British artillery, of course, would follow suit. Meanwhile, he was thinking about his particular examination. How would it be, he thought, if he would expand it—if with each meditation he would offer to the Blessed Mother his death on the battlefield? He had really meant it when he made this offering the night before. It had not been a moment of sentimental feelings of exuberant devotion. He would now renew the same request every time he made his particular examination. From now on this is how his time of mental prayer with Mary culminated. It was to be an offering without reserve. Death might come upon him with all the horrors of battle he knew so well. From now on he renewed the offering of his life eight times a day. He joined to it a prayer of petition asking the Blessed Mother to accept his offering so that a movement might come about from her Schoenstatt Shrine for the religious and moral renewal of the world.

The spirit of recollection and prayerful union with the Blessed Mother had a mysteriously strong influence on his spiritual life. They aroused the most tender promptings of his soul and the noblest sentiments of his heart. The impressions were so vivid and deep that the Blessed Mother actually seemed to be present. But they also called for manly, heroic courage. Nowhere was it put more to the test than in the "drum fire" of Flanders. When a man is surrounded by the horrors of battle and when the fear of death shakes him in violent fits, whatever is not genuine will crumble like a false front from an old building. Then he shows the stuff he is really made of and his real worth becomes apparent. What did Joseph show in these days? His comrades said it was his remarkable coolness, courage, and spirit of self-sacrificing comradeship. At one point he shared with his spiritual director about how this affected his inmost soul. Precisely in the moments of greatest danger he was overcome by an indescribable feeling of shelteredness. His great ideal would then seize him even to the last fiber of his being. He prayed to the Blessed Mother and felt transported to her little shrine. He thought of all those who were called to these same ideals. On May 20 he wrote to his spiritual director:

"I have a day of recollection today. I remember my former zeal for the sodality, the time in Schoenstatt—and I promised my Little Mother to become zealous again. The same shall happen with love of neighbor. Some days ago when the shells hit to the right and to the left of me, I prayed as usual to my Little Mother and placed myself spiritually into the shrine. I had rarely felt so close to my dear Little Mother in my whole life. Her nearness was sweet and lovely; I no longer had any fear of the grenades. It was a happy state and I would have liked to remain in it. How beautiful and exalted, how lovely and encouraging is our dear Mother Thrice Admirable. A great longing for her shrine, for you and for my dear fellow sodalists often over comes me" (May 20, 1918).

The Life-Offering in Writing

On June 3, Joseph was lying in a shellhole on the bank of the Lys River. He was writing a letter to his spiritual director, giving an account of the month of May. He enclosed his spiritual schedule, well-kept and in order. He also felt urged to send a greeting of childlike love to the Sodality Queen in her shrine at Schoenstatt. So on the reverse side of the sheet on which he had recorded his particular examination he wrote a prayer which for some time now was the content of his particular examination and in which he used to offer his life as a offering to Mary:

"Dear Little Mother, Mother Thrice Admirable, I give myself to you anew as your sacrifice. I offer you everything I am and have, my body and my soul with all its abilities, all my possessions and goods, my freedom, my will. I want to be totally yours. I am yours. Use me and whatever is mine entirely as pleases you. But if it can be reconciled with your plans, let me be a sacrifice for the aims which you have assigned to our sodality.

"In humility, your unworthy servant,

"In battle, June 3, 1918, Joseph Engling."

Now the offering of his life was finalized in writing. His dedication to Mary was complete in every respect.

Although the German offensive had gotten a firm foothold on the Lys River, the artillery duels continued. In the first days of June the British even brought heavy mortar batteries to advanced positions. The din of battle rose to a deafening roar. For the poor infantrymen in their ditches and foxholes, even worse things were to come.

In those days the men of the 25th began to feel that the regiment would soon have to withdraw from this sector. They had spent almost six weeks on this fiercely contested piece of earth near Calonne. Heavy casualties had thinned the ranks of the companies. Some had lost a third, others as much as a half their battle strength. Yet the infantry had been absolutely inactive during these six weeks. A day on the offensive probably would have cost them the same number of casualties, perhaps more. Nonetheless, one such day would have been preferred to the weeks of inactivity, huddled here and there, exposed to heavy shelling. It was like a fever consuming their physical and mental strength. It would not take very much more before they were totally consumed and crushed. The war became an indescribably hard test of nerves and character. Besides the heroism of valor in the charge of attack, there developed another kind of bravery in the course of time. It was the heroism of patiently suffering with unbroken strength of soul. Not everyone was capable of such heroic greatness. Most were ready to quit and go home.

While regiment command weighed its options, Joseph lived his new particular examination. The more he lived it, the more the bloody battle seemed to lose even its worst horrors. He familiarized himself more and more with the thought that one day he would have to lose his life in the hail of shells. This state of complete inner peace seemed even to himself a little strange at times. In the midst of heavy shelling he entered in his diary:

"We are in reserve position. 'Tommy' seems to have discovered our position and fires miserably in our direction. I am a strange fellow; I do not even understand myself. Shells may hit right next to me and I am not afraid. I remain calm and composed, 'cool' as we say here. While my companions tremble from fear and others run away, I calmly remain in my hole and imagine that a grenade tears me to pieces and I am not horrified. On the contrary, behind this mental picture a happier state shines through. Even the thought that I might lie miserably mutilated, but alive, does not seize me with trembling. If it comes (so be it), in God's name" (June 5, 1918).

In the last days of June the 15th Reserve Division concluded its activity in the Calonne sector. For eight full weeks they persevered on this blood-soaked battlefield. They urgently needed several

211

weeks of complete rest, so they were moved to a quieter sector facing the Vimy Heights. The eight weeks in the sector of Calonne cost the division almost 2,000 men.

Joseph looked back upon the time near Calonne with limitless gratitude. The battlefield and the hundredfold brushes with death had been a school of training such as he had never experienced. Never in his life had he felt such protection from the sheltering hands of Mary as he had in Flanders. Deeply moved he wrote in his diary:

"It is wonderful how God has protected me. How can I thank him and his holy Mother? Mother, Protectress, Queen! What do you expect of me? Here I am, I submit to your will" (June 26, 1918).

10. The Road to Perfection

On Furlough

In early July 1918, Joseph's regiment was in rest camp at Esquerchin near Donai. Sick soldiers filled every available bunk in the infirmary. For many days now, influenza had been making its cruel rounds on the Western Front. The medical sergeant was at a loss for places to put the newly infirm and said so to the regiment's doctor. "Then we have to make room," said the doctor.

"Anyone who has put the worst of the fever behind him must make room for others. Anyway, this time the influenza wasn't too deadly."

"But it has struck many more soldiers than before," answered the sergeant.

"Yes, and it is no wonder," agreed the doctor. "You have to think of what four years of war will do. The men are undernourished and emaciated by the rigors of war. Years of lying in damp trenches and the incredible effects of modern warfare have worn down the bodies. Their inner resistance is gone and they immediately fall ill when an epidemic strikes."

Then they went from bed to bed. The sergeant carried the sick list and gave a report about each man's progress.

"Private Engling," he now said, "also sick with the flu, here for the last three days."

"How is his temperature?" asked the doctor.

"Dropping since yesterday afternoon; this morning not totally fever free," reported the sergeant.

The doctor felt his pulse and had him stick out his tongue. "When was the last time you were on furlough?" he asked.

"Fourteen months ago," replied Joseph.

"Sergeant, see to it that this man is sent on furlough immediately." The sergeant made a note of this and added one more to the list of beds that would be free in the morning.

The next evening Joseph was already in the train taking him on furlough. In spite of the warm weather, shivers went through his body because of the chills. Carrying his knapsack to the train station had practically exhausted him. Now came the long, long journey all the way across Germany. When he got off the train at Frankenau in East Prussia, he still had to walk two and a half miles to reach his home in Prositten. Being so close to home gave him a second wind. He pulled himself together, tired though he was. As soon as he got home, he had to go to bed. He had a mild case of pneumonia. But the tender care of his mother nursed him back to health after about eight days. Now he could finally enjoy being at home again.

Joseph during his last visit to Schoenstatt, July 1918. Left to right: Wergen, Engling, Fr. Wagner, Hafeneth, Waldbröl.

How warm and cozy the familiar rooms of his parents' home now looked after months of living in foxholes and trenches. The most beautiful moments came in the evening, when the family gathered to talk. He said very little about the front. He mostly talked about Schoenstatt, about becoming a priest, and about what he would do after the war. Life was not easy in Prositten. Almost every family had lost a loved one on the front. Everyone was wearing threadbare clothes. Even the church bells would soon have to be taken down and melted into shells if things went on much longer.

Because of all this, a certain melancholy hung over his furlough. His heart was especially heavy when, after two weeks, it came time to bid farewell. Once more he knelt down before father and mother. Deeply moved, both gave him their blessing. "In God's name," they said. "Until we meet again," said Joseph confidently. It was their last farewell.

All the way to Schoenstatt, Joseph's thoughts were already there. He had saved four of his furlough days for this visit. What a welcome there would be! He had already imagined a dozen times what it would look like when he came. He would soon be kneeling before the picture of the Blessed Mother in the Shrine. He would see Father Kentenich and tell his spiritual director everything that filled his soul. He would even meet the younger sodalists just before they left for summer vacation.

On July 25 he walked the familiar path from the train station in Vallendar to Schoenstatt. He was greeted from afar by the "New House," now filled with wounded soldiers. He could see them sitting at the windows in the typical striped hospital gowns. Below in the valley the two old steeples still raised their towers towards the sky. Not far away, hidden in pine trees, was the little Shrine of Our Lady. Yes, this was Schoenstatt, his beloved second home. He put his gun and heavy knapsack next to the door and entered the shrine. It was a moment that moved him deeply. How often had he come in spirit to this hallowed place! Each day when he made his holy hour he placed himself before this tabernacle. Whenever he presented a great sacrifice to his Little Mother for her "capital of grace," he visited her here in thought. For him this simple home of the Mother Thrice Admirable was the symbol of a great idea. From here a stream of graces would flow in every direction for the religious and moral renewal of his country. It was for this that he had made his life-offering. No wonder the little shrine came to his mind every time death came close to him on the battlefield. Now he entered this holy place in all reality. An inexpressible feeling of shelteredness came over him. He knelt down before the picture of the Mother Thrice Admirable and said a long prayer of thanksgiving.

With a joyful heart he now set out to find the room of his spiritual director. He did not get there right away. In the corridors and stairways of the seminary he met students racing around excitedly. The school year had just ended and the following day they would leave for home. He remembered well the excitement that filled those hours. But he did not remember many of the faces. How pale and gaunt they looked! Not many representatives of the older classes were to be seen. Now even the birth year 1900 had been called to arms. They were barely 18 years old. The former point-man of his Schoenstatt group, Alfons Hoffmann, was one of them. Whenever an acquaintance did turn up, a warm and hearty welcome followed.

Joseph was assigned a room in the seminary nicknamed "the barracks." This room was reserved for soldiers visiting on furlough. He had hardly entered when someone knocked at the door. It was one of the young students. He was assigned to clean his room. With a smile Joseph took the mop and pail from the little fellow's hand and helped him with the clean-up. When they were done, Joseph even gave him a bag of cookies. Overjoyed, the young student took them and left thinking, "What a good soldier!" Meanwhile, the whole building was being cleaned from top to bottom. Father Prefect laid great stress on leaving all the rooms in tip-top shape before going on vacation. All the halls, classrooms and corridors had to be painstakingly swept and scrubbed. When Joseph saw the boys at work, he barely gave it a second thought—he joined in and helped along. The boys doing the cleaning were surprised at such unexpected and efficient help. Most of these did not know Joseph and asked curiously who the soldier was who was so eager to help. Soon the news spread through the whole school: "Engling is on furlough. He is upstairs helping with the cleaning."

It seems that one of the middleclassmen did not receive this bit of news. He later described his first meeting with Engling—whom he had not known previously—this way:

"Vacation was approaching. I was in one of the washrooms when I suddenly heard heavy steps coming from the next room. Looking up, I saw a soldier in his field-gray uniform. He came to me, shook hands and modestly inquired how I was doing, how I liked it in Schoenstatt and if I were looking forward to my vacation. It seemed so unusual to me that a soldier and perfect stranger would have such great interest in a student. My curiosity was aroused and I began to examine the questioner more closely. The first thing I noticed was that he had the ordinary uniform of a private. He had large glasses, the kind worn by soldiers, but instead of regular bows they had field-gray bands which gave his appearance a comical touch. What struck me as odd in a soldier was his posture which was slightly stooped. A winning kindness was typical of him and it prompted me to talk as if he had been a friend of mine for a long time. After he left I thought: 'This is really a kind lay-brother. One can see the goodness in his eyes.' Later in the day, when I came to the dormitory, I was surprised to see the same soldier helping the students clean the dorm. 'This is an ideal brother' I thought to myself, 'I must get to know him.' I inquired about him and received the surprising answer: 'This is not a lay-brother, this is Joseph Engling, the former prefect of the Junior Sodality.' I was, of course, greatly disappointed, for I had imagined that such a famous person would look quite different."

Downstairs in the yard the student prefect of the upper class was loading baggage on a wagon for it to be brought to the train station. Joseph was immediately at his side, lending a helping hand. Then he sat down with him on the loaded wagon and inquired: "Tell me, how is the sodality doing?" Then the prefect told him about his cares and his work on behalf of the sodality during the year just past.

When all the chores around the house had been done, Joseph finally arrived at the room of Father Kentenich. This long-awaited meeting was a heartfelt one. For now, Joseph could not talk long. The young students wanted to hear many things from this soldier sodalist. Only after they had been satisfied was Joseph able to return to his spiritual director for a long conversation. Father Kentenich wanted to hear everything. Everything that had happened in his spiritual life now came back to Joseph. His director approved of everything Joseph had done. At the end, both agreed that three days of his stay at Schoenstatt should be spent in the prayer and solitude of retreat.

Four other soldiers from the seminary's upper classes were visiting Schoenstatt on furlough at the same time as Joseph. They talked long into the evening about their experiences. At first they talked about the conditions on the front. Each had been at a different point in the front lines. Given the failures of the German offensive, all four felt that the situation of the war was critical, if not hopeless.

Now they talked about the religious and moral situation of the nation and the army. One had been in the war since 1914. The others had been drafted one or two years later. All saw a general moral decline. The needs caused by the war were so extreme that they not only wore down the body, but also one's moral resolve. Things were best in the front lines. The farther back one went into the reserve positions the worse things got. Some of the cities used for reserve stations were dens of iniquity. Slackers and deserters hung out. Soldiers waited in long lines to get into houses of ill repute.

Things were not much better at home. Black marketeers, war-profiteers, and opportunists were exploiting the German people. They all agreed that the growing civilian distress was leading to a moral decline, too. One could sense decay and contamination at work everywhere. After the war a tremendous work of renewal would have to take place.

With that they came to the topic of the sodality. What would they have done without it! What a school of character formation it had been for them in younger years! "Who knows," they all honestly admitted, "Would we have been able to resist the general moral dangers? The undertow is so strong that one can be swept away without even knowing it." How much the "MTA" Magazine had helped give the groups support and inspiration! And then they came to the most beautiful part of their sodality: their Marian devotion and the great idea of Schoenstatt as a second Ingolstadt. These warriors, hardened by the storms of war, were not ashamed to talk about Our Lady and how she had protected them in so many dangers. The ideal of her immaculate purity had sheltered them. How different was their attitude to women than so many of their comrades! The one or the other told about other seminarians who had "gone over the edge" as a soldier. They had met others who had become totally discouraged. As sodalists they felt called to a great work. It was clear to them all that Mary had erected her throne of grace in a special way in the shrine in Schoenstatt. From there she would send forth a stream of graces for the religious and moral renewal of the nation. No one knew how that would happen, but the beginnings were already visible. Recently a number of high school students and seminarians from other places had joined the Schoenstatt "External Organization." This sodality was clearly called to something great. Joseph listened to the conversation with mostly silent attention. In his heart he agreed with the others. The closing words about the sodality, their future, and the Blessed Mother had nearly melted his heart. Just like the others, he had experienced the blessings of the sodality, love of Mary, and the capital of grace. A foreboding cloud may have hung over their beloved nation, but the mood of the Schoenstatt soldiers was not one of gloom and doom. They felt that they were at the beginning of a new springtime. Because of it, they looked forward with great confidence to divine victory.

The following days Joseph made his private retreat under the guidance of his spiritual director. He did not need any conferences or many new thoughts and suggestions. Instead, he spent many hours in quiet prayer before the tabernacle and the picture of the Mother Thrice Admirable in the shrine. He talked in great detail with Father Kentenich about how to best shape his spiritual life. Joseph told him how much the biography of Bl. Gabriel Possenti[1] had impressed him. It was especially this saint's way of living in the presence of God that appealed to him. Joseph felt urged to imitate him in this point. This biography had been his spiritual reading in the previous month. His spiritual director sensed that the grace of the Holy Spirit was behind this urging. As a result, his advice to Joseph aimed at supporting this trend in his spiritual life. These suggestions would be of great importance for his future inner development.

During the hours of solitude, his thoughts also turned to his group. In the last weeks, the group members had not been able to devote much time to their group work because of the military offensive. Johannes Dekarski wrote from a hospital that his leg had been amputated. Clemens Meier was in a hospital in Berlin. One after the other was gradually heard from; in spite of the terrible battles, all were accounted for. Fortunately, one of those spending his furlough in Schoenstatt was also the leader of Joseph's section,

---

[1] St. Gabriel Possenti of the Sorrowful Mother (1838-1862), Italian seminarian of the Passionist Fathers who died of tuberculosis. During the lifetime of Joseph Engling he was a Blessed; he was canonized a Saint in 1920.

Rudolf Gross. Joseph discussed his group work with him. Rudolf had given his section the motto "Remain true to our principles, complete the work of self-education, and return home a real man."

Joseph needed a new field of activity for his group. So far they had concentrated on personal sanctification and for this reason had dealt with such topics as the spiritual daily order, the particular examination, spiritual direction and the like. Now these points were practiced by all the members of his group. He considered the time opportune for turning their attention to the apostolate. This was in harmony with the prevailing condition of the External Organization and with his own spiritual growth. From a better understanding of the Mass he had come to a deeper appreciation of the Church year. Now a new reality stood vividly before his soul: the Church. He saw in her the bearer of religious and moral rebirth. His contributions to Our Lady's capital of grace did their share to open his mind still more to the Church and her great needs. So he selected the apostolate for their new field of activity. From Schoenstatt he wrote a long group letter on this topic.

The moment of farewell tolled for Joseph on July 30. He knelt before Father Spiritual Director and asked for his blessing. Then he went down to the shrine. The Iron Crosses earned by Schoenstatt sodalists in the war were displayed on a velvet-covered board. His was one of them. It reminded him of his life-offering. So he renewed his consecration prayer. Then his spiritual director accompanied him to the edge of the Schoenstatt property. *"Nos cum prole pia,"* said his director and Joseph concluded the sentence, *"Benedicat Virgo Maria."* Then he departed. Schoenstatt would never see him again.

High Ideals Great Disappointments

Not long after Joseph left Schoenstatt, his friend Karl Klement arrived on furlough. Father Kentenich received him with the words: "It is too bad that you did not come a little sooner. Then you would have seen Joseph. You surely would have been edified. He has matured and knows what he wants. His views are so clear." Yes, an important development had taken place in Joseph's soul in the last years. And his stay in Schoenstatt had given him the necessary

220

solitude and grace to increase it.

Others too, noticed the change which had taken place in him. Shortly after he returned to his regiment he met one of his Schoenstatt comrades, Joseph Friedrich. Their conversation soon turned to Schoenstatt, the sodality, and religious questions in general. Joseph Friedrich could not help but sense a deep religious atmosphere radiating from Joseph. In Hagenau he had been ashamed to walk with Joseph because he was not enough of a "parade soldier" and even seemed stupid at times. While in Schoenstatt, Friedrich had been some grades ahead and only seen Joseph at a distance. But now Joseph exerted an inexplicable influence over him. His entire being was a mysterious testimony to religious "grippedness," and Friedrich himself felt gripped. Friedrich was long pursued by these extraordinary impressions. This conversation left such a mark on his soul that later he called it his deepest experience of the war years.

Joseph's battalion was sent to the lines again on August 8. They were stationed to the west of Douai in an established network of trenches. They were stretched out on a slight ridge between the villages of Bois-Bernard and Fresnoy. In the distance they could see the bluffs of the Vimy Heights. Joseph was assigned to the "I.B.O." (infantry observation corps) again. He was with Schoenstatter Edmund Kampe, now a petty officer. Their quarters were behind the front lines.

Things did not look good. The German command knew from Allied prisoners that R.I.R. 25 was faced by no fewer than four fresh Canadian divisions. They were some of England's best troops, and it was the sign of a counter-offensive. Since Callonne there had been no replacements, leaving the regiment at about one-quarter strength. German High Command had known since July 18 that the handwriting was on the wall. There were no more reserves. The offensive had to be abandoned. The initiative now went over to the enemy, and High Command could only hope that their fortified positions would hold. The soldiers on the front sensed an impending storm and shivered.

Rumors, conjectures, and personal experience warned the men on the front that they were on the eve of a great catastrophe. Confidence in the High Command was seriously shaken; hope in a victorious end to the war vanished. The ordinary soldier on the front now faced the most difficult psychological test of the war, a test more difficult than all the battles fought so far. Joseph, too, was affected by the fury of events. But in spite of the increasing war-weariness and the poisoning effect of whispered revolutionary slogans, Joseph remained master of the situation. It was not always easy, and after a comrade had spilled out question after bitter question in a conversation with Joseph, he had to wrestle with questions of his own: Was there no other way for peoples to resolve their differences than war? What was he to think of this war? What was he to think of his own government and nation? What should he think of the old slogan that "a soldier's death is a hero's death"?

After long reflection and meditation in the solitude of his heart, he forged the following guiding principle: He must leave the difficult questions of war and nation for later study. For now all he knew was this: A merciful and wise God rules over all world events. In his inscrutable designs He permitted this war. We must accept the approaching total collapse as a difficult trial from God who knows how to turn evil into good at the right moment. The legitimate state authority has called me to arms to defend the fatherland. I confirmed my obligation with an oath, so I must do my duty.

From this principle he drew appropriate conclusions. He wanted to go on fighting valiantly, not because he enjoyed warfare and blood-shed, but because he wanted to obey his God-given authority. In this way he kept his military oath. In like manner he did not want to shirk any military duty; this would be against the spirit of obedience. He wanted to stick to these two norms under all circumstances even if it caused his death so shortly before the end of the war. In the future he wanted to accept the hardships of war without complaint. According to Divine Providence the war remained a means for furthering his progress in sanctity. He made a firm resolution not to complain or grumble about life in the army. On the contrary, he wanted to help his comrades see the war in the spirit of faith. In this way he could counteract the general war-weariness and the spirit of rebellion.

These ideas put solid ground under his feet again. As he wrote to his friend Karl in a letter just a few days before: "God permitted

222

this war and called us to arms by legitimate authority... Like you, I must not shirk my duty. I will gladly fight and bear all kinds of hardship..." To his spiritual director he communicated the result of his reflections with the simple brief words: "It is God's will that I fight—this conviction is enough." Two months later, he wrote to his parents on October 2, "We will hold our position even if Tommy' comes in great numbers." On the same day he could report to his spiritual director, "I have broken entirely with grumbling about army life. In fact, whenever I have a chance, I try to present it in a favorable light and to fight against war-weariness."

This was how he mastered the problem of being in a war in the face of immanent collapse. In the midst of an exhausted and already beaten army he stood as an upright soldier. In contrast to the advocates of rebellion he was the example of loyalty. In the meantime, Joseph's thoughts hastened beyond the present momentary events. He visualized the Church and her mission as the proponent of religious and moral renewal, of the rebirth of mankind and his fatherland through faith and grace. His vision was directed to the little Shrine of the Mother Thrice Admirable in Schoenstatt, the home of his sodality, the symbol of its ideals and endeavors. The sodality needed real saints in everyday life. More than ever this ideal stood out in his mind. In his SDO he applied it to daily life and made it fruitful for Our Lady's capital of grace. From this there could be no turning back. He even connected the aims of the sodality to his life-offering. Especially at this time, when discouragement and despair spread more and more through the masses, the sodality had a chance to conquer souls with undiminished faith. He summarized this idea in the word "apostolate." It was to be his group's new field of activity. He could see two tangible immediate objectives. The members of his group would have to be active as lay apostles in every available field. In addition they must interest suitable comrades in Schoenstatt and have them join the External Organization of the sodality. With these members a Marian League would be formed with the intent of serving as the elite troop of a broader apostolic movement.

Joseph wrote two group letters on this topic. In the first one he dealt with the fundamentals of apostolate, with the spirit of being a lay apostle, and with the sanctification of one's own life. In the second he made practical suggestions. He proposed new fields of activity:

1) The apostolate of good example.
2) Direct work for the good of souls.
3) Combating immorality.
4) Love for the Holy Church.
5) Helping others see the war in a religious light.
6) Education of new apostles.
7) The apostolate of the press.
8) Foreign missions.
9) Social work.

To the various fields of activity he added appropriate explanations. For example, he elaborated on the apostolate of good example with the words "living our faith, military professionalism, and camaraderie." To the paragraph on social work he added: "fostering love for one's family, resisting class struggle, helping comrades to satisfy their thirst for knowledge."

Every point of this extensive program bore the traces of having been already tested in everyday life. It was a concise summary of his own apostolic activity.

The efforts to win new members for Schoenstatt's cause were very dear to his heart. For weeks he had already been making a valiant effort in this area by introducing three comrades to the spiritual world of the sodality. For the time being they would work along in his group. He kept in touch by mail with one; the other two belonged to his company, namely Konstantin Grosse and Paul Süchten, the company tailor. So even while the German army was collapsing around him, Joseph made bold steps forward—believing in Schoenstatt's mission and showing an intrepid spirit of conquest.

One day in early September, Joseph was sitting in the observation dugout. He had just written a letter and now took out his books to do some studying. First came French. His goal for September was to repeat ten pages every week and learn a new chapter of material. He did that mostly in the free time between observation duties. He was uneasy about Edmund Kampe. He just couldn't shake the impression that Edmund didn't have the patience to keep up the observations for hours at a time. As it appeared to Joseph, he was constantly assigning his own observation time to others. This rubbed Joseph the wrong way and made him quietly upset. It would not have bothered him much if it had been someone else, but Edmund was a fellow sodalist from Schoenstatt, and Joseph just couldn't like what he saw. Just now Kampe came rushing into the dugout. Joseph was so engrossed in his studies that he barely heard him. Startled, he heard his name being called. He had to go up to take over the observation post. Joseph murmured: "O, you could sit at the field periscope once yourself, instead of sitting on your duff all day." He didn't really say it with anger; but one could tell there was a subtle protest in the tone of his voice. The other soldiers looked up amused. They found it funny that the fresh petty officer with the boyish face would receive such a rebuttal. The petty officer felt lectured like a little boy, and took it as a questioning of his authority. His face turned bright red with anger. "I can do what I want," he shot back angrily. And in defense of his authority he made Joseph stand at attention and gave him an official dressing down in hard military tones for violating discipline.

Those who saw it were shaken. Kampe and Engling, the two Schoenstatters, no less! The petty officer stormed away and Joseph took his post without speaking a word. But unhappiness reigned in both hearts. Edmund Kampe was in Joseph's vicinity several times in the next hours, but only looked at him shyly. Then they finally met in the dugout alone. Neither of them could stand the state of affairs. They sat down and calmly talked things over. "You have to understand, Joseph," said Edmund, "that I must frequently run to regiment command. I cannot always be on observation duty. And then you cannot just say that in front of the others." Joseph asked forgiveness for his rashness. But Edmund could also see that he had been much too harsh. He also felt that he needed to make amends. They soon put the matter behind them.

Lately, Joseph had been quite busy with group mail. After all, every single member had to be won over to the idea of apostolate. He got together with Paul Reinhold several times a week and discussed these ideas. Of course, it always took quite a while to locate him. Others from the group, however, were beginning to worry him. Three were in a hospital; two of them in Berlin. They were exposed to the dangers of the big city and the moral depravity of the masses. Though they did not abandon their principles, the new experiences threatened to leave them utterly discouraged. Those not in hospitals were not doing much better. The general atmosphere weighed heavily on them and they keenly felt the prevailing discouragement. All of them were troubled by doubts about their ideals; they were in danger of yielding to despair and lack of faith in human goodness. Without others near at hand who shared their ideals, they were oppressed by an unspeakable feeling of loneliness in the midst of an antagonistic world. It seemed to them that they stood entirely alone in a raging flood. As group leader, Joseph wrote many letters during this time about apostolate, moral and religious renewal, and being a positive influence on their surroundings. Joseph sensed the inner affliction of his group brothers and helped them as much as he could, never losing sight of his groups's aim. He wanted to share his ardor and unbroken faith with these friends, so he wrote letter after letter. Not all were answered, but he did not give up. He tried to encourage them and fill them with enthusiasm. But his own apostolic zeal and faith in the goodness of man were soon to be subjected to a severely tested.

His friend Grosse had been on furlough for fourteen days. He had joined Joseph's group some time ago and, to Joseph's great delight, had been quite active. Joseph had high hopes for him. The day came when he was due to return from leave and report to the infantry observation post. But he did not show up. Time passed and no one heard from him. "Funny," remarked Edmund Kampe, "I have to ask the company secretary what's wrong." Joseph, too, was very much concerned.

Edmund Kampe returned from the company office one day with some unexpected news. He knew that it would be a painful disappointment for Joseph. During his furlough, Grosse became weak and fell back into his former vices. Grosse contracted venereal disease and the office had to commit him to an isolation hospital. On hearing the news, Joseph seemed paralyzed, his face grief-stricken. Edmund also said he had brought a card for Joseph from Grosse. But when he searched his pockets, he could not find it. "I must have lost it," he said sadly, "but I know pretty well what it said. He humbly admitted his guilt and signed it, 'Your unhappy friend.'"

This affected Joseph deeply. He spoke no word of contempt or indignation. The only emotions that moved him were sorrow and compassion. He did not want to judge his fallen comrade too severely. He did not even want to desert him. He was set on helping him to rise from his fall and lead a better life. "Edmund," he begged, "look for that postcard again. I need Grosse's address." Edmund turned his pockets inside out, but was unable to find it. The card was lost and he never heard from his friend again.

On another occasion Edmund Kampe brought a surprising message from his customary trips to regiment command. He had been ordered to officer school in Germany. According to instructions Engling was to be in charge of the infantry observation post. The fact that Edmund was to become an officer filled Joseph with sincere joy. Joseph did not begrudge him the honor, even though he, a fellow student, had to remain a private. Edmund, his immediate superior, had always been a good comrade. They had spent many dangerous hours together on the battlefield and had stuck together. Edmund, too, found it hard to say goodbye to Joseph. He would most likely never find such a good comrade and subordinate again.

Around this time the infantry observation post was moved to a new location. Now Joseph and his men had to share a dugout with the liaison personnel of his battalion, where they really fell into bad company. Joseph soon sensed that he was dealing with morally unstable and corrupt men. If they had only realized their deplorable condition and shown signs of remorse! On the contrary, they seemed to feel perfectly satisfied with their depraved lives. Bragging and boasting about their own meanness, they became insufferable. Religion, of course, meant absolutely nothing to them. They were fed up with the clergy and their empty talk, as they said. Why should they believe when the clergy themselves did not believe their own teachings.

Joseph was immediately determined to deal with these men as an apostle would. He despaired of no one. Even in these fellows there must be something good that could be developed. At first he did nothing more than what was expected of a good comrade. He especially focused on keeping the dugout clean. He wanted to keep it habitable and clean. When the sun rose especially beautifully one Sunday morning, he gave the dugout a thorough cleaning and decorated it with pictures. One must see it was Sunday by the appearance of the dugout; was not the Lord's day the day for man to also show exterior worship to God? Most of the comrades liked Joseph's concern for the cleanliness of the dugout. Only the liaison personnel believed they should just be all the more careless. They threw all the trash and rubbish on the ground and acted, according to the opinion of the others, like pigs. Why be different, if there was a numbskull who took a broom several times a day and tidied up the place? Joseph felt their abuse and contempt and began to feel resentment building up in him. Should he, under such circumstances, continue to perform these acts of charity? At first these ruffians misused his services and then ridiculed him as a mute idiot. A little upset, he wrote in his diary:

"This room could be rotting in filth before a single liaison officer would use a broom. And this exterior uncleanliness mirrors the interior one. The word 'swine' is too good for them. For the first time today I did not clean our quarters and I have not been so friendly toward them. One can really despair of one's own idealism and give up at times. However, it is a question of immortal souls; hence, nothing must be too hard for me" (September 24, 1918).

With the last sentence he found his better self again. He was not performing these acts of kindness in order to receive anything in return. He did not expect recognition, gratitude nor any other advantage. He did it to remain faithful to his ideal which expressed the idea of service to immortal souls. If his actions were now repaid with ingratitude and contempt, he served God with an even purer intention.

The Cigar Incident
One day at the distribution of food, the soldiers received their usual allotment of tobacco. "Engling doesn't smoke," was the motto of the liaison personnel, meaning they considered it their duty to hound Joseph for his cigarettes. "Slow down, slow down" he said, "I want to save a few of the cigars for my father." The

rest he gave away. That's how it always was. In spite of the give-aways, he had managed to save quite a few cigars. Soon there would be enough to send a whole box of them home to his father. How happy that would make his father! It was very hard to get cigars at home and his father had certainly earned a few simple joys. He could already imagine his father sitting back on a Sunday and enjoying one, especially as a gift from his son.

Joseph went to his knapsack to get the cigars. He was ready to pack them and send them to his father. But when he opened the box, he found it nearly empty. Only a few cigars were left. He immediately guessed what had happened. The liaison personnel had stolen them. Inside of him a violent anger was beginning to burn: "That's the last straw! Those outlaws! I'll show them! But first they're going to know that I've seen through their thievery." He stormed into the dayroom and hurled the rest of the cigars in front of them. They could have these, too, he told them. Then he went on guard duty. Deep within he was fuming; innumerable questions raced through his mind. Was it really possible to stick to one's ideals under these conditions? Could he become all things to all men when treated so cruelly? Was it prudent to be an apostle when it only earned ingratitude and contempt? Should he try to win the souls of men who act like ruffians? He raised his eyes to the Blessed Mother. Her intercession can work miracles. But in return she demands sacrifices of us, sacrifices of atonement on behalf of others. After all that is what her Son taught and lived. With that his life's ideal gained the upper hand. He pulled out his diary and began to write:

"On guard duty. I wanted to get my anger off my chest and write about it during the first three hours, but then I postponed it until I had calmed down. The cigars which I wanted to send to my dad were stolen. For a moment the idea went back and forth in my head: I will steal anything I can get my hands on from these liaison fellows. I will refuse to do them any more favors. I went up to the dayroom and threw the remaining cigars down saying, Here, take these too!' But I will continue to do favors for them. Perhaps the heavenly Mother will accept my sacrifices on their behalf" (September 25, 1918).

Meanwhile, Joseph was becoming more and more worried about the life of his group. His many suggestions on the subject of the apostolate produced no response. No one seemed to be aroused by his suggestions. The general state of affairs and the spiritual numbness of their surroundings had paralyzed their spirit. They liked to read what their group leader wrote, but they could not brace themselves to do the same. That's why they wrote only scanty and irrelevant answers to his letters. The new group point-man in Schoenstatt was too young and inexperienced to be of any real help. He left Joseph's letters unanswered, just as so many of his group members did. The sad condition of his group lasted until Joseph's death. He had no success in interesting his fellow workers in his new aim. This much, however, he did accomplish: they did not lose their faith in their ideals and in human goodness. The fact that there was one among them who cherished these ideals was a strong support. This was acknowledged many years later by one of his group members: "At a time when I suffered greatly from the existing military conditions, Joseph was almost the only light in dark hours."

Again Joseph was afflicted with trials and failure. He stood alone. None of his Schoenstatt comrades were close to him. The group seemed to have left him in the lurch. Joseph's attempts to win friends and helpers for Schoenstatt's cause had been a dismal failure, especially in the case of Grosse. The apostolate among his comrades was like working a stony vineyard, producing rubble and failure. All around him the subversive spirit and war-weariness increased. In spite of it all, Joseph remained free from bitterness toward his environment, free from discouragement in the face of the sad conditions of the time. He stood firm with unbroken faith in the ideals of his youth.

This fortitude had a secret source. In all trials and failures, even in loneliness, Joseph experienced the most intimate union with God.

Intimate Union With God

The last two months of Joseph's life, August and September 1918, proved to be the climax of the story of his soul. They stood under the sign of grace-filled closeness to God. The days of solitude during his furlough in Schoenstatt proved to be extraordinarily fruitful. Though the conditions on the front were the same when he returned there at the beginning of August, he was a changed man. Something quite new, for which he at first did not have the right word, had transpired in his soul. A little later the biography of Bl. Gabriel Possenti helped him to interpret this new phenomenon. From now on he spoke of the state of his soul as "walking in the presence of God."

On the very first day of his furlough in Schoenstatt he had formulated a new resolution for his particular examination: "Six times a day I want to recall that God is with me and sees me." This was not meant as a mere mental exercise, but as a prayer. In essence, it was the same exercise he had made weeks and months ago toward Our Lady, only now he focused on the all-present God. He proceeded with the new resolution as he had before. First he recollected himself to become aware of God dwelling in his soul. Then he lifted up his mind and heart to God by various affections and offered up the work he was about to do. This prayer was inspired by a mysterious urging. When reading the biography of Bl. Gabriel Possenti he sensed that the saint had experienced the same thing. This biography had a tremendous influence on him and it became his guidepost.

When he returned to the battlefront the last day of July, he did so armed with the new particular examination. Once back in the accustomed conditions of the front, he could not help but notice that something had taken place in his soul. The easiest way to get a clear notion about it was to present the matter to his spiritual director, so he collected his thoughts and wrote:

"Yesterday I arrived safely back in the company. Now after the furlough I feel like a completely changed man. The farewell from home was more difficult than the farewell from Schoenstatt. But I feel the pain of the latter farewell much more keenly than that of leaving my parents, brothers and sisters. I wanted to ask you, Reverend Father, to be more strict with me, but only as you think best. I want to share with you a different fruit of walking in the presence of God. Repeatedly when I was distracted in my prayers, the thought struck me: 'God is with you,' and then my prayer became more devout" (August 1, 1918).

Of course, this "walking in the presence of God," was not totally new to Joseph and his prayer life. It had its first beginnings back in his years in Schoenstatt. God's call had been perceptible in the first blossoming of his personal ideal and in the aims of the sodality. He fought for these ideals because he saw in them a mission from God, to which he wanted to be loyal and faithful. They had not been inspired by special revelation, but by plain, simple faith in Divine Providence. His contributions to Our Lady's capital of grace were an everyday school of how to take seriously the acceptance of God's call even at the price of the greatest sacrifices. His SDO had drawn him into the solitude of prayer. His daily participation in the Eucharistic sacrifice, in person or in spirit, was the center of his daily work and reminded him of the indwelling of Christ in his soul. All these partial experiences now came together in the integrated experience of being a child of God. It brought him inner serenity and the security of being sheltered in God's wings.

How marvelous was God's provident care in the inspirations and guidance of Joseph's past life! It now seemed to Joseph that he had not really seen things so clearly in the past. Just in the last few weeks he really began to see the hand of God working daily in his life. When he was alone on guard duty, he often found time to reflect. On one occasion he wrote to his spiritual director and gave him the gist of one such meditation:

"A few days ago it dawned on me how wonderfully my Little Mother used the virtuous example of her three servants Barbaric, Coassini, and Gabriel of the Sorrowful Mother to lead me to a more perfect life. I still remember well how the life of Peter Barbaric inspired me to faithfulness in little things, to diligent study, and to being a whole-hearted sodalist. From Coassini I learned willpower, the energetic '*Volo!*, I will!,' spiritual exercises and the striving for an all-embracing perfection. The life of Blessed Gabriel showed me the inner life, walking in the presence of God. I read his life a second time, one chapter every day, sometimes only half a chapter, but in every case I meditated on what I had read. Comparing his life with mine, I find so many faults in myself. I thought I had made quite some progress already, and now I find nothing but faults. And if I wanted to take the full scope of his actions seriously in my life, Reverend Father, I would lose courage. For every virtue he practiced I find the opposite fault in myself. But my Mother will and must help me. I want to become a saint, one even greater than Blessed Gabriel. Blessed Gabriel, obtain for me a great love for my beloved Mother, I beseech you, and I will become as holy as you!" (September 1, 1918).

How loving God's providence had been by calling him at such a youthful age into the school of Our Lady! Love for her stirred him to good and gave his efforts the aroma of God's blessing. Everything he treasured in his spiritual life he owed to her. That's why his heart now burned with the desire to increase and intensify his love for Mary. Because of this he soon broadened his particular examination. Every time he paused to recall the presence of God, he would ask Him for the grace to love Mary more fervently. The gift he received from his Little Mother in return was growth into a deeper childlikeness toward God. From now on he recalled the presence of God not only six times a day but every hour. Although he had formulated his resolution differently, the thought of Mary remained in the new formula: "Every hour I will recall that God the Father, Creator of my Mother, my Creator, and Creator of the entire world surrounding me, looks upon me with interest. I want to converse with Him."

In those days he felt more and more drawn into prayerful solitude. He probably reached the pinnacle of faithfulness to his SDO in the last two months of his life. He practically never omitted any exercise through a fault of his own. He was also keeping some extra exercises. Every morning he renewed his personal ideal: "To become all things to all men and Mary's very own." It summed up his whole life in a single thought. His desire was to bring the entire day under its influence. It was, in fact, a personalized form of the good intention, consecrating the entire day to a higher purpose. In addition, he added a prayer for the St. Boniface Society to his SDO. In the last few years, it was plain that the intentions of holy Mother Church had become very near and dear to his heart. This was especially true of the intentions of the Church in his fatherland. The care for her well-being and mission played an important role in his apostolic endeavors. The prayer for the St. Boniface Society was to remind him of that. In like manner he inserted in his spiritual daily order the prayer for the Confraternity of the Scapular. Although he had said both prayers for years, from now on they belonged to his daily program. Lastly, he resolved to say five decades of the rosary instead of his usual one. As a result, his spiritual schedule now contained a total of seventeen exercises.

From then on he examined himself twice a day (instead of once) on the performance of these exercises. The accuracy with which he checked them increased with the number of exercises. In fact he wrote down the hour when he made the examination. The irregular life at the front often reversed the waking hours during a twenty-hour period. Quite often nighttime was used for working and daytime for resting. The nightly examination of conscience generally took place sometime between 10 pm and 1 am at night. He made the second one at midday, generally between 11 am and 2 pm. All in all, it was quite an achievement to keep such a schedule amid the extraordinary conditions of military life on the front.

Still, Joseph could not say that his schedule required extraordinary effort. Neither the 17 exercises nor the two examinations of conscience, nor the day of recollection held every Sunday caused him any appreciable difficulty. In no case did they ever require a forceful or great exertion of the will. It almost seemed to him that everything moved along with a certain ease. The deeper his recollection, the more varied his day's work could be. He felt that a great evolution was taking place in his life. Formerly, he had to use great willpower to strive for the realization of his ideal. He had to stress his self-activity. Now God's invisible hand seemed to have taken over the guidance of his soul and he felt permeated by God's activity so that now everything went faster and easier. When he looked back, it seemed to him that he had been like a boatman who was forced to ply the oars; at present, however, a strong wind seemed to swell the sails and move the boat over the water with ease. He continued to row, perhaps even more zealously than before, but his contribution seemed insignificant when compared to the rapid progress made through the force of the wind.

To be precise, he presently only had one thing to really focus his efforts on—listening to the voice of God and promptly following the inspirations of grace. Influenced by such experiences, he formulated a new particular examination. It read: "The Holy Spirit abides in me, is near to me with his gifts. I must, therefore, make an effort to respond to his grace just as you, dear Little Mother, did. I will think of it every hour!" It was indeed true: The Holy Spirit, this great Divine Teacher, ruled his spiritual life in a tangible way. To be submissive to His inspirations was his special concern. Whenever he clearly perceived the will of God, he felt obliged to follow it unconditionally. Of course, reason enlightened by faith had to discern if the inspiration came from God. For example, he read in the life of Blessed Gabriel how he had done certain hard and extraordinary penances. Was he to do something similar? Before making a definite decision he wrote to his spiritual director:

"The life of Bl. Gabriel has made me think. Especially his way of practicing detachment from the world, his penitential zeal, his obedience, has given me much food for thought. Father, he was a real saint. At times, however, it seemed to me that he went too far. Until now I have only made the resolution to strive for sanctity with all my might. What is decisive is that I always say 'Yes' to the question, 'Is it God's will?' even in the smallest things. I have long asked myself if it is possible to also practice perfect obedience, humility, and love of poverty in the world—as perfectly as Bl. Gabriel did, but I have not been able to find a decisive answer. One thing is sure, I can practice these virtues more perfectly in the army than before. My love for my beloved Little Mother must become at least as fervent as his. I want to especially practice it this week" (August 19, 1918).

From this point on, his favorite particular examination was: Did I joyfully obey the will of God as I have recognized it? It was along this line that he wrote to his spiritual director:

"I am sending you my spiritual report, the first one after the grace-filled days in Schoenstatt. Being the first, it should have been flawless. Unfortunately, this was not the case. Until the last three days, I had responded to grace rather well. On the 13th, 14th and 15th I was guilty of more than ordinary transgressions. I do not remember now exactly what they were. I was also careless in keeping my particular examination, though I did not omit any of my exercises. Father, please impose a penance for these transgressions. I have kept the vow of chastity and renewed it for the next half of the month" (August 19, 1918).

His hourly practice of "walking in the presence of God" made him quick to hear and obey God's holy will. It also had another effect. The more he was at home in the solitude of prayer, the clearer his vision became for small and even the smallest imperfections in his soul. It was almost as if he opened his eyes for the first time. Things he had scarcely noticed or at least not particularly felt now aroused a deep sense of remorse. Often he could not put his finger on anything definite, but sensed a broad range of inordinate tendencies to self-love. For this reason he suffered the pangs of knowing he was a sinful man who was often driven by inordinate desires. He wrote:

"I know now for sure that I have offended the all-present God not only a few times but repeatedly. Despite these offenses—and he is sadly aware of them—He remains in my presence."

The mental suffering he endured because of sins and faults he had committed was no morbid inferiority complex. This, as a rule, produces restlessness, downheartedness or increased selfishness. Instead, his soul always remained in the peace of divine security brought about by perfect confidence in God. Yet the smarting pain inflicted by his many faults and imperfections burned in his soul like a consuming fire.

His intensified awareness of flaws and imperfections and his heightened sense of remorse were accompanied by a deep sensitivity to the need to do penance. Such penance is practiced by self-denial and sacrifice. "There is only one way," he wrote in his diary, "the way of self-denial and mortification." From now on he did not want to miss a single opportunity. Every day offered him countless possibilities to do penance. The meager food rations often left him feeling hungry; living with rough men tested his patience every day; he had to put up with their rudeness and ridicule; failures in the apostolate and lack of success put his perseverance to the test; many of the military orders he received demanded great sacrifices and continuous obedience. In the future all these countless opportunities were to be a continuous way of the cross. After he had walked this way of the cross for some time with great severity toward himself, his soul was stricken by a sudden horror. Deep inside he seems to have drawn back and been tempted to rebel against such a life. In prayer form he wrote in his diary:

"Mother, help me to continue; help me to overcome the horror that holds me back" (September 17, 1918).

The Holy Spirit, this Divine Teacher who guided Joseph's inner life, drew his soul more and more into a mysterious closeness to God. Under His guidance, Joseph sought God in the most hidden recesses of his soul. His attention was directed to the Son of God dwelling in him. So he formulated his resolution for the particular examination: "Every hour, while awake, I want to think of God the Son dwelling in my soul." In one of the succeeding weeks it was formulated this way: "God the Son, my self-sacrificing Savior, and Son of my Mother, is with me." Then he turned once more to the Triune God. This also found expression in his practice for the particular examination: "Every hour I want to recall that the most holy Trinity is always with me, while at rest or at work." In the following week he expressed the thought of union with God even more clearly: "I want to become fully conscious of the presence of the Triune God, at least once every hour, and recall that one day I will be united with him, and that the least imperfection hinders and delays this union." It was through prayer and penance, conditions essential for any spiritual progress, that Joseph's inner growth took place. Thus he reached a high degree of union with God. His whole being, even his feelings, were influenced by the presence of the Most High. He experienced in a tangible way the nearness of God.

At this point in Joseph's spiritual life the Divine Educator made a new move. He let his soul become confused in judging the morality of his actions. It became extremely difficult for him to decide whether a movement of the heart came from God or from self-love. Once he discovered an imperfection, he felt overwhelmed by an acute sense of guilt. God gave him the guidance of a priest to help deal with both the uncertainty of judgment and the sense of guilt. Joseph admitted his failings and asked for help. Joseph wrote to his spiritual director:

"I have kept the vow of chastity and renewed it for the next half month. In September and October I want to abstain from alcohol, smoking, and card playing. This shall remain in force as long as it is not an obstacle to my personal ideal 'all things to all men.' The renunciation shall oblige me under venial sin, dependent on you, Reverend Father. The temptations to selfishness were more frequent in recent days. In order to fight them, I omitted several times writing down accounts of my work for the group and entries in my diary. Reading the life of Bl. Gabriel brought to my attention my inordinate inclination for sweets. On one day, for instance, I consumed a whole pound of imitation honey. On another occasion I ate all my jam and sugar as soon as I received them. I fought this somewhat. Sometimes, however, I tried to suppress the thought of the presence of God and gave in to the passion. The suppression of the thought of God's presence was most shameful. Father, please impose a severe penance for that. Walking in the presence of God is the best means to advance on the road to perfection. I will bring it ever closer to the ideal of my life" (September 1, 1918).

The spiritual director read his penitent's letter with careful attention. He, too, realized that the extraordinary guidance of the Holy Spirit was at work in Joseph's soul. On principle, his director had previously exercised great reserve toward Joseph. He considered it his main task as spiritual director to present the community ideal and the idea of the Schoenstatt Sodality in a convincing and attractive manner. Then he made a constant effort to be in living personal contact with the spiritual children entrusted to his care. It was also this way with Joseph. As long as Joseph lived in Schoenstatt, his development in the direction of the given ideal was so natural that Father Kentenich hardly ever had to intervene in his spiritual life. Even his letters to Joseph on the front were limited to a few lines. In most cases they consisted of just a few short sentences written in the margins of the letters sent to Joseph by other students. But in the face of this new situation in Joseph's spiritual life, he changed his approach, for now Joseph needed special priestly guidance. His uncertainty of judgment demanded a sure norm. While preserving Joseph's delicate conscience, the director could not let him become the victim of scrupulosity. And the wish for a penance from the hand of the priest for the faults committed had to be moderated. So he gave Joseph the following advice:

"I give my approval to your binding yourself under venial sin this month to abstain from alcohol, smoking and card playing. Presupposed that your personal ideal does not counsel you otherwise. It is good and necessary that our ideal be decisive in all indifferent matters. Of course we have to guard against attacks of self-love and human respect. You know what I mean. But to protect yourself against unnecessary qualms of conscience, I would rather that you drink, smoke, and play cards in doubtful cases and show me your self-denial in prudent moderation. 'Every man must choose his way, know the place where he must stay, so where he stands he does not fall.' *What may be good for one is not good for all.*

"I do not think it is a good idea for you to omit marking your schedule in order to protect yourself from selfishness; some compulsion may easily slip in in this manner. Perhaps you remember the example of St. Bernard. Once when preaching he had the idea: Bernard, you did a fine job. He answered the tempter: 'I did not start the sermon for your sake; I will not stop it for your sake.

"I approve very much the inspiration of grace which urges you to be strict with yourself because you see very clearly that you could be more advanced due to all the graces which the dear God and our dear Mother have given you. I see as one of the greatest blessings that you strive with your old vigor and enthusiasm toward your old goal to become a saint in spite of the many difficulties which you face in military life. Cultivate the longing and the desire for this goal with inner warmth and with prayer. If it is not too difficult for you, you could renounce the imitation honey twice as atonement for the reported faults of your palate or give it to a comrade" (September 9, 1918).

In the meantime the guidance of the Holy Spirit directed Joseph's spiritual life a step further, making him realize his moral weakness and helplessness once more. He was even deprived of the consolation of feeling God's closeness. The shortage of food and desire for sweets caused these tests of humility. As a penance for his faults, his spiritual director had asked him to give his honey away twice. The letter reached him just before the arrival of an allotment of honey. After a brief struggle he postponed the penance for the next two times. Out of weakness he did not immediately follow the promptings of grace. The following week he postponed his penance once more and thus gave in again to his weakness. In a different field he sustained another defeat. The orders of a corporal offended his sense of justice. An inner voice told him to be quiet about it. In spite of it he complained about military life in the presence of his comrades. God punished him for these faults against obedience by immediately depriving him of the consolation of feeling God's closeness. Experiencing deep sorrow, he entered in his diary:

"Mother, I was very careless the day before yesterday and today. Today I even failed grievously. By giving in to inordinate inclinations, I lost the intimate union with God which I attained through my striving for mortification. Please, obtain forgiveness for me. This, your unworthy servant asks of you" (September 26, 1918).

Joseph took these events as deep humiliations, and rightly so. For weeks and months he had proved his spirit of mortification and courage under the most trying of circumstances. Now he failed in trifles. This made him keenly aware of his human weakness and dependence. In all frankness he confessed his guilt to his spiritual director:

"On Thursday we had honey again. At first I wanted to forego it. But I hesitated and then became weak. I experienced real satisfaction only on Friday when I could offer my dear Mother some acts of self-denial as penance for the faults committed on Thursday. This week I have controlled myself perfectly. I often quake at the thought of having to lead such a life of constant penance if I want to become a saint" (September 23, 1918).

Joseph was again on the high road of penance. In his particular examination he also took this into account and formulated the resolution: "I want to recall the presence of God hourly, my loving Father, and consider that he sees my conduct toward others."

On October 1 and 2 Joseph wrote his last letter to his spiritual director. In it he could inform him that he had mastered the existing difficulties:

"I have kept the self-imposed penances mentioned in the last letter... I have broken entirely with grumbling about the military life. In fact, whenever I have a chance I present it in a good light, but of course, only as far as truth permits" (October 1-2, 1918).

Calm and peace entered his heart once more. As before, he was filled with the happiness of being a child of God who knows he is secure in the love of the heavenly Father.

11. Homeward Bound

The Final Hours

For more than a month, German troops had felt a mounting tension. A British offensive was expected at any time. On the evening of October 1, R.I.R. 25 was suddenly ordered to the front. "This cannot bode well," said the men in Joseph's regiment. "We are rested and will land in a dangerous spot." Transport vehicles waited in Flers, not far from Douai, to take them to the train station at Pont de la Deule. The haste of this action made the troops more certain of their fate. Which faltering sector were they being called on to defend?

The Germans had been on the defensive for two weeks. A major attack on Ypres was in progress. The whole Lys River was lost. St. Quentin was occupied on October 1. Now the British had Cambrai in the pinchers, attacking from the left and right. If Cambrai fell, the entire Siegfried Line would collapse. German high command faced a desperate situation. Gaps caused by enemy attacks had to be closed on all sectors. But when one was closed, two or three more appeared elsewhere. The army's strength was rapidly ebbing away.

The British had formed a bulge in the line north of Cambrai. It was clear that they wanted to take Cambrai from the north. For some days a Swabian division had held them off and even pushed them back, but the British were getting reinforcements. Joseph's division was being sent to back up the defense at Eswars. The train stopped in Bouchain. The signs on the road read "Cambrai, 10 miles." The division set up camp. A hailstorm of enemy shells fell on Bouchain. During the night of October 3, an order was suddenly given: "Alarm! Everyone ready to move out!" Under the protection of darkness the troops began to move toward Cambrai. They had been ordered to a position between Eswars and Bantigny.

Silently and bent under the weight of their knapsacks, the exhausted soldiers walked along. Two heavy and four light machine-guns and the necessary cases of ammunition had to be carried. The men took turns carrying the extra load. How much the size of the companies had diminished! In spite of added reserves, they had

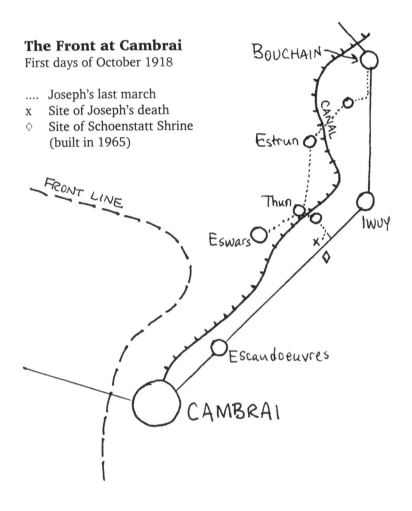

The Front at Cambrai
First days of October 1918

.... Joseph's last march
x Site of Joseph's death
◊ Site of Schoenstatt Shrine
(built in 1965)

FRONT LINE

BOUCHAIN

CANAL

Estrun

Thun

Eswars

IWUY

x

◊

Escaudoeuvres

CAMBRAI

at the very most 60 guns per company. Joseph marched in the 4th company. His infantry observation unit had been dissolved when they left the Vimy Heights. The companies needed every available man. Joseph found his comrades in a very glum mood. In the haste of their departure for the front, they had been given only the most necessary provisions. The edginess caused by the constant shellings only made matters worse. The heavy machine-guns and cases of ammunition cut into their shoulders. And they felt the paralyzing effect of fighting what they felt was a lost cause. "We cannot go on fighting anymore; we are at the end of our strength," they thought and said. The desperate condition of his comrades touched Joseph's heart deeply. He changed his particular examination to fit the situation: "Every hour I will say out loud: God, the loving Father of mankind, is with me. He sees how I make use of my innate urge to help serve others." He applied his particular examination by helping to carry the heavy cases of ammunition more than he had to. He encouraged his comrades and tried to convince them that the position had to be held. Only the day before he wrote to his parents: "We will hold our position, even if Tommy' comes in great numbers."

Toward morning they arrived at the village of Eswars. The soldiers tiredly collapsed in the hedges and ditches along the road. Some dug a hole into the embankment, others fell asleep on the spot. Autumn mists rose over the already harvested fields. It was 6 o'clock in the morning. On the edge of the village Joseph found shelter under a protecting hedge of thorns. The troops were supposed to stay here until nightfall. After the previous night's meager supper and the long night march, hunger gnawed at them, but no warm meal could be expected until they reached the front line. They would have to be patient. Joseph pulled out the diary from his knapsack and began to write:

"In Eswars, 5 kilometers from Cambrai... We sit here prepared, ready for any eventuality, while 'Tommy' is constantly shelling our vicinity. Fifty meters from me is a military cemetery and former Church cemetery where some open graves are waiting for us. But we are not quite that far yet. Today I observe an involuntary fast. The company which is to bring provisions has received food for only two [of the 4 from the I.B.O. unit] and, because of our change of position, nothing else can be supplied. Thus none of us has anything to eat and we reach the kitchen only later this evening."

When noon arrived he pulled out his spiritual daily order and checked it. He had kept all the morning exercises. The particular examination, too, got a positive check mark. His present resolution was to walk in the presence of God and help his comrades. He was writing the "amen" of his life's work. The hero of everyday life answered the last roll call.

On the afternoon of October 4 Joseph visited his Schoenstatt comrade Paul Reinhold. They chatted together for quite some time. Paul had the impression that Joseph was in a pensive, melancholy mood. Was he affected by a presentiment that this might be his last farewell from a member of his Schoenstatt group?

When they parted, Joseph's thoughts were occupied with the problem of how to help his comrades of the former infantry observation post get over the worst hunger. There was a potato field on the other side of the road. Although it had been harvested, there were many potatoes lying around. He gathered a potful of them and started a fire in the nearby shed of the farmyard. The potatoes were soon swirling in the boiling water. At that moment he heard a call from outside. His comrade Nicholas Gilgenbach was looking for him. Joseph learned that he had been ordered to join an advance commando and they would set off at once. Joseph got ready to march and checked his boiling potatoes. They were not quite ready. The men of the advance commando were already standing on the road, ready to march. "Yes, yes," called Joseph," I'll be right along. Just let me eat my potatoes." The half-raw tubers crunched between his teeth. Then he hurried off.

As he began to walk away, he remarked to Gilgenbach, "Well, now I have eaten enough, though it may be for the last time. In case I do not return, I wish to say to you 'until we meet again,' if not in this world, at least in the next. And if you see Edmund Kampe again, give him a last greeting from me."

Surprised, Gilgenbach looked up. He was not used to this kind of talk from Joseph. To dispel such melancholy thoughts Nicholas remarked, "We have gone into the line of fire many times and nothing has ever happened to us."

With a quiet smile Joseph replied, "Man always has some presentiment. And I feel something, I don't know what it is, but whatever God wills, his will be done." Joseph suddenly shook Nicholas' hand and hurried after the advance commando.

Darkness was falling. In the meantime, British artillery shelled the rest quarters and strafed the roads on the German side of the front. The advance commando first marched back to the village of Thun-St. Martin. From there they tried to advance to the main road to Cambrai. On the horizon the big guns of the English batteries were rumbling. Here and there the flashes of exploding shells were seen. A ruddy glow hung over the front.

The spot where the secondary road from Thun-St. Martin joined the main road seemed to be a favorite target of enemy artillery. About 200 yards before reaching the intersection, the commando leader lead his men to the right into an open field. They threw themselves against an embankment about three feet high and watched the exploding shells dancing around the intersection.

"If only we come out of this fire alive," ventured a corporal close to Joseph. "Oh," said Joseph, "Everything has gone all right so far. Let us hope it will continue this way." In a break in the shelling the troop set out again and tried to reach the main road while keeping a safe distance from the dangerous intersection. Suddenly a new volley came rushing in from the British batteries. As though a whimsical hand were guiding the shells, they struck about 200-300 yards from the road instead of on the road itself. In the flash of bursting shells one could see a man collapse at the head of the column. The others scattered. When the sudden gunfire ceased Sergeant Einig and a few comrades ran at once to the scene of the accident. A man was lying in his blood. At once they recognized their comrade Joseph Engling. He had suffered severe wounds in the head and chest from the shrapnel of the shell. He was already dead. According to the recollection of his comrades, it was the evening of October 4, sometime between 6 and 7 o'clock.

The scattered men of the advance commando wandered aimlessly in the fields through the night. Only at about 5 o'clock in the morning did they begin to find their way back to the 4th company and report that Joseph Engling was killed in action and lay not far from the meeting of the roads. Nicholas Gilgenbach heard the report, too. What Joseph had guessed just a few hours earlier had come true. Nicholas and many of his comrades were deeply affected by the report. "Oh, our good Joseph," they remarked, "He was a loyal and God-fearing comrade."

The battalion's medical sergeant sent out some of his men to find the fallen man at the supposed place of death and bury him. In all likelihood they buried him in one of the many shell holes. The confusion of the front almost certainly prevented them from bringing his body back to one of the established military cemeteries. The company later sent Joseph's parents his diaries and personal belongings. Joseph had them in his knapsack. His grave remains undiscovered until today.

Beyond Death

Joseph Engling's earthly life ended on the battlefield near Cambrai on October 4, 1918. But it also marked the beginning of a new and unexpected activity on his part. The memory of his person had made a lasting impression on those who knew him. The Apostolic Movement of Schoenstatt which began to blossom and prosper in Germany after World War I saw in him and in his generous life-offering for Schoenstatt a pioneer in the truest sense of the word. When the "MTA" Magazine began to publish excerpts from his diary, many wanted to know more about his life and striving. At the instigation of Father Kentenich, who had carefully collected all the documentation about Joseph Engling's life, a first biography was published in 1932 by Fr. Heinrich Schulte SAC under the title *Omnibus Omnia* (All things to all men). In 1938 the biography which you now read appeared in its first edition, drawing on an even broader range of historical sources.

Joseph Engling's charism exerted a great influence in the circles of the growing Schoenstatt Family. His life became a school of Schoenstatt's founding history, of its most central sources of life, of its approach to self-education and striving for the ideals of sanctity. Not a few venerated Joseph Engling as a genuine saint and entrusted to him their prayers to God in many matters. This veneration was cultivated through novenas, prayer cards, and the publication of answered prayers. The widespread conviction that he led a saintly life and the growing veneration led to the opening of the process for his beatification and canonization in Trier on October 4, 1951. The diocesan investigation was brought to a close in the summer of 1964 and later that same year the official documentation was brought to the competent authority in the Holy See for the further steps toward this goal.

It is understandable that more and more Schoenstatt members

became interested in visiting the places Joseph lived during the war and to especially walk in the footsteps of the final hours of his life. A first detailed search for his mortal remains was undertaken in 1934, but this and subsequent searches failed to find his body. In 1937 a simple stone cross was erected at the general location of his

Stone cross at the site of Joseph's death near Cambrai, France.

death in the field near Thun-St. Martin northeast of Cambrai. It bore the inscription in German and French:

"Joseph Engling, born January 5, 1898, killed in action October 4, 1918. His heroic death crowned a saintly life in the service of his neighbor and of the Mother Thrice Admirable of Schoenstatt."

In the 1950s the Schoenstatt Family acquired land near this site

247

See in the month of Schoenstatt's 50th anniversary (October 1964). It was also connected with a fervent petition to Our Lady of Schoenstatt to reunite the founder, still living in exile in Milwaukee, with his family. In spite of many obstacles and under the capable leadership of the Schoenstatt Brothers of Mary, the shrine could already be built in 1965 and dedicated on September 12, 1965 by Archbishop Jenny of Cambrai. Already on the following day came the telegram calling Schoenstatt's founder back to Rome, a sheer work of grace through the intercession of Joseph Engling.

Joseph Engling was chosen by Divine Providence to fulfill an exciting mission for our times. This simple farmer's son became a preeminent instrument for the founding of an international Catholic movement. He gives witness to everyday sanctity, to a striving for holiness befitting our times, and to a deep love for Mary. Not least of all, he gives living witness on behalf of Schoenstatt's founder, himself a candidate for sainthood. When the official papers for Joseph's beatification were presented in Rome, he became, as it were, Father Kentenich's precursor, telling the world of his heroic striving for the ideal of sanctity and the educative personality of the Father and Founder of the Schoenstatt Family.

Whatever happened to...?

Joseph's family:
(parents):
August—died in Prositten in 1934 at the age of 76.
Maria (nee Masuth)—died in Prositten in 1939 at the age of 78.
(brothers and sisters:)
Maria—1892-1948, married and had 7 children.
August—1894-1915, killed in action in Russia.
Valentin (Valentine)—1896-1945, tailor, married and had 7 children.
Joseph—1898-1918, killed in action in France, process of beatification begun in 1951.
Elisabeth—1900-1946, married and had 8 children.
Johann (John)—1902-1988, farmer, emigrated to Brazil in 1924, married and had 5 children.
Luzia (Lucy)—1904-1988, single, buried in cemetery of the Schoenstatt Sisters of Mary in Koblenz-Metternich.

Joseph's spiritual director:
Father Joseph Kentenich (spiritual director of the Schoenstatt seminary and Joseph spiritual director)—founder of the Schoenstatt Movement, died in Schoenstatt, Germany, September 15, 1968, process of beatification begun 1975.

Joseph Engling's class:
Joseph Engling—killed in action October 4, 1918, memorial erected in his honor behind the Original Shrine in Schoenstatt, Germany in 1935/36, process of beatification begun 1951.
Karl Klement (Joseph's best friend)—ordained a Pallottine 1926, after World War II a priest in Communist East Germany. His priestly work was blessed because of his friendship with Engling. He died in Germany, June 13, 1981, at the age of 82.
Fritz Esser (the likeable friend of Joseph who could sense the troubles of others)—carved the light frame around the MTA picture in the shrine with the famous motto *Servus Mariae nunquam peribit* (A child of Mary will never perish), Pallottine novice 1919-21, died in Germany, January 18, 1924 of bad health resulting from the war.
Hans Wormer (who took his prize as "primus" in the second year)—killed in action July 15, 1917, his mortal remains were

transferred from France to behind the Original Shrine in 1934.

Paul Reinhold (master of comedy in the seminary)—missing in action and presumed dead October 1918.

Adolf Baldauf (leader of the Eucharistic Section of the Junior Sodality)—ordained a Pallottine 1926, missionary in Chile, died in Chile, February 25, 1954.

Gustav Rischewski (from Warmia like Joseph)—unknown.

Otto Boenki (from Warmia like Joseph)—transferred as seminarian to the United States 1924, ordained a Pallottine 1925, superior of the Midwest Province and promoter of Schoenstatt, became a Schoenstatt Father in 1965, died in New York, December 21, 1969.

Nicholas Wilwers (one of the frequent letter-writers among the sodalists)—as a seminarian transferred to the United States in 1924, ordained a Pallottine 1926, promoter of Schoenstatt, died in Milwaukee, August 6, 1979.

Class younger than Joseph Engling:

Alfons Hoffmann (one of the leaders in this class)—ordained a Pallottine 1926 and worked with the Girls Youth. He died in Germany, May 11, 1933 at the age of 34.

Alex Menningen (author of this book)—ordained a Pallottine 1926, close associate of Fr. Kentenich's in building up Schoenstatt Movement, first postulator of Joseph Engling's cause for beatification 1951-64, became a Schoenstatt Father in 1965, died in Germany, May 19, 1994, at the age of 93.

Joseph's wartime Schoenstatt Group:

Paul Reinhold—Wounded, British prisoner-of-war, missing and presumed dead.

Eduard Struth—After WWI did not return to seminary

Florin Rüber—After WWI did not return to seminary

Johannes Dekarski—Wounded in action, May 1918 (shrapnel in leg, leg had to be amputated). Did not return to seminary.

Clemens Meier—Became a Pallottine Father. Wounded in action, May 1918 (three bullets in the shoulder). Because of war injuries he remained sickly for the rest of his life. Died 1929.

Alfons Hoffmann—See above.

Karl Klement—See above.

Chronology

1898	January 5	JOSEPH ENGLING BORN in Prositten, Germany
	January 9	Joseph Engling baptized
1904	Spring	Joseph enters the first grade in village school at Prositten
1910	May 1	Joseph begins a diary in preparation for his First Communion
	June 29	Joseph receives his FIRST COMMUNION
1912	Spring	Joseph experiences his call to become a priest and missionary
	September 24	Joseph joins the course of studies of the Pallottine Fathers and BEGINS STUDIES AT SCHOENSTATT
1914	October 18	Fr. Kentenich proposes his idea to the Senior Sodality to turn the St. Michael's Chapel into a Shrine of Mary (SCHOENSTATT'S FOUNDING)
	December 8	Junior Sodality Founded
1915	April 11	Joseph accepted as member of the Junior Sodality
	May 13	Joseph becomes prefect of the Junior Sodality
	May	Joseph becomes a promoter of the "Ingolstadt-Schoenstatt Parallel"
	October 6	Joseph's oldest brother August killed in action in Russia
	December	Annual retreat in Schoenstatt seminary: Joseph begins his diary with the solemn words "I want to become a saint."
1916	February	Joseph experiences great inner turmoil in his soul
	April	Over Easter vacation Joseph makes a private retreat; He formulates his Personal Ideal as "All things to all men and Mary's very own"
	May	MAY BLOSSOMS; Joseph offers the Blessed Mother 1712 prayers and sacrifices
	June	Third Class takes over leadership of Junior Sodality, end of Joseph's term as Prefect
	August 13	Joseph and two other sodalists meet in Dietrichswalde, hoping to win outside students to Schoenstatt

	November 16	JOSEPH DRAFTED INTO THE GERMAN ARMY
	November 20	Joseph arrives in Haugenau for boot camp
1917	May 2	Joseph leaves Haugenau on furlough (visits his family, Schoenstatt)
	May 16	Joseph returns to Hagenau
	May 20	Schoenstatt Sodalists make pilgrimage to Marienthal to renew consecration to Mary
	June 6	Joseph's company finishes boot camp and leaves Hagenau for THE EASTERN FRONT
	June 8	Arrive in Jablonna, near Warsaw
	July 15	Hans Wormer killed in action
	July 18	Recruits transferred to Bendzin (Upper Silesia, Poland); Joseph becomes leader of a Schoenstatt group of soldier Sodalists
	July 25	Joseph ordered to nearby Grodziec (soldiers stricken with dysentery)
	August 6	Joseph's company leaves Bendzin for Jablonna
	August 9	Joseph's company leaves for the Eastern Front in Galicia near Tarnopol—in the next month Joseph does not keep an SDO or PE
	August 20	Joseph's company reaches assigned position in Probudzna, Galicia
	September 9	Joseph repents his laxity and begins a new phase of spiritual striving
	December 6	General cease-fire is reached on the Eastern Front
	Before Christmas	Joseph's company begins march back from the Eastern Front
	Late December	Joseph's company begins transport from Galicia to the Western Front
1918	January 6	Joseph's company arrives in France (Dun-Rémonville) on THE WESTERN FRONT
	January 8	Joseph plays cards through the night at Rémonville
	January 9	Joseph writes his "Poor Sinner Letter" to Father Kentenich
	January 20	Joseph is able to attend his first Holy Mass in four months
	February 5	Joseph assigned to shock troop
	February 24	Shock troop raids French lines (Operation February I)

March 10	Shock troop raids French lines, Joseph volunteers "because Karthaüser was there" (Operation February II)
March 20	Joseph's regiment moved to "Camp Magdalene"
April 6-16	Shock troop sent to front line at Forges Creek again
April 24-25	Joseph's regiment transferred to Flanders
May 2-7	Joseph's battalion in readiness position at Lestreme (2½ miles behind the front line); Joseph leads daily May devotions
May 7	Joseph's company advances to front line position at Calonne; Joseph given the dangerous task of the nightly runs to the field kitchen
May	Joseph volunteers to take the place of a comrade assigned to spy patrol
May	Schoenstatters Clemens Meier and Johannes Dekarski are seriously wounded
May 19 (Pentecost)	Joseph's diary contains prayer ". . .Oh Little Mother, intercede to the Holy Spirit for me so that he will grant me the seven gifts . . ."
May 29	Joseph's infantry moves once again to the front; courier and signal post located close to Lys River behind front line
May 31	JOSEPH OFFERS THE BLESSED MOTHER HIS LIFE: "If it can be reconciled with your plans, let me be a sacrifice for the aims which you have assigned to our sodality."
June 3	Joseph makes his life offering in writing
June 26	Joseph's Division concludes its activity in Calonne sector after eight weeks and 2,000 deaths; Joseph records in his diary his gratitude for the Holy Mother's protection
Early July	Joseph's regiment retreats to rest camp at Esquerchin near Donai
July	Joseph suffers from influenza and is released on furlough; Joseph goes home to Prositten, his mother nurses him back to health
July 25-30	Joseph uses his last four days of furlough to visit Schoenstatt
July 30	Joseph receives parting blessing from Fr. Kentenich and leaves Schoenstatt—JOSEPH'S LAST VISIT TO SCHOENSTATT
August 1	Joseph writes to his spiritual director concern-

	ing distraction in prayer and "walking in the presence of God"
August 8	Joseph's battalion sent to the front west of Douai with only one-quarter strength in their regiment and facing four new Canadian divisions. There are no more reserves; the German army is collapsing
September 25	The "Cigar Incident"—Joseph discovers cigars he had saved for his father were stolen
October 1	R.I.R. 25 ordered to the front; the strength of the German army severly diminished. Joseph and troops sent to back up the defense at Eswars
October 1-2	Joseph's last letter to Fr. Kentenich
October 2	Joseph's division sets up camp in Bouchain, ten miles from Cambrai
October 3-4	Joseph's division moves in the night to Eswars
October 4	Joseph ordered to join advance commando and march toward Cambrai
October 4	JOSEPH ENGLING CALLED HOME TO GOD. Killed by a stray shell near Cambrai, France

Index

257